Childhoods in context

This book is part of the series *Childhood* published by The Policy Press in association with The Open University. The four books in the series are:

Understanding childhood: a cross-disciplinary approach (edited by Mary Jane Kehily)

ISBN 978-1-447-30580-4 (paperback)

ISBN 978-1-447-30927-7 (ebook)

Children and young people's cultural worlds (edited by Sara Bragg and Mary Jane Kehily)

ISBN 978-1-447-30582-8 (paperback)

ISBN 978-1-447-30925-3 (ebook)

Childhoods in context (edited by Alison Clark)

ISBN 978-1-447-30581-1 (paperback)

ISBN 978-1-447-30924-6 (ebook)

Local childhoods, global issues (edited by Heather Montgomery)

ISBN 978-1-447-30583-5 (paperback)

ISBN 978-1-447-30926-0 (ebook)

This publication forms part of the Open University module E212 Childhood. Details of this and other Open University modules can be obtained from the Student Registration and Enquiry Service, The Open University, PO Box 197, Milton Keynes, MK7 6BJ, United Kingdom (Tel. +44 (0845 300 60 90, email general-enquiries @open.ac.uk).

www.open.ac.uk

Childhoods in context

Edited by Alison Clark

Published by
The Policy Press
University of Bristol
Fourth Floor, Beacon House
Queen's Road, Clifton
Bristol BS8 1QU
United Kingdom
www.policypress.co.uk

in association with
The Open University
Walton Hall
Milton Keynes MK7 6AA
United Kingdom

First published 2003. Second edition published 2013

Edited and designed by The Open University.

Typeset by The Open University.

Printed in the United Kingdom by Bell & Bain Ltd, Glasgow.

British Library Cataloguing in Publication Data:
A catalogue record for this book is available from the British Library.

Library of Congress Cataloging-in-Publication Data

A catalog record for this book has been requested

ISBN 978-1-447-30581-1 (paperback)

ISBN 978-1-447-30924-6 (ebook)

2.1

Contents

Series preface

The books in this series provide an introduction to the study of childhood. They provide a cross-disciplinary and international perspective which develops theoretical knowledge about children and young people, both in the UK and overseas. They are core texts for the Open University module E212 *Childhood*. The series is designed for students working with or for children and young people, in a wide range of settings, and for those who have more general interests in the interdisciplinary field of childhood and youth studies.

The series aims to provide students with:

- the necessary concepts, theories, knowledge and skills base to understand the lives of children and young people

- relevant skills of critical analysis

- critical reflection on and analysis of practices affecting children and young people

- an understanding of the links between children's experiences on a global and local level

- an understanding of the analytical, research and conceptual skills needed to link theory, practice and experience.

The readings which accompany each chapter have been chosen to exemplify key points made in the chapters, often by exploring related data, or experiences and practices involving children in different parts of the world. The readings also represent an additional 'voice' or viewpoint on key themes or issues raised in the chapter.

The books include:

- **activities** to stimulate further understanding or analysis of the material

- **illustrations** to support the teaching material

- **summaries** of key teaching points at appropriate places in the chapter.

The other books in this series are:

Kehily, M. J. (ed) (2013) *Understanding Childhood: A Cross-disciplinary Approach*, Bristol, Policy Press/Milton Keynes, The Open University.

Bragg, S. and Kehily, M. J. (eds) (2013) *Children and Young People's Cultural Worlds*, Bristol, Policy Press/Milton Keynes, The Open University.

Montgomery, H. (ed) (2013) *Local Childhoods, Global Issues*, Bristol, Policy Press/Milton Keynes, The Open University.

Professor Mary Jane Kehily

Series Editor

Contributors

Alison Clark

Alison Clark is a Senior Lecturer in Childhood Studies in the Faculty of Education and Language Studies at The Open University. Her research interests include children's experiences of place, school design and the development of participatory research methods across the life course. She developed the Mosaic approach, a visual, participatory research framework with Peter Moss, first published in 2001. Recent studies have included involving young children and adults in the design and review of schools, and a study of the impact of post-war school design on contemporary design and practice.

Mary Jane Kehily

Mary Jane Kehily is Professor of Childhood and Youth Studies at The Open University, UK. She has a background in cultural studies and education, and research interests in gender and sexuality, narrative and identity and popular culture. She has published widely on these themes.

Heather Montgomery

Heather Montgomery is a Reader in the Anthropology of Childhood at The Open University, UK. She has carried out research with young sex workers in Thailand and written extensively on issues of children's rights, global childhoods and representations of childhood.

Sarah Crafter

Sarah Crafter is a Senior Research Officer at the Thomas Coram Research Unit in the Institute of Education (University of London). Her background is in cultural-developmental psychology. Her research interests include home and school learning, parental involvement in mathematics, culturally diverse childhoods, and cultural identity development. Her work also examines the concept of 'normal' childhoods in relation to children who work; particularly young carers and language brokers.

Lesley Gallacher

Lesley Gallacher is a lecturer based in the Moray House School of Education at the University of Edinburgh. She has a background in human geography. Her research interests fall broadly into two categories: materials, bodies and spaces in early childhood; and the international reception of Japanese popular culture. Lesley has published on socio-spatial relations in childcare settings, the practices of reading manga and methodological issues in childhood research.

Martyn Hammersley

Martyn Hammersley is Professor of Education and Social Research at The Open University. His early research was in the sociology of education. Later work has been concerned with the methodological issues surrounding social and educational enquiry. These include objectivity, partisanship and bias, and the role of research in relation to policymaking and practice. More recently he has investigated ethical issues in social research and how the news media represent social science research findings.

Peter Kraftl

Peter Kraftl is Senior Lecturer in Human Geography at the University of Leicester. He has published over 40 articles and book chapters on children's geographies, geographies of education and architecture. He co-edited *Critical Geographies of Childhood and Youth* (published by Policy Press in 2012) and his newest book, *Geographies of Alternative Education*, will be published by Policy Press in May 2013. He is an editor of the *Children's Geographies* journal and Chair of the Geographies of Children, Youth and Families Research Group of the Royal Geographical Society-IBG.

Lindsay O'Dell

Lindsay O'Dell is a Senior Lecturer in the Faculty of Health and Social Care at The Open University. Her research interests focus on 'different' childhoods, including intersections of gender, ethnicity, culture, disability and generation. Specific research projects include work with young carers, language brokers, children with a visible difference and young people with autism. She is interested in constructions of normative childhoods and children who are seen to be 'different'.

Introduction

Childhoods happen in context. Children's and young people's lives are often discussed in such abstract terms that take for granted the *spaces*, *places*, *objects* and *practices* that make up the everyday world of the child. Throughout this book, we will be considering childhood in relation to contexts that have a significant impact on young lives, principally the institutional contexts of family and school. Against this backdrop, we will bring into focus the spaces and places of childhood, adopting geographer Chris Philo's definitions of spaces as 'types of setting for interaction' and places as 'specific sites of meaning' (Philo, 2000, p. 245). The settings in which children interact, and the meanings that they ascribe to these settings, offer a further way of understanding childhood from the perspective of the child. Throughout the book, childhood is productively explored and made visible through attention to the range of places and objects encountered in childhood. While there is an established history of childhood documented through toys, in this book we will cast our net wider to explore objects encountered in a range of contexts, including domestic and public spaces, work and school. As well as the materiality of childhood, we will explore how practices emerge as children and young people interact in these diverse spaces and places in local and global settings.

We will be exploring childhood through the following three themes:

- **Childhood is always located *somewhere*.** Some places are assumed to be more natural for children, or are more strongly associated with them, than others. Which places are seen as natural will depend on many factors, including the age of the children, their gender and the cultural context in which they are living. By drawing these contexts into focus, further understandings can be gained of childhood in the past and present.

- **Childhood** does not involve only abstract qualities such as innocence or laughter, but **is experienced through objects, people and places** and through everyday routines. The discussions about childhood in this book will be rooted in the details of children's lives. This will lead us to look at school, for example, through discussions about food and eating practices which include examining the dining room and the lunch box.

- **Childhood and adult identities are relational.** Who one can be depends on how the other is defined and understood. Looking at places – homes, institutions, public spaces and sites of work – can tell us more about how children and adults are defined in different contexts, and about relationships between them.

The opening chapter of the book provides a conceptual background to thinking critically about the importance of context in the lives of children and young people. Alison Clark and Lesley Gallacher begin by discussing the interactions between processes, on a global and local scale, which influence children's everyday lives. The chapter looks at the kinds of places that adults produce and set aside for children, as well as the territories that children develop for themselves. Examples are explored of conflicts over spaces and places, between adults and children, and among children themselves. Drawing attention to contexts can bring into sharp relief tensions that are mapped out in the physical environment. The chapter investigates examples of young people's narratives about these contested places.

The home is an important context for childhood and one that is very closely related to the concept of the family. Together, these two institutions can profoundly shape children's and young people's experiences, expectations and world views. Chapter 2 provides a critical framework for examining our own assumptions about home and family. Alison Clark and Mary Jane Kehily examine the social and material organisation of domestic life in a range of cultural contexts. For example, they look at preparing for motherhood, using images taken by mothers. They explore the idea of family as created by practices of 'doing' rather than necessarily of biological relationship. The home is the site where family practices are developed and repeated, but home and family may become disconnected. The chapter discusses alternative ways of 'doing family' through young people's accounts of residential care and youth homelessness.

In Chapter 3, we move from the domestic sphere to consider children in public spaces (although, as the case of youth homelessness illustrates, the lives of children and young people do not necessarily comply with such neat academic definitions). In this chapter, Peter Kraftl looks at how children and young people inhabit public spaces, building on the concepts and examples introduced in the opening chapter. He probes further into the contested nature of some young people's relationship to the public. The chapter shows how the geography of childhood is constructed across time and place, revealing an oscillation across localities and contexts in which the same young people are constructed as either 'children' or 'yobs' and 'youth' (Nayak, 2003).

Alison Clark, in Chapter 4, explores schools as particular contexts for childhood. Schools can be highly charged emotional environments, in which many children and young people spend an increasingly large percentage of their childhoods, while others do not have access at all. The chapter considers the different ways in which children are shaped by their learning environments and how they can shape these spaces. The chapter begins by considering influential examples of school and preschool design, and examines what changes in the physical layout and material culture of school can tell us about how children, childhood and learning are viewed. Moving beyond bricks and mortar, the chapter considers the relationships between adults and children, among children themselves, and between indoor and outdoor spaces, which different environments support or hinder. Children's control or lack of control over time in school is examined by exploring how food and eating practices are approached in schools.

Chapter 5 takes children and work as its central theme. Lindsay O'Dell, Sarah Crafter and Heather Montgomery illustrate the forms of work that children do and the sites in which work takes place, which includes revisiting contexts discussed in earlier chapters: the home, the street and the school. The chapter discusses issues of risk that children can face in undertaking work, but the authors also explore questions of children's agency, and argue that it may not be work itself that is harmful for children but the working conditions. This reinforces the importance of looking at issues about childhood in real contexts, considering the local alongside the global and not relying on abstract judgements.

The final chapter is methodological. This stems from our belief that the task of reconceptualising childhood, in which we are engaged, involves a re-examination of methods employed to understand children's lives in context. Drawing on examples throughout the book, Martyn Hammersley focuses on the use of visual material, both on and off screen. The chapter considers the different purposes for which such data can be used, how it can be produced (e.g. by an adult researcher or by children as participants), its relationship with other research material, and ethical issues that can arise.

To summarise, this book examines childhoods in context. In doing so, it draws on local and global examples across a wide age range, from prenatal to youth, emphasising where childhoods are lived, with whom and with what materials.

This book is the third of four volumes in the Childhoods series. We would like to thank the consultants who have contributed to the preparation of this book; Professor Chris Philo (University of Glasgow) for his insightful comments on draft chapters in his role as external assessor; Professor David Messer (The Open University) for his support throughout; and Lara Knight (The Open University) for her perseverance in seeing the book through to production.

Alison Clark

The Open University, 2012

References

Nayak, A. (2003) '"Through children's eyes": childhood, place and the fear of crime', *Geoforum*, vol. 34, no. 3, pp. 303–15.

Philo, C. (2000) 'The corner-stones of my world', editorial introduction to special issue on spaces of childhood, *Childhood*, vol. 7, no. 3, pp. 243–56.

Chapter 1

Children in and out of place

Alison Clark and Lesley Gallacher

Contents

In this chapter, you will:

- gain an understanding of the importance of spatial contexts for children and young people's lives
- critically analyse the social and material aspects of space and place in childhood and youth
- develop an awareness of the interaction between processes, on global and local scales, in children and young people's everyday experiences
- discuss how conflicts over spaces and places arise and are resolved between adults and children, and among children themselves
- critically evaluate information from a range of sources about the spaces and places of childhood.

1 Introduction

This chapter is concerned with the spaces and places in which children and young people live their lives, and the role that these spaces and places play in shaping their experiences. This is a growing area in the sociocultural study of childhood and youth, which has been particularly associated with the emergence of 'children's geographies' as a distinctive subdiscipline within the broader field of geography. This is not to say that the spatial contexts of children and young people's lives are only of interest to geographers: researchers in a range of disciplines – including anthropology, sociology and education – have attended to what might be called the 'geographies' of children and young people's lives. We will begin by discussing definitions of space and place. We will be asking, where do children and young people fit in, where are they seen as in or out of place? And we will explore such terms as 'children as weeds' and ideas about 'adult-only' or 'child-free spaces'. Moving from thinking about how adults define space, we will explore examples, from literature and practice, of children's agency in creating spaces. We will end by focusing on the tensions that can arise between adults and children, and among peers, in negotiating space.

2 Spaces and places

Before we can explore the spatial contexts of children and young people's lives, we need to be clear about what we mean when we talk about 'spaces' and 'places'. Yi-Fu Tuan (1977) reminds us that 'space' and 'place' are very familiar terms. We use them every day and often without really thinking about what we mean when we use them. Indeed, the meanings of the two words often seem to merge. We may think of a child's bedroom as both a space in the family home and a place in its own right. When we make a distinction between the two terms, we often think of 'space' as a more abstract concept than 'place'. We think of space as a container filled with things and people, and the backdrop against which things happen. 'Place' is what becomes of space when it is invested with meaning and comes to have some kind of identity in its own right. In this sense, space becomes a surface on which individual places can be pinpointed and mapped.

However, these familiar and taken-for-granted understandings of space and place are not necessarily useful for understanding the geographies of children and young people's lives. Many geographers have argued that space is not an inert surface over which we move and on to which we impose meaning. Ed Soja (1980) argues that space simultaneously shapes and is shaped by social relations; he terms this the 'socio-spatial dialectic'. Doreen Massey (2005) sets out some key principles for understanding space in this way:

1 Spaces do not pre-exist and contain social action; they are produced through the practices and processes of social life.

2 Spaces are always relational; that is, they are produced through all manner of interactions between people and things.

3 Spaces are always heterogeneous; individual spaces are produced from many different relations at the same time, and alternative trajectories exist within them.

4 Space is always under construction; it is never complete, but always in the process of being made through new interactions and new practices or processes.

Starting from these principles, Massey describes space as 'a simultaneity of stories so far' (2005, p. 130). Spaces are always the sum of the practices and processes that make them up. Massey argues that places are never imbued with stable or singular identities, but are continually being remade and reformed through a range of social practices and processes. As she explains:

> If space is rather a simultaneity of stories-so-far, then places are collections of those stories, articulations within the wider power-geometries of space. Their character will be a product of these intersections within that wider setting, and of what is made of them. And, too, of the non-meetings-up, the disconnections and the relations not established, the exclusions. All this contributes to the specificity of place.
>
> (Massey, 2005, p. 130)

Jay's box

When Jay was 12, she travelled to school on the London Underground. One Underground station in particular became a popular gathering point after school for her and her friends. At one end of the platform, there was a metal box that was large enough to sit on. This became the meeting point for her group of friends each day, where they would talk endlessly and begin to add their own markings to the box. Through these repeated interactions and practices, the box became a significant landmark in the shared childhoods of Jay and her friends, a safe place between home and school.

The box could also become embroiled in other practices – for example, its official use by Underground staff. However, these other practices, experiences and 'stories-so-far' didn't necessarily result in the box ceasing to be a special place for the girls, although these other actions may have affected them and altered their interactions in all kinds of ways.

While places can come to have some specificity based on the endurance of the kinds of interaction from which they emerge, they can never have clearly defined boundaries. Places are necessarily porous to other influences and connections on a variety of scales.

Figure 1 The journey to school, Brasov, Romania

Activity 1 Seeing global influences in local places

Allow about 30 minutes

In the extract below, Doreen Massey (1993) gives a short description of her local high street in the early 1990s. She presents Kilburn High Road as a multicultural place that is intimately connected with other places around the world, in both obvious and more subtle ways.

Read the extract, then try to write a similar sketch of the connections between your own local high street today and other places both in the UK and more globally.

Take, for instance, a walk down Kilburn High Road, my local shopping centre. It is a pretty ordinary place, north-west of the centre of London. Under the railway bridge the newspaper-stand sells papers from every county of what my neighbours, many of whom come from there, still call the Irish Free State. The postboxes down the High Road, and many an empty space on a wall, are adorned with the letters IRA. The bottle and waste-paper banks are plastered this week with posters for a Bloody Sunday commemoration. Thread your way through the almost stationary traffic diagonally across the road from the newsstand and there's a shop which, for as long as I can remember, has displayed saris in the window. Four life-sized models of Indian women, and reams of cloth. In another newsagent I chat with the man who keeps it, a Muslim unutterably depressed by the war in the Gulf, silently chafing at having to sell the *Sun*. Overhead there is always at least one aeroplane – we seem to be on a flight-path to Heathrow and by the time they're over Kilburn you can see them clearly enough to discern the airline and wonder as you struggle with your shopping where they're coming from. Below, the reason the traffic is snarled up (another odd effect of time–space compression!) is in part because this is one of the main entrances to and escape-routes from London, the road to Staples Corner and the beginning of the M1 to the north. These are just the beginnings of a sketch from immediate impressions but a proper analysis could be done, of the links between Kilburn and the world. And so it could be for almost any place.

(Massey, 1993, p. 66)

Comment

Your sketch is likely to be very different from Massey's. She provides a snapshot of a very multicultural area of London that was deeply inflected by the broader political landscape of the time. Your sketch may not present such an overtly politicised landscape, but it is likely to reflect elements of the contemporary social, cultural and political landscape in more or less subtle ways.

Author Lesley Gallacher's sketch of Gosforth High Street in Newcastle upon Tyne includes, among other things, a boutique children's shoe shop. The shop stocks fashionable, branded shoes which are popular among the (predominantly middle-class) parents in the local area, and which reflect ideas about the need to support children's growing feet with well-designed and expensive shoes. The shoes are produced by a range of companies based in Norwich, London and Milan (among other locations), and are manufactured in an even wider variety of locations, in Europe, Latin America and Asia. Massey argues that it is impossible to unpick the geography of Kilburn High Road 'without bringing into play half the world and a considerable amount of British imperialist history' (Massey, 1993, p. 66). Similarly, Lesley's sketch of Gosforth High Street, while less obviously multicultural and globally connected, is inextricably caught up in the complex relations that make up the contemporary global political economy. Massey stresses that these are not only 'ritualistic' or tokenistic connections to wider systems, but 'real relations with real content – economic, political, cultural – between any local place and the wider world in which it is set' (Massey, 1993, p. 67).

While Massey wasn't writing specifically about children and young people, her ideas are useful in thinking about how children and young people's lives are affected by a range of processes and forces operating on a variety of scales, even as these processes and forces are experienced in particular times and places, and through practices and interactions peculiar to them.

2.1   Collecting lichen in the Indian Himalayas

Thinking about how processes and ideas circulate on a global or national scale – such as the value of education for all children and young people, or ideas about class, gender or caste within a region or country – can become implicated in the everyday practices and experiences of children and young people in particular places. In the remainder of this section, we are going to think about this through the example of young people's work collecting lichen in the Indian Himalayas.

In 2003, Jane Dyson (2008) carried out an ethnographic study of young people's experiences of gender in the far north of the Indian state of Uttarakhand. Villagers in Bemni, like those in most villages in the Chamoli district, are predominantly reliant on agriculture for survival. In addition to farming crops, villagers also collect lichen in the surrounding forests to sell at the local markets. This work is often carried out by young people in the village, whose access to and activities within the forest are contingent on a wide range of influences, including local gender roles, the caste system within India, and the global circulation of ideas about education and marriage. These factors affected individual young people within the village differently, depending on their particular circumstances.

For example, Saka was a 16-year-old girl from a higher-caste family within the village. Like most women of her generation in Bemni, Saka's mother had received no formal education and had been married at 12. In contrast, Saka had been educated up to age 14 in a local school and did not expect to marry until she was 18. In this respect, Saka was not unusual within the village. Indeed, many of her peers had been educated beyond the age of 14. Dyson explains that this extended period of education was creating a period of youth between childhood and adulthood that had not previously existed within the village. As unmarried young women, Saka and her friends remained within their natal homes and were able to carve out free time and space for themselves through their work collecting lichen in the forests, as well as generating income for their families.

The girls viewed the forest as a place for fun, where they could be free of the demands placed on them at home and in the village. This aspect of the trips often took precedence over the 'official' business of lichen collection, as Saka explains:

> If we don't want to, we do nothing all day and collect a little later. If we come back with very little lichen, we make up a story for everyone to tell her parents. We say we met a bear and we had to run away quickly. When we all have the same story, nobody will know what really happened. Our mothers don't go for lichen, so they don't know what we do.
>
> (Quoted in Dyson, 2008, p. 170)

The girls used their trips into the forest to play and to discuss puberty and their emerging sexual desires (topics that were never openly discussed in the village). They spoke of the forest in terms of 'our spaces' and explained that both their freedom and their attachment to the place came from their newly defined status as 'young women'. Saka and her friends had not yet needed to migrate to their (future) husbands' villages and they had no mother-in-law to fear. As Saka explains:

> When we go for dry leaves or dry wood, we are always with young married women and they are afraid of being late because their mothers-in-law will punish them. So we have to collect the leaves quickly and can't sit and chat. But when we go for lichen, we are just girls. We only have our parents and we are not afraid of them. We don't have mothers-in-law to be afraid of, so we can do as we like.
>
> (Quoted in Dyson, 2008, p. 170)

However, for young women from lower castes within Bemni, the experience of the forest was very different. They were often required, from the age of nine, to go on long journeys to remote jungles to collect lichen. Once there, they worked closely with their parents and were keenly aware of the necessity to earn money for their families. These young women did not benefit from the freedom and flexibility that Saka and her friends enjoyed; rather, they viewed the forest as a place of hardship and danger. Dyson reports that two lower-caste girls had died on these lichen gathering trips in the previous five years: one suffered from hypothermia and the other had been eaten by a leopard. For lower-caste girls in Bemni, then, the forest was 'malevolent, dark and terrifying' (Dyson, 2008, p. 172).

While lichen collection was often the preserve of young women in Bemni, some young men also engaged in the practice as a means of supplementing the family income. Sixteen-year-old Rakesh came from a higher-caste family in the village. He described lichen collecting as a 'job'. Rakesh and his friends played together before going to collect lichen; but, once in the forest, they worked diligently to collect as much lichen as possible. He explains the differences between the approaches to lichen collection taken by young men and women in the village:

> Girls hang around beneath our trees and steal the lichen that falls. Anyway, they just go for fun, for passing time (timepass). But the boys are serious and go just for lichen.

> (Quoted in Dyson, 2008, pp. 172–3)

Yet Rakesh and his friends did not begrudge the girls their free time in the forest. Gender norms in Bemni allowed boys and young men far more freedom within the village. Unlike boys, who were expected and encouraged to be 'lazy', girls were expected to work diligently and with skill. For Rakesh, 'young women need this time [in the forest] to mess around' (quoted in Dyson, 2008, p. 173).

The forest surrounding Bemni was experienced in very different ways – as a place of labour, fear or fun – depending on young people's social situations and the everyday practices in which they were engaged. This example illustrates how multiple social, economic, cultural and political processes circulating on a global scale can coalesce in particular places and can inform the experience of individual children and young people in distinctive ways, depending on their circumstances.

Summary of Section 2

Spaces and places can be understood as contingent and heterogeneous outcomes of social processes, practices and interactions between people and things.

Children and young people's experiences in particular places and times are influenced by social, political and economic processes operating on a variety of different scales.

3 Children as weeds?

The sociologist Chris Jenks argues that children and young people's spatial contexts can usefully be understood through the horticultural notion of 'weeds'. For gardeners, a weed can be defined as 'any plant that is growing in the wrong place' (Jenks, 2005, p. 74). He explains that, like dandelions and Japanese knotweed, children and young people are particularly noticeable because of where they are.

Figure 2 Play-parks are one environment in which young children are not seen as 'out of place'

In the minority world children are generally placed in designated settings, such as schools, their own bedrooms or play-parks. When children and young people are found outside of these settings, they become noticeable because they are 'out of place', particularly if they are not accompanied by adults:

> Childhood, then, is that status of personhood which is by definition often in the wrong place, like the parental bedroom, Daddy's chair, the public house or even crossing the busy road. All people in any society are subject to geographical and spatial prohibitions, whether delineated by discretion, private possession or political embargo, but the child's experience of such parameters is particularly paradoxical, often unprincipled and certainly erratic. In terms of social space children are sited, insulated and distanced, and their very gradual emergence into wider, adult space is by accident, by degrees, as an award or as part of a gradualist *rite de passage*.
>
> (Jenks, 2005, pp. 73–4)

Children and young people are not uniquely noticeable in relation to their location, but spatial prohibitions and limitations do seem to be particularly fundamental to children's experiences.

This argument has much in common with those of anthropologist Mary Douglas, about social pollution and social order. Douglas argues that the avoidance and elimination of 'dirt' in human cultures is not fully explicable in relation to notions of hygiene or germs. Instead, she explains that dirt is simply 'matter out of place' and the existence of dirt implies both 'a set of ordered relations and a contravention of that order' (Douglas, 1999, p. 109). Cultural practices that aim to eliminate dirt, then, can be understood as an attempt to maintain social and cultural orders and systems of values against anything that threatens to confuse or contradict them.

Building on Douglas's ideas, the geographer David Sibley explains that there is a continuing need for 'ritual practices', even in secular societies, which enable social groups to maintain order and 'purify' space (Sibley, 1995, p. 72). The guardians of this social order are likely to be parents or judges rather than priests, who police public institutions, spaces of commerce and even the home. He argues that there is a need to produce an 'anthropology of space' (p. 72) which focuses on the nature and effects of the various practices and 'curious rituals' through which sociospatial orders are maintained. It is useful to ask whose needs and values are privileged and supported by the environments in which we live (Malone, 2002). The same environment can support groups differently, as the example of the young people in the Himalayas illustrates.

3.1   What are adult spaces?

Chris Jenks argues that children and young people often become 'conspicuous by their inappropriate or precocious invasion of adult territory' (Jenks, 2005, p. 74). But what exactly constitutes adult territory? Gill Valentine argues that, for the most part, space tends to be understood as adult by default. This is particularly true of so-called 'public spaces' which, by definition, should be open and accessible to anyone and everyone. Children and young people are very often perceived to be vulnerable to a wide range of dangers in public space. Parental fears about 'stranger dangers' and busy road conditions, among other things, mean that children are often prevented from accessing public spaces alone, and are encouraged to spend more time in their homes or engaged in adult supervised activities. Valentine explains that 'parents' repetitive actions to limit children's activities congeal to produce the appearance that public space is "naturally" or "normally" an adult space' (Valentine, 1996, p. 209).

[handwritten margin note: Valentine parental fear stranger danger]

Children and, particularly, young people are not only perceived as vulnerable in public space. Their activities are often viewed with suspicion by the adults around them. Indeed, they are often viewed as a danger themselves. In Reading A, Gill Valentine explores how young people are constructed as a polluting presence in public space.

Activity 2   Reading A
Allow about 40 minutes

Go to the end of this chapter and read Reading A, 'Contested productions of public space', by Gill Valentine. As you read, make notes in response to the following questions:

- According to Valentine, how do young people threaten public order? What measures are taken to mitigate against this threat?
- To what extent do you think the 'problem' lies with the young people or with the adults around them?

Comment

Valentine argues that young people's activities are often overtly concerned with asserting their independence, and that this can lead to conflicts over the use of public space. When young people contravene the established social order, either deliberately or without realising it, they are often viewed as a threat to the personal safety of others (particularly of groups such as young children and the elderly, who are perceived as especially vulnerable) and to the peace and order of the area. Accordingly, young people are subject to a range of interventions, intended to restore social order and protect others, which determine where they can go, when they can go there and how they must conduct themselves. According to Valentine, these processes of curfew and 'moving on' work to exclude young people from public space and to render their activities as 'deviant'.

She explains that the blame for this problem can be attributed either to parents and wider society or to young people, depending on your point of view. Some commentators Valentine refers to – for example, Jamieson and Toynbee (1989) and Ambert (1994) – argue that parents have moved so far away from models of 'traditional authority' that some are reluctant to make any attempt to control their children's behaviour. This liberalisation of parenting is mirrored in changes to the state's approach to disciplining children and young people. Valentine quotes parents and police officers who lament that pressure from the children's rights lobby has resulted in a situation where adults can do nothing to control young people's behaviour. Jamieson and Toynbee (1989), among others, argue that the erosion of sanctions against children and young people has caused a breakdown in proper relations between the generations. They argue that young people are no longer afraid of authority and have no 'respect' for their elders. For Valentine, these types of comment expose the assumption that public space is adult by default.

Children and young people often complain that adults frequently assume they are 'up to no good' and move them on, regardless of what they are actually doing. For example, in Susie Weller's (2003) study of children's citizenship on the Isle of Wight, some boys aged 13–14 described their experiences:

[Weller]:   Do you ... do you ever get moved on from where you hang out?

Bob Stevens: Sometimes.

Agnuz: Yeah.

Loki: Mmm.

[Weller]:   Who ... who by?

Loki: Police. Old people mostly.

[handwritten margin notes: Inequality. Certain places only accessible if I am an adult. Children not feeling welcome. Being Moved on]

[Weller]:	Do they tell you why you shouldn't be there?
Loki:	No. They go 'move on, move out the way. You're causing trouble' or we're loitering.
Agnuz:	'Cos you're thinking you're not doing anything wrong and they just chuck you out 'cos down [supermarket] we're just sitting on the wall there eating crisps and stuff and they like come out and go stop skating there. … and we didn't even have skateboards with us! And they went and phoned the police.

(Weller, 2003, pp. 166–7)

Children and young people were not only moved on from outside the shops. They didn't feel any more welcome playing in the local countryside:

There's tons of big fields. We go and play manhunt in 'em, but the old people, I think it's the farmers probably all walk their dogs through and they tell us to clear off. They tell us to 'F' off and 'go away you little *** … 'cos you run along the footpaths and they come running off the fields …' we don't smash up the crops or nothing. We just find tracks and jump in and hide.

(Loki, aged 13, quoted in Weller, 2003, p. 164)

In Faith Tucker and Hugh Matthews' (2001) study of recreational activities in rural Northamptonshire, some girls aged 13–14 described how they also found themselves moved along from their local leisure centre and supermarkets when they weren't swimming or shopping. They admitted that some young people's activities were problematic, and understood that staff and the police wanted to prevent this, but they felt they were often stereotyped as 'troublemakers' because of their age and treated accordingly:

We haven't actually had any trouble with them [supermarket staff], if you're in the cafe and you're having a drink. But if you are wandering around 'cos there is quite a few people that do steal things, and obviously they presume everyone's like that.

(Natalie, aged 13, quoted in Tucker and Matthews, 2001, p. 164)

Figure 3 A private property notice

Another of the girls, Rebecca, felt that illegal and antisocial behaviour by some young people, mostly older teenagers, had a detrimental effect on her own activities. She felt that the police were restricting all access to particular areas based on the activities of some young people at certain times of the day:

> People [older teenagers] come here [the shelter at the edge of the recreation ground] to smoke and drink and to take drugs as well. Everyone knows that they come down here to take drugs ... The police come round here regularly 'cos this is a known place ... where things happen, like break-ins and blowing up cars and things like that ... You do get moved on from here as well if they [adults] see you hanging around here [at a different time of the day when the older group of children do not use the site].
>
> (Rebecca, aged 14, quoted in Tucker and Matthews, 2001, p. 163)

Karen Malone (2002) suggests that a popular strategy for dealing with the 'problem' of young people in public spaces is to restrict their activities to separate, 'youth-specific' spaces. Malone refers to this as a '"not seen and not heard" strategy' (Malone, 2002, p. 164). She describes the development of a skate park in the Australian city of

Frankston. Young skaters were perceived as a nuisance in the city and their activities often damaged the street furniture. The development of a separate skate park appeared to be a 'win-win' strategy, as it enabled the skaters to get on with their activities without upsetting or inconveniencing more 'legitimate' users (and uses) of public space. Despite this, the skate park was not a success. Situated in a marginal area of the city, with poor lighting and providing no shade, drinking water or toilets, the skate park was only used by the keenest skaters. The area was also generally unsafe, not least because it lacked the kind of natural oversight found in normal public spaces. Girls were particularly reluctant to go there. Far from pleasing everyone, the creation of the skate park served to reinforce the position of young people as a problematic group in society, and justified the need to separate them from other members of society. It also completely ignored the fact that young people want to be included in wider civic life rather than excluded from it.

3.2   'Adult-only' or 'child-free'?

Henry Giroux (2001) has commented on the emergence, in the USA, of a political movement known as 'child-free', which has since spread internationally. Organisations like 'No Kidding!', which sets up social events for adults who do not have children, and a range of websites, with names like 'Bratz!' and 'We Kid You Not', support and promote this movement. Those involved explain that it is a reaction against the assumption within society that all adults should be parents. Instead, the 'child-free' want to emphasise that they are not missing out because they have chosen not to have children, as the *childfree.net* website asserts:

Who are we?

We are a group of adults who all share at least one common desire: we do not wish to have children of our own. ... We choose to call ourselves 'childfree' rather than 'childless', because we feel the term 'childless' implies that we're missing something we want – and we aren't. We consider ourselves childfree – free of the loss of personal freedom, money, time and energy that having children requires.

(www.childfree.net)

Of course, many adults who are not parents (by choice or otherwise) would not describe themselves as 'child-free'. It is worth noting that, as an aspect of identity, 'child-free' is still defined by its relation to children; it is a movement defined by being without children. The child-free movement is not only an attempt to show that adults do not have to want to have children in order to be 'normal'; it is also caught up in the construction of all public space as intrinsically adult. Giroux (2001) describes how many of those involved in the movement 'view the presence of young people as an intrusion on adults' private space and rights' and perpetuate 'the growing assumption in the popular imagination that young people are, at best, a social nuisance and, at worst, a danger to social order' (Giroux, 2001, pp. 65, 70). These sentiments are expressed in the growing number of 'child-free' restaurants, holidays and even residential complexes to be found in the minority world.

Activity 3   Child-free communities

Allow about 20 minutes

In 2006, the Australian government held a parliamentary inquiry on the topic of 'Children and Young People and the Built Environment'. The extract below is from a submission to this enquiry by Brendan Gleeson.

Read the extract and make notes in response to the questions listed below it.

The emergent will to brush children aside may reflect in part the cults of individualism and materialism that have flourished during the era of neo-liberal reform. Children necessarily restrain the lure of individualism – they are by nature dependent. They remind us that we are of *Nature*. Their upkeep dilutes the material flow and their care reduces the time for self. Every social prohibition has its geography and thus we will surely witness the surfacing of new islands of *demographic* exclusion, such as Aurora, the child free 'community' proposed for Queensland's Gold Coast region by the developer Craig Gore. Aurora was scuttled in 2003, after raising the ire of the state's Children's Commissioner, but its proposal raised a semaphore warning of the new archipelago of exclusion lying on the horizon of selfishness that we are steadily approaching.

(Gleeson, 2006, p. 2)

- How does Gleeson explain the rise of child-free or adult-only spaces in Australia? Do you agree?
- What do you consider to be the positive and negative aspects of child-free living?

Comment

Gleeson very forcefully argues that this kind of desire for 'demographic exclusion' is rooted in the promotion of individualism and materialism promoted in neoliberal societies. If values are based on the advancement of individual pleasure and economic well-being, then there is little incentive to share with others. These 'others' may be people from different backgrounds or different generations. The development of child-free communities challenges views about community as a meeting of people across the generations. There are communities, such as religious orders of monks or nuns, which are composed only of adults. However, a child-free community is different in that it is naming itself and constructing its identity around the exclusion of a section of society. Here Gleeson parallels Giroux's overtly political and provocative argument that the impetus towards 'child-free' living reflects and exacerbates the subordination of democratic ideals, and of society itself, to 'the ethos of self-interest and self-preservation in the relentless pursuit of private satisfactions and pleasures' (Giroux, 2001, p. 67).

You may or may not agree with the politics underlying these arguments, and you may feel that the argument unfairly makes villains of adults who want to live and socialise in child-free spaces. Most of those who self-identify as 'child-free' are not antipathetic to children in principle. Even if you are a parent yourself (perhaps especially if you are a parent yourself), you may well be able to imagine several advantages to child-free living, and you may sympathise with complaints about toddlers making a fuss and running around in restaurants or teenagers chatting among themselves and texting in the cinema. Many young people will themselves acknowledge that some of their peers' behaviour (and probably some of their own, too) is annoying or otherwise problematic for other people. The management of children and young people's access to space, and of their experience and use of it, is therefore very ambiguous.

Ward 1990 - used as a
play area - used as a part
distraction so adults
can socialise

Summary of Section 3

Regulation and control of children and young people's use of space is implicated in the maintenance of social order.

The perceived vulnerability of children and young people has contributed to an understanding of public space as adult by default.

Children and young people are often perceived as a 'problem' because their activities and purposes conflict with those of adults.

The 'child-free' movement is an example of the explicit exclusion of children from a community.

---

4 Children and young people's spaces and places

The anarchist and architect Colin Ward began the final chapter of his seminal book *The Child in the City* (1990, first published in 1978) with a quotation from George Sternlieb. In it, Sternlieb compares the city to a sandbox or sandpit in which children are quarantined off and 'parked':

> A sandbox is a place where adults park their children in order to converse, play or work with a minimum of interference. The adults, having found a distraction for the children, can get on with the serious things of life. There is some reward for the children in all this. The sandbox is given to them as their own turf. Occasionally, fresh sand or toys are put in this sandbox, along with an implicit admonition that these things are furnished to minimize the level of noise and nuisance. If the children do become noisy and distract their parents, fresh toys may be brought. If the occupants of the sandbox choose up sides and start bashing each other over the head, the adults will come running, smack the juniors more or less indiscriminately, calm things down and then, perhaps in an act of semi-contrition, bring fresh sand and fresh toys, pat the occupants of the sandbox on the head, and disappear once again into their adult involvement and pursuits.

(Quoted in Ward, 1990, p. 176)

For Sternlieb, the sandbox, and the formal playground in which it is situated, is a quarantine for children, masquerading in part as a play space and coming with a whole set of adult-imposed rules for behaviour and proper play. In this way, the sandbox appears to work to ensure that children do not interfere with the real business of city life undertaken by the adults around them. Similarly, Roger Hart argues that the containment of children was a key motive for planners involved in the development of playgrounds in New York in the early twentieth century. However, this motive of containment was not simply concerned with the repression of children: Hart explains that 'tears of children' combined with 'fears for children' in the development of playgrounds (Hart, 2002, p. 138). Fears for children included concern for their physical safety, particularly in the case of young children who would otherwise play on dirty streets which accommodated ever-increasing volumes of vehicular traffic. These physical dangers were matched by social reformers' concern over the moral dangers faced by children on the streets, who may be corrupted and transformed into an uncontrollable force to be feared.

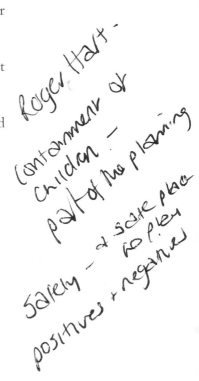

[handwritten margin note: Roger Hart - Containment of children - part of the planning. Safety - a safe place to play. positives + negatives]

Figure 4   A play-park with slides and climbing walls designed as a pirate ship

Playgrounds or play-parks can, therefore, represent adult visions of, and agendas for, childhood (Laris, 2005), but these visions and agendas are riddled with contradiction. As the historian Roy Kozlovsky argues:

on the one hand, modernity has conceptualized play as a biologically-inherited drive that is spontaneous, pleasurable and free. It valorized the subjective experience of play as an attribute of the autonomous, individual self. On the other hand, modern societies began to rationalize and shape children's play from the outside to advance social, educational and political goals. Thus playgrounds are very much about censoring and restricting types of play deemed undesirable and displacing them from places deemed dangerous or corrupting, such as the street.

(Kozlovsky, 2008, p. 171)

These tensions have been present throughout the history of organised and designated play spaces for children. The Playground Association of America, formed in 1907, explicitly focused on preparing citizens of the future by establishing playgrounds in which children could demonstrate athletic success by participating in adult-organised games and dancing. These playgrounds were resolutely *not* to be spaces for free play. Elizabeth Gagen (2004) argues that the social reformers involved in the playground movement were explicitly concerned with training children into being socially useful subjects; the playground was to be synonymous with improving physical exercise and to protect against the corrupting influences of the city. Social reformers viewed this as especially important for immigrant children who might otherwise pose a threat to civil society.

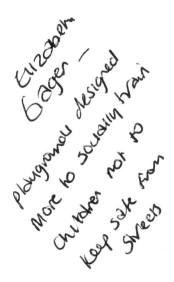

Department of Education, New York City
A Souvenir Postal Card for the Playground Children to Send to Their Friends to Give to Them a Desire for a Playground for Their Own Neighborhood

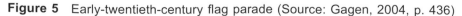

Figure 5 Early-twentieth-century flag parade (Source: Gagen, 2004, p. 436)

Activity 4   Reading B

Allow about 30 minutes

Go to the end of the chapter and read Reading B, which is an extract from Colin Ward's book, *The Child in the City* (1990). As you read, make notes in response to the following questions:

- What does the phrase 'fenced-off child-ghetto' tell you about how Ward felt about playgrounds?
- What does Ward propose instead?

Comment

As an anarchist, Colin Ward did not promote the building of purposely designed play spaces for children. In the reading, he explains that the idea of the adventure playground emerged from observations of children's own play on waste land and derelict areas. However, these play activities became formalised and sanitised in the process. Ward argues that playground design, with its rigid structures and obsession with issues of safety, has taken all the excitement out of the park. He also laments the way that the playground, which he describes as a 'fenced-off child-ghetto', increases the social separation between adults and children. He advocates, rather, that we should strive to create flexible community spaces that can accommodate the needs of both adults and children and, in doing so, bring them closer together.

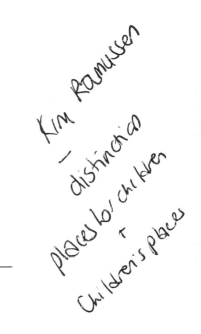

4.1   Informal spaces and places

Kim Rasmussen makes a distinction between 'places for children' and 'children's places', where officially designated areas can be described as 'places for children', while 'children's places' describes those places that children and young people produce for themselves, often by adapting the environment around them:

> One could say that while 'places for children' display adults' ideas about children (toys, fences, etc), 'children's places' make clear that children develop meaningful relationships to other places. This assessment takes place on the basis of what children tell, show and do themselves …
>
> (Rasmussen, 2004, p. 166)

Figure 6 Children playing football in a primary school compound in Kolkata, India

First, we will explore how children and young people are able to appropriate spaces and places for themselves, and how these spaces and places come to be important to them.

Activity 5   The sand-hill

Allow about 20 minutes

In the letter below, the social and political commentator William Cobbett describes a sand-hill where he used to play with his brothers in southern England in the 1820s. Read through the extract and then make notes in response to the questions below.

Odiham Hampshire

Friday 27th September, 1822

We went to this Bourne in order that I might show my son the spot where I received the rudiments of my education. There is a little hop-garden in which I used to work when from eight to ten years old; from which I have scores of times run to follow the hounds, leaving the hoe to do the best that it could to destroy the weeds; but the most interesting thing was a *sand-hill*, which goes from a part of the heath down to the rivulet. As a due mixture of pleasure with toil, I, with two brothers, used occasionally to *desport* ourselves, as the lawyers call it, at this sand-hill. Our diversion was this: we used to go to the top of the hill, which was steeper than the roof of a house; one used to draw his arms out of the sleeves of his smock-frock, and lay himself down with his arms by his sides; and then the others, one at head and the other at feet, sent him rolling down the hill like a barrel or a log of wood. By the time he got to the bottom, his hair, eyes, ears, nose and mouth, were all full of this loose sand; then the others took their turn, and at every roll, there was a monstrous spell of laughter.

(Cobbett, 2010 [1830], p. 11)

- How does this differ from George Sternlieb's account of the sandbox in the section above?
- Can you remember any important 'children's places' from your own childhood?
- Can you find evidence of them in your local area today?

Comment

Sternlieb's account presents the sandbox as a somewhat repressive place in which children are contained and kept busy while their parents or carers get on with more important things. Cobbett's account of the sand-hill is full of joy; it was a place for him and his brothers to play, to roll down and get covered in sand. You may remember all kinds of similar places that were of particular significance to you and your friends or siblings during your childhood.

Author Lesley Gallacher's primary school playground featured all manner of 'children's places'. For example, three trees on the hill at the far end of the sports pitches formed the 'hidden cities', a place where children would go to sit and talk in some privacy away from the rest of the playground. The infants' playground (for children in the lower years of the school) featured a 'squashing corner' (a designated space for 'squashing' your peers by pressing them into the corner). Like many children's places, this squashing corner was often invisible to adult eyes; it looked like any other corner in the playground. Its purpose and meaning may have been lost on the teachers and other school staff. Indeed, Lesley can no longer remember what the point of the squashing corner was, or why she and her peers wanted to squash each other. For this reason, it may be difficult for you to recognise children's places in your local area unless you have children acting as guides.

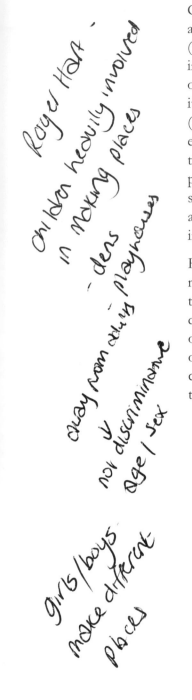

Geographers have been interested in the production of children's spaces and places, and the experience of them, since the 1970s (Valentine, 1996). For example, Roger Hart (1979) conducted an influential two-year study of children's experience of place, based on observing and working with children in a small New England town and its environs. In the study, he meticulously documented how children (aged between 4 and 12 years old) engaged with the physical environment. Hart commented that children of both genders and across the age range were heavily involved in 'making places' (Hart, 1979, p. 205). Often, the structures they constructed – dens, treehouses and such like – were temporary in nature and remained largely invisible to adults. These transitory structures often involved leaps of the imagination rather than actual, physical modification of the landscape.

Hart describes a range of mainly natural materials used by children to make places, including trees, bushes, long grass, cut grass and cut timber, as well as cardboard boxes and other manufactured items. He describes how many children enjoyed building 'houses' and 'forts', either on the ground beneath trees or in the branches of trees. He commented on some of the age and gender differences in the approaches that children took to place making. Girls in the study referred more often to tree houses, and the boys to tree forts:

> Girls make places as frequently as boys, but there [they?] are quite different in structure. Whereas boys concentrate on building structures with walls, and roofs, with little detail in the interior of the places, the girls' emphasis is almost entirely upon interior detail. Also, like younger boys and girls (under eight years), the older girls are much more willing to modify their places in their imagination. These imagined elements may exist in boys' structures also, but they are not consensual like those of the girls', that is to say they do not communicate these imagined elements to each other or to me. The girls often name all of these elements for each other. 'Paradise' is an example of the kind of creative place-naming I occasionally came across. I accidentally stumbled across this place, built by two girls with the help of their out-of-town boy cousin on my last day in this town. One of the girls quickly sketched a plan for me [see Figure 7]. The place names are each

made up from combinations of three children's surnames and first names.

(Hart, 1979, p. 213)

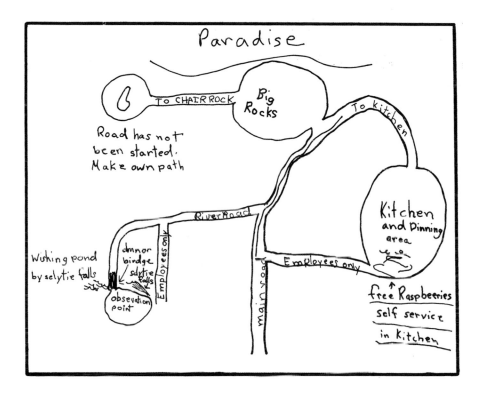

Figure 7 'Paradise' on Plum Hill, drawn by a child aged 9 (Source: Hart, 1979, p. 483)

Research of this kind allows us to discover more about children and young people's experiences of place, but making these spaces and places visible also poses ethical challenges. As in other areas of childhood research, greater understanding of children and young people's worlds can increase our knowledge as adults, but it could also be a form of surveillance used to better regulate those worlds.

4.2   Childhood cities?

A growing number of initiatives seek to subvert the assumption that space is adult by default. They do this by foregrounding children and young people's needs, purposes and interests in the design process. Colin Ward's description of the creation of a 'Childhood City' (Ward, 1990, p. 179) provided a starting point for a range of initiatives, including the 'Child-Friendly Cities' movement (Lynch, 1977; Chawla, 2002; Driskell, 2002).

At several points in this book, we will explore the involvement of children and young people in the design of their locality. In Chapter 3, we will discuss young people's participation in urban design and, in Chapter 4, young children's involvement in the design of learning environments. Here, however, we will examine how young children have been foregrounded in the design of a housing cooperative in northern Italy.

Coriandoline is situated on the outskirts of the small town of Correggio in northern Italy. Here the designs of the houses and landscaping are the result of a long-standing engagement between the architects, 12 nursery and infant schools, and two child psychologists. The development is described in Italian as 'le case amiche dei bambini e delle bambine' which translates as 'friendly houses for girls and boys'. The project began by exploring what the children valued in a house.

This is how I would like my house to be:

Transparent
…so I can look outside if it is sunny or if it's raining

Hard outside
So it will never break.
If a bad man comes along he will hurt himself on it.

Soft inside
…The house is lovelier, it would be soft and warm.

Decorated
I would put precious stones, so that the house is nicer.

Intimate
I would like a secret place to go into and come out of whenever I liked.

Peaceful
…not trafficky.

Playful
A house with stairs and slides.

Big
So that when Emanuel and Mattia come they can stay over. So they can ride around it with their bikes.

Childsize
I would like a bell button with my name on it.

Magic
I want a special wall with ...
So that when I put my hand on it it took me on journeys.

(Malavasi and Pantaleoni, 2008, pp. 8–9)

Figure 8   Coriandoline, a housing development on the outskirts of Correggio in northern Italy

The project also involved the 'invasion' of the public square by numerous child-designed cardboard houses: 'the kids' town occupies the grown-ups' city, and the kids symbolically take over the city with their imagination' (Malavasi and Pantaleoni, 2008, p. 5). These activities informed the design of the real houses in Coriandoline so as to create a community in which children and living with children were placed centre stage:

> We used the 'child's point of view' as a measurement of quality. These are 'real houses' in which families have constructed life projects and have invested their economic resources. ...
>
> Giving importance, legitimacy and interest to the contributions and ideas of children is the most revolutionary aspect of the research. Listening to their needs and taking in their comments: welcoming, playful ... richness, transparency ... These are the words that have

> disappeared from the vocabulary of those who actually make houses.
>
> (Malavasi and Pantaleoni, 2008, 'Manifesto delle esigenze abitative dei bambini [Manifesto of children's living needs]', pp. 23, 33)

Designing environments around the needs and interests of children raises questions about how this may benefit or impede adults who are invariably co-dwellers in these environments. The list of design principles followed in Coriandoline, including transparency and intimacy, may support both children's and adults' sense of place. But designing a whole city along this model may result in some adults feeling marginalised and excluded.

Summary of Section 4

Spaces and places created for children and young people often reflect adult ideas about and agendas for childhood and youth.

Children and young people are able to create spaces for themselves within other landscapes, and to adapt spaces and equipment to their own ends.

Some initiatives have attempted to place children and young people at the heart of the process of designing spaces and places.

---

5 Negotiated spaces

The Coriandoline example from the previous section indicates that privileging the needs and purposes of children and young people can be as problematic as privileging the needs of adults. It may be more useful to consider both adults and children as equally implicated in the production of spaces and places through their interactions and activities. In the remainder of this chapter, we will consider how adults and children interact with one another to produce negotiated space, and how conflicts over space can occur among children and young people just as they can arise between adults and children.

5.1   Adult–child negotiations

Many spaces and places are occupied and used by a range of people of
all ages. Those spaces are usually produced through interactions
between adults and children in the course of their shared activities. One
example where this was explored was Lesley Gallacher's (2005) study of
the sociospatial relations in the toddler room of a Scottish day nursery.
It is, to some degree, possible to think about the nursery as a conflict
between two separate worlds and agendas – that of the adult staff and
that of the children – but this may not be the most useful way to
understand the nursery.

Adult / children
sharing spaces /
places

The toddler room had an 'official' structure and a very definite spatio-
temporal routine. The staff set the room up in a variety of
configurations, and moved the children around throughout the day so as
to facilitate a range of different activities that supported children's
educational and personal care needs. This spatio-temporal routine was
supported and enabled by a set of rules and practices that guided the
smooth running of the nursery day. Alongside this routine of 'official'
activities, the toddler room also had what could be described as a peer
culture 'underlife'. In his study of mental asylums, Erving Goffman
(1968) argued that institutions invariably support a range of 'unofficial'
practices through which inmates are able to get around or even break
the rules. The young children in the toddler room were able to adapt
the use of equipment and spaces in various ways, and to work around
the official system and routine to produce their own peer culture
routines and activities.

However, this is not simply a case of adults versus children. Although
there were times when the children's activities and purposes were not
tolerated, in general the 'official' routine and the children's activities did
not stand in opposition to each other. Instead, the adults and children
usually worked together and negotiated the use of space throughout
their everyday interactions. The children would improvise new games
and adapt activities, and the staff would respond to and take advantage
of these adaptations and activities. For example, one member of staff
responded positively to the children's attempts to turn a table into a
tunnel, and even acted to ensure that the game was not disrupted:

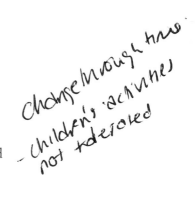

Change through the
- Children's activities
not tolerated

> Nuala was trying to read to some children in storybook corner but
> the children were more interested in crawling under a small red
> table. She decided to abandon the story and organize what the
> children were doing instead, encouraging the children to take turns

and imposing a one-way system. Charlotte noticed the game and joined in. On his turn, Max decided to lie down under the table disrupting the game. Nuala warned him that she would move the table unless he moved so he started crawling again. Abbie and Liam began to push in front of each other but Nuala stopped them explaining, 'It's not nice to push'.

(Gallacher, 2005, p. 260)

As such, we can think of the nursery as a thoroughly negotiated space which is contingent on the emergent practices of both adults and children within it. We can think of the examples in Section 4, of children carving out spaces to play, in the same way.

These kinds of negotiations are not limited to the play activities of younger children. Young people are able to make use of official channels and processes so as to negotiate their own uses of space and to enable their own activities. In Susie Weller's (2003) study of young people on the Isle of Wight, 14-year-old Kat described the conflict there had been between some local teenagers and other local residents over the disused bus shelter in their village. Known as 'the busie', it had become an important place for many local teenagers, but many of the other villagers were concerned about it becoming covered in graffiti. Kat became involved in a campaign to save the bus shelter from demolition, through which the young people obtained a council grant to remodel the shelter in a way that was more acceptable to everyone:

The bus shelter was going to get knocked down because everyone was writing horrible words in it and none of the people round the estate really liked it so we made the decision that we were going to keep it tidy and we were going to paint it so all the graffiti and so the council gave us money to buy the spray paint.

(Quoted in Weller, 2003, p. 163)

5.2   Negotiations among children and young people

In the same way that they can come into conflict with adults, children and young people can also come into conflict with each other over the use of particular spaces and places. Barry Percy-Smith and Hugh Matthews argue that many children and young people experience their local environments through a 'hidden geography of fear' (Percy-Smith and Matthews, 2001, p. 50) based on all manner of intergroup and interpersonal conflicts. These 'tyrannical geographies' can sometimes be described in terms of bullying. For example, a 13-year-old boy from the East Midlands described how a group of local friends barged in and took over his games in a particular area:

> At the top of Craven Street there's Adam and Luke … and there's like their friends, there's Mickey and that [other] boy … Jamie that's it, they're all round there, and if you go there and you've got a football … , they'll just come round and say 'let me kick the ball around', and if you say no you're beaten up. You get no choice. And like once when I was playing pogs they walked up … and nicked my pogs.

> (Quoted in Percy-Smith and Matthews, 2001, p. 55)

In another study of girls and young women in Northamptonshire, Faith Tucker and Hugh Matthews (2001) found that conflicts over the social ownership of 'micro-spaces' (such as bus shelters, climbing frames and steps) often occurred between children of different ages. Younger children were often excluded from play spaces by the presence of older children:

> I don't like walking past the bus shelter … All the people [boys and girls aged 14–16] shout at you.

> (Helen, aged 11, quoted in Tucker and Matthews, p. 165)

> Me and my friend used to have a den [in the park], but we don't use it anymore. We went back one day and [there were] … all these smashed beer bottles and everything, so we just left it because they'd ruined it. They [a group of older teenagers] were going to come in there again.

> (Eleanor, aged 11, quoted in Tucker and Matthews, 2001, p. 165)

My brother and my mum went down to the park and my brother wanted to have a go on the swing, but there were some teenagers our age down there, spinning it around so it was really high up and my brother couldn't even get on it ... which was really bad.

(Joy, aged 13, quoted in Tucker and Matthews, 2001, p. 166)

Conflicts over social places

Conflicts over particular spaces and places also occur between girls and boys. This was particularly the case for the younger girls (aged 10–13) in Tucker and Matthews' study, who preferred to socialise in single-sex groups. Indeed, two of the girls who socialised in mixed-sex groups described as 'tarty' and 'rough', Sophie (aged 13) and Chloe (aged 11), told how they didn't really have any spaces of their own, unlike the boys:

Sophie: The girls don't really have a hang out place like the boys do [the boys have a tree house]. They just go to each other's houses ... You never see them out unless they are walking to each other's houses.

Chloe: ['Boy places' are] the dens across the road.

Interviewer: Do the boys not allow girls to go there, or do the girls choose not to go there?

Chloe: Sometimes, when they're not there, we go in. And when they're there we don't go in because the boys will just fight with us and tell us to get out.

Interviewer: Are there any places where just girls hang out?

Chloe: No. Just on the path, they like sitting on the path.

(Tucker and Matthews, 2001, p. 167)

Skelton – teenage girls – wrong age & gender

This parallels Tracey Skelton's argument that teenage girls often found themselves in the 'uncomfortable position of being the "wrong" age, being the "wrong" gender and being in the "wrong" place' on the streets of South Wales (Skelton, 2000, p. 80).

Activity 6   Gang territories

Allow about 30 minutes

Figure 9 shows two maps of the same area of Glasgow. The maps were drawn by two 11-year-old boys who lived in the area. The boys were in the same class at school and shared very similar interests.

Figure 9   Two maps of the same area of Glasgow, made by two 11-year-olds (Source: Kintrea et al., 2008, p. 37)

- What do you notice about the two maps?
- Consider the sketch of your neighbourhood which you wrote earlier, in Activity 1. What differences do you think young people of the same age might point out in your area?

Comment

The two maps are very similar in that they portray many of the same features of the boys' local area. Both boys have indicated territories on the map that would otherwise be invisible to anyone not involved in the local gang cultures. The boys were members of rival gangs in the area, and this gang affiliation restricted where they could safely go within their local area. The areas that each boy designated as 'safe' and 'don't go' are almost exact opposites, such that the maps almost mirror each other. Kintrea and colleagues explain how the boys lived their lives within these mirrored territories: 'they existed very much on different sides of the same road, rarely crossing over to the other side' (Kintrea et al., 2008, p. 36). The boys feared violence from members of rival gangs if they strayed into the wrong territory, and preferred to remain within their own gang's territory where they could rely on their fellow gang members for protection. This fear of leaving their own territory was so acute for some Glaswegian gang members that they would refuse to take part in leisure activities in other areas, even when transport was provided to them. The irony is that, in joining a gang for safety reasons (sometimes because gang membership offers them protection from the gang operating where they live), young people are exposing themselves to far more violence than they would otherwise have encountered.

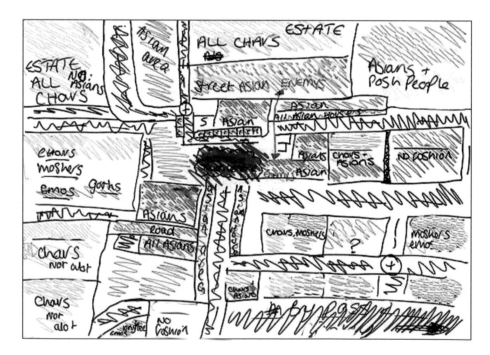

Figure 10 Territorial restrictions in Bradford

Kintrea and colleagues studied gang territoriality in six British case study locations: Bradford, Bristol, Glasgow, Peterborough, Sunderland and Tower Hamlets. They found that gang activities were most pronounced in the deprived areas of cities and were particularly acute in Glasgow, a city dominated by multiple deprivation which means that most areas have a gang presence. Gang affiliation and territoriality in the English cities were often focused around tensions between ethnic groups (Figure 10 shows a map of gang territories drawn by a 15-year-old white young woman in Bradford). This was not the case in Glasgow, and interviewees were keen to stress that gang activities there were no longer centred around religion and sectarianism.

The core age for gang membership in the UK is between 13 and 17 years of age, although some younger children are involved (particularly in Glasgow). Most young people tend to move on from gangs after 17, and to focus instead on jobs or long-term relationships. In the study, gang activities in most cities were not affiliated with organised crime, but gang membership was more likely to be prolonged into early adulthood in Bristol and Tower Hamlets, where gangs were more strongly linked to criminal activities.

The Kintrea et al. study showed that involvement with gangs had a detrimental effect on young people's movement around all six cities. Young people who are heavily involved with gangs have a more limited range of mobility and are able to participate in fewer leisure activities than those who do not become involved with gangs. This can have long-term effects on their aspirations and opportunities, as one of Kintrea and colleagues' interviewees explained:

> If your horizons are limited to three streets, what is the point of you working really hard at school? What is the point of passing subjects that will allow you to go to college or university if you cannot travel beyond these streets? What's the point of dreaming about being an artist, a doctor, etc., if you cannot get on a bus to get out of the area in which you live?
>
> (Quoted in Kintrea et al., 2008, p. 35)

In this way, the territorial behaviour associated with gang membership often serves to further disadvantage young people. Although gender does not prevent young people from becoming involved with gangs, girls and young women often find that they are less restricted by gang territoriality than boys and young men.

Territorial negotiations between different groups of children and young people are not always characterised by violent activities, and the boundaries of their 'territories' are not always so rigorously policed.

[Handwritten marginal note: Kintrea study / gang culture / restricting movement.]

Groups can come into conflict in much less overtly 'tyrannical' ways. In addition to indicating the territories of Asian gangs in Bradford, Figure 10 also shows areas that are occupied by a range of subcultural groups, including 'emos', 'moshers', 'goths' and 'chavs'. There are also a couple of areas marked 'no fashion'. Similarly, in Susie Weller's study of young people on the Isle of Wight, 13-year-old Bob noted the rivalries between different groups:

Bob: Townies just sit on the bins outside McDonald's, and wear Adidas and Nike and stuff like that all the time.

[Weller]: Is there quite a lot of rivalry between the skaters and the townies?

Bob: Yeah.

[Weller]: Are there any other groups there?

Bob: There's the BMXers and the Goths.

[Weller]: So there's lots of rivalry between all those groups?

Bob: No. Umm ... the skaters get on with the Goths and the BMXers, so it's just there's Townie Goths that like walk round pretending ... going 'Oh yer I'm a Goth' but they're wearing Adidas and all that ... and there's townies that wear Adidas on skateboards, which gets on my nerves and there's townie BMXers as well. Townies just act like they're like us and that's why they get on my nerves.

(Weller, 2003, p. 168)

These different groups do not seek to defend a clearly delineated territory through violent means; rather, they choose to associate with their own subcultural grouping in different places. These groupings may not fear each other at all. It may simply be that they do not want to occupy the same place. Young people may choose to avoid particular areas because they do not want to be associated with the people who hang out there, or because they do not want to be associated with their activities. For example, 13-year-old Loki told Weller that he avoided certain areas of the school playground that were used by smokers:

Loki: Yeah we've got our own little places. We … we hang around the back of the school. We hang around on the grass. We go down to the other field. We play football and stuff like that. We just round the back … and then you've got the smokers' hedge down the bottom of the field. We don't go down there … everybody just smokes. Um … and then you've got the tree they smoke behind there. We don't go there.

Weller: Is that the farthest bit from the school?

Loki: Yeah the bit down by the hedge … yeah they go down there and there's a tree at the front. They go behind there and they used to throw stuff at us when we used to play near there.

(Weller, 2003, p. 161)

Children and young people's experiences of a neighbourhood may involve complex negotiations with adults and other groups of other young people. These relationships among groups or gangs may be violent, involving what Percy-Smith and Matthews (2001) refer to as 'hidden geographies of fear'. Accounts by young people discussed in this section highlight some of the sharp contrasts between how the same neighbourhood can be experienced.

Summary of Section 5

Spaces are very often contingent outcomes of negotiations and interactions between adults and children.

Conflicts over space occur among children and young people as well as between adults and children.

---

6 Conclusion

This chapter has explored the importance of spatial contexts in the lives of children and young people. Children and young people are often particularly noticeable in relation to their spatial contexts because their place making practices and activities conflict with those of the adults around them. This place making can occur through practices that are seen as 'play', 'work' or 'learning'. This can lead to conflicts between adults and children, as well as among children themselves. In this way, spaces and places can be usefully thought of as carefully negotiated outcomes of interactions between adults, children and their material environments. These environments are always contingent on the everyday activities and practices of those who use them and the wider networks to which children and adults belong.

References

Ambert, A-M. (1994) 'An international perspective on parenting: social change and social constructs', *Journal of Marriage and the Family*, vol. 56, pp. 529–43.

Chawla, L. (ed) (2002) *Growing Up in an Urbanising World*, Paris, UNESCO/London, Earthscan.

childfree.net, 'Who are we?', *www.childfree.net* (Accessed 22 November 2012).

Cobbett, W. (2010 [1830]) *Rural Rides* (ed I. Dyck), London, The Folio Society.

Douglas, M. (1999) *Implicit Meanings: Selected Essays in Anthropology* (2nd edn), London, Routledge.

Driskell, D. (2002) *Creating Better Cities with Children and Youth: A Manual for Participation*, Paris, UNESCO/London, Earthscan.

Dyson, J. (2008) 'Harvesting identities: youth, work, and gender in the Indian Himalayas', *Annals of the Association of American Geographers*, vol. 98, no. 1, pp. 160–79.

Gagen, E. (2004) 'Making America flesh: physicality and nationhood in early twentieth-century physical education reform', *Cultural Geographies*, vol. 11, no. 4, pp. 417–42.

Gallacher, L. A. (2005) '"The terrible twos": gaining control in the nursery?', *Children's Geographies*, vol. 3, no. 2, pp. 243–64.

Giroux, H. A. (2001) 'Mis/education and zero tolerance: disposable youth and the politics of domestic militarization', *Boundary 2*, vol. 28, no. 3, pp. 61–94.

Gleeson, B. (2006) 'Australia's toxic cities: modernity's paradox', a submission to the New South Wales Parliamentary Inquiry into Children, Young People and the Built Environment, available from

http://www.parliament.nsw.gov.au/Prod/parlment/committee.nsf/0/
5B225478C667A832CA25719200113229 (Accessed 24 May 2012).

Goffman, E. (1968) *Asylums: Essays on the Social Situation of Mental Patients and Other Inmates*, Harmondsworth, Penguin.

Hart, R. (1979) *Children's Experience of Place*, New York, Irvington.

Hart, R. (2002) 'Containing children: some lessons on planning for play from New York City', *Environment & Urbanization*, vol. 14, no. 2, pp. 135–48.

Jamieson, L. and Toynbee, C. (1989) 'Shifting patterns of parental authority, 1900–1980', in Corr, H. and Jamicson, L. (eds) *The Politics of Everyday Life*, London, Macmillan.

Jenks, C. (2005) *Childhood* (2nd edn), London, Routledge.

Kintrea, K., Bannister, J., Pickering, J., Reid, M. and Suzuki, N. (2008) *Young People and Territoriality in British Cities*, York, Joseph Rowntree Foundation, available from http://www.jrf.org.uk/publications/young-people-and-territoriality-british-cities (Accessed 24 May 2012).

Kozlovsky, R. (2008) 'Adventure playgrounds and postwar reconstruction', in Gutman, M. and de Coninck-Smith, N. (eds) *Designing Modern Childhoods: History, Space, and the Material Culture of Children*, New Brunswick, NJ, Rutgers University Press.

Laris, M. (2005) 'Designing for play', in Dudek, M. (ed) *Children's Spaces*, London, Architectural Press.

Lynch, K. (1977) *Growing Up in Cities: Studies of the Spatial Environment of Adolescence in Cracow, Melbourne, Mexico City, Salta, Toluca, and Warsaw*, Cambridge, MA, MIT Press.

Malavasi, L. and Pantaleoni, L. (2008) *Coriandoline: le case amiche dei bambini e delle bambine* [Friendly houses for girls and boys], S. Paolo, Andria.

Malone, K. (2002) 'Street life: youth, culture and competing uses of public space', *Environment & Urbanization*, vol. 14, no. 2, pp. 157–68.

Massey, D. (1993) 'Power-geometry and a progressive sense of place', in Bird, J. (ed) *Mapping the Futures: Local Cultures, Global Change*, London, Routledge.

Massey, D. (2005) *For Space*, London, Sage.

Percy-Smith, B. and Matthews, H. (2001) 'Tyrannical spaces: young people, bullying and urban neighbourhoods', *Local Environment: The International Journal of Justice and Sustainability*, vol. 6, no. 1, pp. 49–63.

Rasmussen, K. (2004) 'Places for children – children's places', *Childhood*, vol. 11, no. 2, pp. 155–73.

Sibley, D. (1995) *Geographies of Exclusion: Society and Difference in the West*, London, Routledge.

Skelton, T. (2000) '"Nothing to do, nowhere to go?": teenage girls and "public" space in the Rhondda Valleys, South Wales', in Holloway, S. L. and Valentine, G. (eds) *Children's Geographies: Playing, Living, Learning*, London, Routledge.

Soja, E. W. (1980) 'The socio-spatial dialectic', *Annals of the Association of American Geographers*, vol. 70, no. 2, pp. 207–25.

Tuan, Y-F. (1977) *Space and Place: The Perspective of Experience*, Minneapolis, MN, University of Minnesota Press.

Tucker, F. and Matthews, H. (2001) '"They don't like girls hanging around there": conflicts over recreational space in rural Northamptonshire', *Area*, vol. 33, no. 2, pp. 161–8.

Valentine, G. (1996) 'Children should be seen and not heard: the production and transgression of adult's public space', *Urban Geography*, vol. 17, no. 3, pp. 205–20.

Ward, C. (1990) *The Child in the City* (2nd edn), London, Bedford Square Press.

Weller, S. (2003) '"Teach us something useful": contested spaces of teenagers' citizenship', *Space and Polity*, vol. 7, no. 2, pp. 153–71.

Reading A
Contested productions of public space

Gill Valentine

Source: 'Children should be seen and not heard: the production and transgression of adults' public space', 1996, *Urban Geography*, vol. 17, no. 3, pp. 213–16.

Spaces are never, however, produced in a singular or uniform way. Rather the identities of spaces, like the identities of individuals, are performances that are 'frequently riven with tensions and conflicts' (Massey, 1991, p. 276). Although adults produce public space as an environment that young children are too incompetent or too vulnerable to negotiate alone, their spatial hegemony is more openly contested by teenagers struggling to assert their independence.

Children and teenagers have little privacy relative to adults. At home or school they are subject to the gaze of teachers, siblings, and relatives (Wolfe, 1978; Parke and Sawkin, 1979), who often try to channel them into organized activities that conflict with youngsters' own agendas (Qvortrup, 1994). The space of the street, particularly after dark, when many adults have retreated to the sanctuary of the home, therefore is often the only autonomous space that many teenagers are able to carve out for themselves (Corrigan, 1979). In this sense, young people often paradoxically experience the home as a public space and the street as a private space. This paradox further justifies the growing unease many academics are expressing about the use of the term 'public' to describe everyday spaces such as the street, the suburb, and the mall, and indeed about the validity of the public–private dichotomy.

Hanging around on street corners or in parks, underage drinking, petty vandalism, and larking about and other forms of nonadherence to order on the street become (deliberately and unconsciously) a form of resistance to adult power. This strategy of resistance is read as a threat to the personal safety of other children and the elderly and as a threat to the peace and order of the street (Valentine, [1996]).

> I've seen a um, standing, with cans of lager outside the shop. Now I'm not saying that we didn't sort of buy a bottle of Strongbow cider or something but we wouldn't ever do it blatantly in front of adults like that, outside a shop. … They're a lot less frightened of authority than we were, we'd never have done certain things that

they do, I'm sure of that. … I tend to keep away from them because I find them threatening myself when they're in a group and like I say they don't have much respect for authority or older people (Mother, nonmetropolitan town, Cheshire).

As Cahill has argued, 'the very presence of groups of preadolescents or adolescents in a public place is apparently considered a potential threat to public order' (Cahill, 1990, p. 398). He has noted that 'while adults treat younger children in public places as innocent, endearing yet sometimes exasperating incompetents, they treat older children as unengaging and frightfully undisciplined rogues. Among other things, the very violations of public etiquette that adults often find amusing when committed by younger children are treated as dangerous moral failings when the transgressor is a few years older' (Cahill, 1990, p. 399). Although adults are supposed to accompany young children in public space to keep them safe, they also are expected to be on hand when teenagers are on the street in order 'to protect public order from the dangers of their charges' amoral ways' (Cahill, 1990, p. 395). Cahill points out that in public places, adults are quick to step in with a frown or a comment to point up the perceived inadequacies of those whose youngsters are considered 'out of control'.

Teenagers, unaccompanied by adults, are considered a polluting presence on the street (Baumgartner, 1988). They are subject to adult regulatory regimes, including suspicious glances on the street, having their movements curtailed by spatial and temporal curfews, and being constantly pushed from one public space to another by the police in response to requests from residents and shop keepers to 'get rid of them'. As one officer explained:

> I worked there for four years in a police car. … Your busy shift would be the afternoon shift till late in the evening. And you would on a busy day perhaps get 20 plus incidents. And maybe 7 or maybe more dealing with what we call Youth Causing Annoyance. And it would sometimes be young people gathering together and it might be an old lady disturbed by the noise they're making. And she makes a phone call can you come down and move them on. We go down and do that but when we've gone they come back again. Or maybe its running across gardens and setting hedges on fire, general vandalism. I would think if we

didn't have that problem our job would be a lot easier. Its
incessant. It goes on and on (Greater Manchester Police Officer).

Public space therefore is not produced as an open space, a space where
teenagers are freely able to participate in street life or to define their
own ways of interacting and using space, but is a highly regulated – or
closed – space where young people are expected to show deference to
adults and adults' definitions of appropriate behavior, levels of noise,
and so on – to use the traditional saying, 'children should be seen and
not heard.' This process of regulating the production of public space to
exclude teenagers, who may perform their identities in a more anarchic
way than adults and therefore produce a more chaotic, noisy, space, is
being facilitated by various processes of surveillance that are
contributing toward 'privatizing' formerly publicly accessible spaces
(Stenning and Shearing, 1980; Davis, 1990; Johnston, 1992). These
include, for example, the growth of private security services and closed
circuit television that allow groups labelled as 'deviant', such as gangs of
teenagers, to be tracked, targeted, and excluded from everyday spaces
more easily (Davis, 1990; Fyfe and Bannister, 1995).

Parenting, like childhood, is a cultural invention, an ideology that is
(re)constructed and (re)produced (Valentine, [1997]). Although parenting
has a long and complex history (see, for example, Ambert, 1994) in
which different sociohistoric contexts have produced different standards
for the relationship between parents and their offspring, set down
formally in law but also established by popular 'norms' (Jamieson and
Toynbee, 1989), adults traditionally have claimed a 'natural' authority
legitimized by their age and size and have maintained a hierarchical
social distance from children. Contemporary social scientists, however,
now are arguing that 'the configuration of Western adolescence has
changed (Modell and Goodman, 1990) in directions that may increase
parental difficulties and/or lead to a restructuring of parenting'
(Ambert, 1994, p. 536). There is an extensive body of sociological
research that suggests that in contemporary Western societies we are
witnessing a decay in childhood as a separate category and that the
distinction between children and adults is becoming increasingly blurred
(Seabrook, 1987). For example, Ambert's research led her to conclude
that 'it is probably true to say that many contemporary parents are
closer to their children and treat them in a less authoritarian way than
their own parents did. Indeed, there is a good deal of evidence
supporting the claim that parents have become more child-centred. It

appears that many of today's parents have given up being distant and dignified, voluntarily relinquishing the trappings of traditional authority, which has become increasingly difficult to sustain'.

The extent to which parents have moved away from 'traditional authority', as Jamieson and Toynbee claim, is exemplified by changed attitudes to 'cheek'. They have argued that 'whereas any kind of "talking back" or questioning of parental authority was considered a heinous crime in former times, parents nowadays appear to invite "discussion", viewing the talking-over of any problems as part of caring and sharing in family life' (Jamieson and Toynbee, 1989, p. 97). On the basis of their research, they claim (1989, p. 86) that 'parents in contemporary Western industrialised societies are less able or willing to control their children's behaviour than those of previous generations'; Ambert is more forthright, stating that 'daily life offers evidence to the effect that adolescents have become less tolerant of parental supervision' (Ambert, 1994, p. 536).

Parallel to this (re)negotiation of parent–child relations (and hence regulatory regimes within the household), the state has adopted a more liberal approach to defining appropriate ways in which young people can be disciplined, largely as a result of pressure from the children's rights lobby, as these parents and police officers describe:

> They don't discipline them anymore. You know, they're not allowed to touch them any more, so they can get away with a lot more. There's no corporal punishment and I think that's wrong, that is wrong. They're making their own decisions in life, that's what it is – the parents are not making the decisions for children. We were brought up to respect the elders – honestly, I mean I sound old fashioned but that is the way we were brought up at school. Like now they just do what they want to do and like no-one can change what they do (Father, nonmetropolitan area, Greater Manchester).

> I think it's getting to the stage where you can't control children. You know you daren't smack 'em, you daren't reprimand them in front of somebody else, otherwise they've only got to utter a word in school and you've got the Social Services knocking on the door. So I think children are allowed to get away with more because we're so frightened of Social Services. So I think that's why children are like they are, because the schools can't give 'em the cane anymore; you daren't smack 'em anymore, so they know that

they're going to be able to get away with it, so they just do it because they know there's nothing you can do to stop it (Single mother, metropolitan area, Greater Manchester).

I know if I ever got into trouble, I mean you hear it in the papers now a copper's clipped a lad's ear and he's in court. I know when I were a lad, if a copper clipped my ear and I'd told me mother she'd have given me another one you know, it's all sort of changed now (Father, rural area, Derbyshire).

I just think there's a whole different, you know, they're a lot less frightened of authority than we were, we'd have never done certain things that they do now I'm sure of that. ... I don't think that they do have much respect for authority or older people now at all. ... But like I say when I've gone down to the off licence and they're all hanging around I find it really intimidating and to be, to feel like that about kids really, it's not nice to think that, not nice (Mother, nonmetropolitan area, Cheshire).

I've been in the Police 12 years and I've certainly found a difference in their [teenagers'] attitude to the police and to people. I mean I can I know it sounds a bit corny or whatever but I remember when I was a lad I would never dream of shouting at some person walking down the street. But now they don't bother and that they do all sorts (Police Officer, Cheshire).

It is a liberalization charged with leaving adults shorn of the one sanction that they once had for the exercise of absolute power over children (particularly teenagers) in public space – violence – without replacing it with other regulatory regimes underwritten with the same 'authority' or regulatory power. Adults and police, echoing the cries of previous generations (Valentine, [1996]), claim that respect has been eroded and asymmetrical deference across the generations has gone, resulting in a breakdown in the subtle regulatory processes by which adults maintain their authority in public space. As the quotations above demonstrate, many feel disempowered and advocate corporal punishment and more aggressive policing, including curfews, to return the street to adult control. This backlash was played out on an international stage in 1994 when a U.S. teenager, Michael Fay, was sentenced to a flogging in Singapore for vandalism. Rather than calling for clemency, as usually happens in cases where a national is sentenced by a foreign judiciary, a large section of the U.S. and the British popular media, and some politicians, proclaimed that he was getting no more than he deserved and advocated the (re)introduction of similar sanctions for comparable offenses committed by teenagers in the United States and United Kingdom. The ensuing opinion polls and talk shows suggested that these pundits were in step with popular feeling.

In advocating such fierce controls of teenagers, the media and politicians, and the police and parents interviewed in this project, expose the underlying adult assumption that public space is not a space shared on an equal footing by all generations, but rather is a space that has been repetitively produced within a regulatory framework as an adult space to such an extent that it is assumed to be 'naturally' or is taken for granted as the realm of grown-ups. The hostility and aggressiveness of adults towards young people's exertion of difference neatly articulates adult insecurities about their inability to maintain this regulatory regime.

References

Ambert, A-M. (1994) 'An international perspective on parenting: social change and social constructs', *Journal of Marriage and the Family*, vol. 56, pp. 529–43.

Baumgartner, M. P. (1988) *The Moral Order of the Suburb*, New York, Oxford University Press.

Cahill, S. (1990) 'Childhood and public life: reaffirming biographical divisions', *Social Problems*, vol. 37, pp. 390–402.

Corrigan, P. (1979) *Schooling the Smash Street Kids*, Basingstoke, Macmillan.

Davis, M. (1990) *City of Quartz*, London, Vintage.

Fyfe, N. and Bannister, J. (1995) 'The eyes of the street: surveillance, citizenship and the city', paper presented at the Association of American Geographers Annual Conference, Chicago.

Jamieson, L. and Toynbee, C. (1989) 'Shifting patterns of parental authority, 1900–1980', in Corr, H. and Jamieson, L. (eds) *The Politics of Everyday Life*, London, Macmillan.

Johnston, L. (1992) *The Rebirth of Private Policing*, London, Routledge.

Massey, D. (1991) 'The political place of locality studies', *Environment and Planning A*, vol. 23, pp. 267–81.

Modell, J. and Goodman, M. (1990) 'Historical perspectives', in *At the Threshold: The Developing Adolescent*, Cambridge, MA, Harvard University Press.

Parke, R. D. and Sawkin, D. B. (1979) 'Children's privacy in the home', *Environment and Behaviour*, vol. 11, pp. 87–104.

Qvortrup, J. (1994) 'Childhood matters: an introduction', in Qvortrup, J., Bardy, M., Sigritta, G. and Wintersberger, H. (eds) *Childhood Matters: Social Theory, Practice and Politics*, Aldershot, Avebury.

Seabrook, J. (1987) 'The decay of childhood', *New Statesman*, 10 July, pp. 14–15.

Stenning, P. and Shearing, C. (1980) 'The quiet revolution: the nature, development and general legal implications of private security in Canada', *Criminal Law Quarterly*, vol. 22, pp. 220–48.

Valentine, G. (1996) 'Angels and devils: moral landscapes of childhood', *Environment and Planning D: Society and Space*, vol. 14, no. 5, pp. 581–99.

Valentine, G. (1997) '"My son's a bit dizzy." "My wife's a bit soft": gender, children and cultures of parenting', *Gender, Place and Culture: A Journal of Feminist Geography*, vol. 4, no. 1, pp. 37–62.

Wolfe, M. (1978) 'Childhood and privacy', in *Children and the Environment*, New York, Plenum Press.

Reading B
Adapting the imposed environment

Colin Ward

Source: *The Child in the City* (2nd edn), 1990, London, Bedford Square Press, pp. 72–4.

The city parks, which are among the best monuments and legacies of our later nineteenth century municipalities – and valuable, useful, often beautiful though they are – have been far too much influenced by the standpoint natural to the prosperous city fathers who purchased them, and who took them over, like the mansion house parks they often were, each with its ring fence, jealously keeping it apart from the vulgar world. Their layout has as yet too much continued the tradition of the mansion-house drives, to which the people are admitted, on holidays, and by courtesy; and where the little girls may sit on the grass. But the boys? They are at most granted a cricket-pitch, or lent a space between football goals, but otherwise are jealously watched, as potential savages, who on the least symptom of their natural activities of wigwam building, cave-digging, stream-damming, and so on – must instantly be chivvied away, and are lucky if not handed over to the police.

Now, if the writer has learned anything from a life largely occupied with nature-study and education, it is that these two need to be brought together, and this through nature activities. But ... we have been stamping out the very germs of these natural boyish instincts of vital self-education, however clumsy and awkward, or even mischievous and destructive when merely restrained, as they commonly have been, and still too much are. It is primarily for lack of this touch of first-hand rustic experience that we have forced young energy into hooliganism; or even worse, depressed it below that level.

(Patrick Geddes)

One thing that observation of the behaviour of children makes clear though it has only recently entered the world of reports and textbooks, and has yet to affect environmental policies, is that children *will* play everywhere and with anything. The provision that is made for their needs operates on one plane, but children operate on another. They will play wherever they happen to be, for as Arvid Bengtsson says, 'play is a constant happening, a constant act of creation in the mind or in practice'. A city that is really concerned with the needs of its young will make the whole environment accessible to them, because, whether invited or not, they are going to use the whole environment.

The concept of the adventure playground grew out of observation of what children actually did on patches of waste land and on derelict areas and bomb sites. Joe Benjamin, a tireless pioneer in this field, laments that even the adventure playground concept has hardened into a kind of ideology in which 'the swings and slides of the engineer have been replaced by those of the scrap merchant: the tubular steel climbing frame of the equipment manufacturer by the old telegraph pole or railway sleeper; the chain by the rope, the wood swing seat by an old tyre'. Similarly, Lady Marjorie Allen complained that American playgrounds were designed for insurance companies, and Paul Friedburg remarks that 'we have taken the romance out of our parks because of our mania about maintenance'.

Parks and playground designers who usurp the creative capabilities of the very children who are intended to use their work by building play sculptures instead of providing the materials for children to make their own, or who have earnest conferences about the appropriate kind of fencing to use, should pause and think about the implications of Joe Benjamin's remark that 'ideally there should be no fence; but when we reach that happy state we will have no need for adventure playgrounds.' For the fenced-off child-ghetto sharpens the division between the worlds of adults and children, while Benjamin's whole case is that we should share the same world. 'No matter how *we* might consider play potential in our present and future designs, children will continue to interpret this in their own way. The point is that the streets, the local service station, the housing estate stairway, indeed anything our urban community offers, is part of the natural habitat of the child. Our problem is not to design streets, housing, a petrol station or shops that can lend themselves to play, but to educate society to accept children on a participating basis.' This explains why it is possible for Dennis Woods of North Carolina State University to deliver a paper with the title 'Free the Children! Down with Playgrounds!'

Hermann Mattern of Berlin underlines his point: 'One should be able to play everywhere, easily, loosely, and not forced into "playground" or "park". The failure of an urban environment can be measured in direct proportion to the number of "playgrounds".' Of course such an approach could easily be seized upon as justification for *not* adapting the city parks to the needs of contemporary citizens, or for *not* creating pocket parks in vacant city sites, and for not redressing the glaring imbalance in the areas of public open space available to the inhabitants of rich and poor districts in the city. But it underlines the fact that we would have a clearer idea of the way the environment could be adapted for use by children if we looked at the way children actually use it.

If you ask adults about their happiest or most vivid recollections of city childhood they will seldom talk about the park or playground, but they will recall the vacant lot, the secret places behind the billboards or hoardings. They will describe the delights of sand in the city, not so much in the sandbox in the playground but the transient pile of sand dumped by builders in the street. In the Parc Monceau in Paris piles of sand are dropped in the avenues by the authorities, apparently expressly for the needs of children and are subsequently shovelled away for use elsewhere.

Chapter 2

Home and family

Alison Clark and Mary Jane Kehily

Contents

In this chapter, you will:

- consider the way in which children's experiences are shaped by the context of family and home
- develop an understanding of the family as a fluid and flexible concept which is differently lived and which differs in form across cultures and across time
- explore family practices and the materiality of the home as a way of 'doing' family
- demonstrate that children take an active role in family and kinship practices, whether living together or apart.

1 Introduction

In this chapter, we consider childhood from the perspective of family and home. We will discuss what makes a family, the ways in which families differ and the place of children within families. Within the context of differing family forms, the chapter also explores the concept of home, what constitutes a home and the experiences of children within the home. Children's earliest memories are rooted in family and home. Sociologists locate the family as a primary site of socialisation for children – the place where children first learn the cultural norms, values and expectations of the society in which they live. In the chapter, we will look at the twin concepts of family and home as locations that give shape to children's experience; in doing so, we will generate meanings about childhood and parenting. Drawing on sociological, cultural studies and geographical ideas, the chapter examines family and home as spatially bound concepts that become sites for the enactment of relationships and practices that play a part in bringing the family into being. We will also consider the materiality of home as a site where relationships, everyday social practices and objects may be imbued with significance. In considering what a family is and how it works, we suggest that family and home can be seen as lived ideas that become meaningful through the shared practices of the people who inhabit them. Our main interest is in the relationship of family and home to childhood and its implications for children.

1.1 Who is family?

Ideas about family and home are, of course, emotive and may generate highly charged feelings. Family and home link people to the past and to the future, and can be filled with idealised versions of what has been lost or what could be. They may be strongly linked to personal memories about one's own family history and to emotional investments in the future. It is extremely hard to remain detached about families; personal experience seems to get in the way. Discussions surrounding family life may be pleasurable or distressing, bringing up happy or painful memories and sometimes unresolved issues. We gesture towards the expansive emotional landscape of family life, but do not offer right answers or models of how the ideal family should be. This chapter does not attempt to look at family policy or the psychological impacts of issues such as divorce on children; rather, it examines the fluidity of family structures, the meanings attached to home and the diversity within contemporary communities. In doing this, it aims to provide an analytical framework for understanding the emotive responses that discussions about the family inevitably raise. While acknowledging how sensitive discussions of family can be, the chapter seeks to examine the assumptions that lie behind beliefs about what is a family, what is a home and what connects children to parents. Family is central to understanding childhood. Beliefs about childhood are strongly connected to expectations of family, and children's experiences are shaped by family.

Activity 1 Who is my family?

Allow about 10 minutes

The quotes below are from children interviewed by members of the module team (the authors of this chapter). We asked them who they thought their family were, and why. Read through the quotes and come up with a list of things that these children see as important in their families.

> **Sophie** is 12 and lives in Oakland, California. She is the child of divorced lesbian parents.
>
> > The people in my family are, I've two Mums and I don't have any Dads ... I call them Mummy and Mumma. And Mummy is ... my biological Mum and she kinda looks like me ... And Mumma, she's kinda, she adopted me. And

my parents they divorced even though they weren't really married but they split up and like I was about five going on six. And then I've got my animals.

Family means like just really close, none of them biological but really close people to you, I mean I even consider my best friend Eve family pretty much. So it's just I think it's just people really close to you, that you are really close to and you really love.

Figure 1   Sophie with her biological mother

Moni is 13 and lives in Bangladesh with her parents and grandmother. She has several uncles and aunts nearby.

I have so many relatives around me they all live around us and I really like it. I feel very close to them. If they go away I miss them so I really like that they are here … My grandmother is right by us … if something happens to the family she is always there. She takes care of us. When my mother can't do it, she always asks us about things and she is always looking after us.

Figure 2 Moni and her family

Shane is about 14 and works on the streets of Cape Town, South Africa. He is talking about his friend Wilfred, to whom he is distantly related.

Figure 3 Shane, Steven and Wilfred

I don't know he was family for me and he didn't know I was family for him, then I hear from my parents he's my family and he hear by his parents he's my family, now [whcn] I saw him have a fight with big boys in Cape Town then I help him – when he saw I have a fight then he help me … so that's why we together. … We can't go away from each other, we can't forget each other, 'cos …, 3 years we are together.

Comment

These children are actively thinking about what makes families. For all of them, although they claim different people as their family, they all list the same qualities: families are based on love, on people who look after you and protect you. Some, like Moni, place more emphasis on biology, and Shane and Wilfred clearly feel that the blood link between them is important. Sophie, on the other hand, who obviously has thought about biological links because of her situation, sees ties of affection as much more important than biological facts. Sophie's quote is particularly interesting because it is easy to misread. On first reading, many might assume that, when she talks about her parents being divorced, she is referring to her biological mother and father. In fact, she is talking about her two mothers getting divorced. Assumptions about the nature of parenthood run very deep, and such a misreading is quite understandable. What is interesting about all three children is how important nurture and care are to them. They are all concerned not only with what makes family ties, but also about what families do, how they act.

This emphasis on affective ties has other implications for who children view as part of their family. Children often have distinct views of who is in their family. An important example here is pets. Pets are often seen by children as being very much a part of the family. Even though some adults might see children's relationship with their pets as irrelevant to family structure, when researchers speak directly to children about pets, their responses indicate that pets may be seen as significant family members:

> In a way, [pets are] sort of part of the family, so you respect 'em, love them (Jade, 11)

> My hamster is important to me because he is the only one in the family who I can trust because I can talk to him but he won't speak back (John, 13)

> *(Quoted in Morrow, 1998, pp. 222–3)*

It would be interesting to know how universal this view is, or whether it is specific to the minority world. Certainly pets exist in many societies, but there is little research on whether they are important to children everywhere or are always seen as part of the family.

2 Experiences of family

2.1   Family forms and idealisations

It is important to acknowledge that families come in a variety of forms: they may exist as extended families where several generations of the same family live together; families where several husbands share one wife or vice versa; gay or lesbian families; nuclear families where two parents live with their children; single-parent families where one adult cares primarily for their children; reconstituted or blended families where a combination of parents, step-parents, siblings and half-siblings live together. It is important to note, too, that not only do general family forms change over time, but there may also be significant changes within many children's family history. Thus a child may be part of a nuclear family, a single-parent family and a stepfamily during his or her childhood. Some may repeat the process a number of times. There is no such thing as a universal family, just as there is no such thing as an ideal family.

The ideal of a 'normal' nuclear family, where two married parents raise their biological children together, is questionable, both at the ideological level and at the level of lived experience. A national charity with a mission to support 'strong family life' claims that 'Stepfamilies are the fastest growing family type in the UK. Over one third of us are part of the stepfamily experience' (Tufnell, 2012). Nor is this a peculiarly modern phenomenon. Despite widespread fears about the ill effects of absent fathers, stepfamilies and working mothers, these have long been a feature of Western family life. In the nineteenth century, the average marriage lasted about ten years (Stark, 1985) and, although curtailed by death rather than divorce, the situation meant that many children were raised in stepfamilies, and many children grew up without one or other of their parents.

2.2   What makes family?

The sociologist Anthony Giddens defines the family as 'a group of persons directly linked by kin connections, the adult members of which assume responsibility for caring for children' (Giddens, 1998). Anthropologists and sociologists use the term 'kinship' to mean the 'connections between individuals, established either through marriage or through the lines of descent that connect blood relatives (mothers, fathers, offspring, grandparents, etc.)' (Giddens, 1998, p. 140). Although some people might say that a family is based on biological relationships, this is far from straightforward.

Figure 4　Three women and a child in the East End of London, 1950s

Within the sociological research tradition, Young and Willmott's (1957) study of family and kinship in the East End of London demonstrates the ways in which a sense of place intersects with ideas of family. Young and Willmott spent three years observing and documenting a working class community in Bethnal Green, an area that, at the time, was renowned for poor-quality Victorian housing conditions that were cramped and lacking in modern amenities – the 'classic white slum' as one commentator put it. Young and Willmott's study presents a detailed and intimate portrait of family and kinship patterns and their associated community values at a time of rapid social change in the UK:

> Since family life is so embracing in Bethnal Green, one might perhaps expect it would be all-embracing. The attachment to relatives would then be at the expense of attachment to other. But in practice this is not what seems to happen. Far from the family excluding ties to outsiders, it acts as an important means of promoting them. When a person has relatives in the borough as most people do, each of these relatives is a go-between with other people in the district. His brother's friends are his acquaintances, if

not his friends; his grandmother's neighbours so well known as to be his own. The kindred are, if we understand their function aright, a bridge between the individual and the community …

In Bethnal Green the person who says he 'knows everyone' is, of course, exaggerating, but pardonably so. He does, with varying degrees of intimacy, know many people outside (but often through) his family, and it is this which makes it, in the view of many informants, a 'friendly place' … that is a feeling of solidarity between people who occupy the common territory.

(Young and Willmott, 1957, pp. 104, 112–13)

Young and Willmott suggest that the strong and supportive nature of the community is forged through the numerous connections between people in the locality. Raymond Williams conjures up a similar picture of family life in the novels *Border Country* (1960) and *Second Generation* (1964), set in the Welsh borderlands where he grew up. Williams uses the term 'structures of feeling' to capture the sense of solidarity and common purpose emanating from being known by and knowing others over generations. We could ask how children fit into this picture? Do they have a special place or are they community members in the making, learning the appropriate forms of sociality from their family? Young and Willmott's description indicates that young people form a point of continuity with their parents, renewing family ties and relationship networks within the community. There is a residual danger of romanticising life in working-class communities by overlooking the fact that solidarity is commonly a response to poverty and lack of resources. An aspect of Young and Willmott's concern to document working-class life was motivated by the desire to document change brought about by welfare initiatives to move families into new social housing. Their study suggests that, in many ways, the improved living conditions did not compensate for the losses incurred by the break-up of community.

Late-modern social theory has further documented how the family and kinship patterns identified by Young and Willmott have been disrupted by a bigger wave of social change. Large-scale socio-economic changes such as deindustrialisation and globalisation have disrupted many long-established working and living patterns. Contemporary Bethnal Greeners are more likely to be a diverse mixture of second- or third-generation immigrants, new migrants as well as East Enders with a history of settlement in the area. A study from the Institute of Community Studies of 'the new East End' (Dench et al., 2006) reports on the area Young and Willmott researched 50 years previously, and particularly on relations between the relatively new Bangladeshi community and the poor white population. The flexible economies of new times place increasing emphasis on fluidity, change and the need for a mobile workforce. This has led some commentators to suggest that family ties and regional identities are weakening as individuals pursue 'choice' biographies at a distance from family and with fewer social obligations. This may apply to a particular, aspiring and upwardly mobile, class-cultural cohort, however. Minority ethnic and religious communities in urban areas point to the limitations of this trend, as patterns of family life and responsibility may more closely resemble those of the East Enders of the 1950s.

Activity 2   Reading A

Allow about 40 minutes

Go to the end of the chapter and read Reading A, 'Jamaican transnational families', by Elaine Bauer and Paul Thompson. This is an extract from a study of Jamaican families separated by successive waves of migration to different parts of the world. Noting that migration is common and even ordinary for many Jamaicans, Bauer and Thompson use the term 'transnational families' to describe this experience of family, and discuss how family relations are sustained across distance.

As you read the extract, make notes in response to the following questions:

- How does the description of transnational families contrast with the portrait of family life in the East End of London as documented by Young and Willmott?

- How would you explain these differences and the effect they may have on children?

- What are the emotional costs of separation as outlined by Bauer and Thompson?

Comment

Obvious points of contrast can be found by drawing up couplets such as 'absence/presence', 'connected/distant', 'together/dispersed'. The East End of London in the 1950s was populated by families who had lived in the area over generations and who had seen each other regularly. Young and Willmott describe a close-knit community with shared values, sustained by familial and regional ties.

The experience of Jamaican family life appears disrupted in comparison, marked by distance and severed connections. The two accounts can be read against the backdrop of colonialism and patterns of migration that create local communities and a global diaspora. Bauer and Thompson document the enduring commitment to family that Jamaicans have developed in adverse circumstances. They document the way family relations survive, indicating that the idea of family adapts to the circumstances of transnational experience, finding ways of reconceptualising relatedness while maintaining family ties and cultural heritage over distance.

Summary of Section 2

Beliefs about childhood are closely linked to ideas about family.

Family is a fluid and enduring concept that differs across cultures and across time.

Children's ideas about family are highly personal and may include significant others such as pets.

Family forms adapt to accommodate the impact of colonialism and migration.

3 Changing conceptualisations of family

Social researchers have pursued new ways of understanding the family in the context of social change. Recognising the diversity of family forms and practices, some scholars suggest that family is understood more in terms of 'doing' than 'being', much as childhood is discussed as an active rather than a passive state. Sociological perspectives, for example, have turned to a more cyclical understanding of family-as-activity; that is, as sets of practices that take on particular meanings associated with family, at particular points in time (Finch, 2007, p. 66). 'Family', on this account, is a facet of social life, not a social institution; it 'represents a quality rather than a thing' (Morgan, 1996, p. 186). In an influential paper, 'Displaying families', Finch (2007) argues for the need to develop the notion of family practices which includes an awareness of the ways in which a family must engage in display in order to negotiate the dispersal of the family over time and space and the uncoupling of family and neighbourhood. Members of the modern family may not see each other every day, but may develop new ways of feeling connected and seek to achieve recognition for the validity of these practices. For the family to have 'social reality', to be recognised as a family, Finch argues, it may be necessary to perform specific practices and to have these acknowledged.

3.1 'Doing' family

Finch employs the term 'display' to focus on understanding families through what they do rather than what they are. Her definition of display incorporates a range of embodied and visual practices, including family narratives, photographs, celebrations and naming practices that provide insights into how the family members see themselves. Finch's account does not engage explicitly with the wider cultural landscape of cultural and visual representations of the family. For Finch, the concept of 'display' is used to encourage us to think about the audience, reception and recognition of family practices, consistent with the sociological framing of stories outlined by Plummer (1995). Plummer's analysis demonstrates the importance of stories to individuals as a way of making sense of the world and their place within it. Plummer pays attention to the way personal experience is narrated and how some stories, such as the sexual 'coming out' story, take on a particular genre with a set of shared features. Plummer argues that the conditions for a story to be articulated depend on the existence of an audience and their willingness to hear and recognise a story. Yet the notion of 'display' as a way of storying the family brings with it the potential to connect family practices to wider landscapes of representation – those imagined families which circulate within popular culture and which incite and discipline our desires, ideas and practices (Smart, 2007). The idealised families of advertising campaigns and televisual representations provide templates of family that may be both aspirational and regulatory. Moreover, it may be that, in particular moments, the visual and the embodied become heightened elements of personal experience and governance.

In the following activity, you are invited to think about these ideas through an extract from Michael Ondaatje's autobiographical novel, *Running in the Family* (1982). The book is a creative reconstruction of the author's family history. A mixture of fact and fiction, the novel chronicles Ondaatje's attempt to gain insight into his own identity by better understanding his parents and the place they came from.

'photographs'
'doing family'

Activity 3   Running in the family

Allow about 30 minutes

Following his parents' divorce, Ondaatje had moved to England with his mother. In the novel, he returns to Ceylon for the first time since his childhood to meet relatives and learn about his family. The novel blends the stories of his aristocratic family with accounts of his experiences in the present. As he meets friends and relatives, finds old photographs and listens to their stories, Ondaatje's lost childhood in Ceylon remains an enigmatic and unresolved part of his identity.

Look at the photograph below and read the extract from the novel which follows.

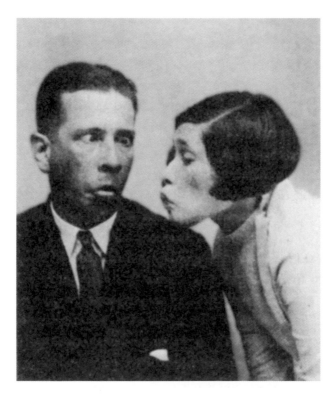

Figure 5   'They both begin to make hideous faces. My father's pupils droop to the south-west corner of his sockets. His jaw falls and resettles into a groan that is half idiot, half shock … My mother … has twisted her lovely features and stuck out her jaw and upper lip so that her profile is in the posture of a monkey … On the back my father has written "What we think of married life" … It is the only photograph I have found of the two of them together.' (Source: Ondaatje, 1982, p. 48)

Truth disappears with history and gossip tells us nothing in the end of personal relationships. There are stories of elopements, unrequited love, family feuds and exhausting vendettas, which everyone was drawn into, had to be involved with. But nothing is said of the closeness between two people: how they grew in the shade of each other's presence. No one speaks of that exchange of gift and character – the way a person took on and recognized in himself the smile of a lover. Individuals are seen only in the context of these swirling social tides. It was almost impossible for a couple to do anything without rumour leaving their shoulders like a flock of messenger pigeons …

Where is the intimate and truthful in all this? Teenager and Uncle. Husband and lover. A lost father in his solace. And why do I want to know of this privacy? After the cups of tea, coffee, public conversations … I want to sit down with someone and talk with utter directness, want to talk to all the lost history like that deserving lover.

Now make notes in response to the following questions:

- What does the photograph tell you about Michael Ondaatje's parents?
- What do you think Michael Ondaatje is looking for when he returns to Ceylon (now Sri Lanka) as an adult in his thirties?
- How does this account resonate with your own experience of family? Describe any similarities or differences, and the feelings you have about your own family history.

Comment

The photograph of Ondaatje's parents is both amusing and disturbing. Memorialised as a couple making faces at each other, they display a playful and ironic attitude to intimacy and romance. Comically lampooning their commitment to each other, the image captures a couple whose relationship is marked by both comfort and contempt. The message is underlined in the caption under the photograph, 'What we think of married life'.

The extract considers the traces left by parents which 'run in the family' through stories, photographs and shared memories. It asks what family connections mean over time. Where do they start and end? And why is it all so hauntingly compelling? The author is thinking not only about the connectedness of parents and extended family but the larger history of broken ties and geographical and cultural locations. Visiting relatives and revisiting the buildings and locations that his family once called home are powerful and evocative. Ondaatje suggests that, as adults, we have an opportunity to re-evaluate our relationship with our parents and think afresh about who they were beyond the parental identity, as people drawn together by things other than us.

Responding to this activity, author Mary Jane Kehily writes:

The image generates a wave of contradictory emotions in me. I applaud their daring. Their refusal to be adults, resisting the usual couple pose: the arms around each other and smile of the photographic genre. Admitting so publicly that relationships are difficult is a brave thing, even as a joke. At the same time there's a hint of disrespect and possibly something more that may signal the break-up to come. I wonder what inspired the caption and did they both feel the same way?

Thinking about the extract in relation to my own family, Ireland is my Ceylon – the place of my parents where I have never lived but remain connected to in a deeply ambivalent way. Lots of stories emanate from there, and lots of secrets too. The story that shapes my parents' relationship is an unspoken one. There's a photograph of a wedding – a bride whom no-one in the family knows, in an impossibly beautiful dress, flanked by bridesmaids in iridescent shades of turquoise. It's the wedding my mother should have had, the bespoke gowns she had ordered before my father 'disappeared' in the weeks leading up to the wedding. For her own wedding (amazingly, to my father), she wore a grey herringbone suit. She looked nice but not like a bride. I was in my forties before I fully realised the significance of this event – the hurt and the anger that consumed my mother, and the realisation that the marriage was fated before it began. This event makes sense retrospectively as the backdrop to my childhood; the unhealed wound underpinning family dynamics, infusing parental and

> sibling relationships with the feelings generated by the
> photograph.

3.2   Brave new families

New reproductive technologies have had a profound effect on family formation. As adoption of infants has become more difficult, it is often medical intervention rather than adoption that many people turn to in the UK if they cannot conceive a child. Assisted conception has refocused attention on biological ties and has emphasised them as the true markers of kinship. Seemingly every day, new moral dilemmas are thrown up as a result of reproductive technology, and science is far ahead of public opinion, and understanding, in this field. Assisted conception creates many moral dilemmas and forces us to look at very fundamental questions about childhood, parenthood and, indeed, life itself. Should postmenopausal women be allowed fertility treatment? Should parents consider the best interests of the child before they undertake assisted conception? Should surrogacy be allowed? Is cloning ever acceptable as a form of human reproduction?

In 1986, the government became very concerned about issues of surrogacy and the donation of genetic material, and commissioned a report from a group led by philosopher Dame Mary Warnock, which would look at the implications of assisted conception. This report also shed light on the assumptions that many people in the UK had about parenthood in the 1980s, and it raised very interesting issues about the 'naturalness' of these techniques. Technology has broken down the concept of a single biological mother. Birth, conception and family ties are not simply universal facts but have cultural meanings attached to them which, when disrupted, can cause profound moral disquiet. Other societies view the nature of family ties very differently, and social scientists have often studied these as part of looking at the families of people across the world. However, in the minority world, the new reproductive technologies have made many look again at family ties, and have forced people – whether in the government, on Royal Commissions or as laypeople – to ask questions about kinship and to examine the question of what is it that makes a parent.

In vitro fertilisation (IVF) and other forms of assisted conception are now very widely practised and widely accepted. The trend towards late motherhood in the West places reproductive technologies as part of a repertoire of 'choice' for women seeking to synchronise having a family with personal readiness, finding the 'right moment' to fit with career and relationship (Thomson et al., 2011). As scientific advances increase, other issues such as human cloning replace assisted conception as a locus of concern. Indeed, the concept of a single genetic mother has itself broken down, as medical breakthroughs meet science fiction by producing embryos that realise the possibility of conception and birth outside of the body, as depicted in the film *Children of Men* (2006, directed by Alfonso Cuarón).

Activity 4   Who is the parent?

Allow about 30 minutes

In the light of the discussion above, think about the issue of who is a parent in the following scenarios.

- A married woman is implanted with eggs donated from her sister which are then fertilised by a sperm donor. When she gives birth, which woman do you believe has the strongest claim to be the child's biological mother?

- A woman carries a baby as a surrogate for a couple, using the commissioning couple's eggs and sperm. When the baby is born the surrogate does not want to give the baby up. What moral claims could the surrogate make in this situation? How valid do you think these claims are?

- In 2023, a child turns 18 and discovers that he was born by a sperm donation. He has always wondered why he looked so different from his father. Because the UK ended anonymous sperm donation in 2005, he has a right to trace the sperm donor. What would be the advantages and disadvantages of letting this boy trace his genetic father?

Ask someone else the same questions and compare notes. On what points do you disagree? Why do you think this might be?

Comment

A central point that emerges from these scenarios is that who a child 'belongs to' is not a straightforward, indisputable 'fact of life' but depends on our belief system informed by the cultural setting in which we grew up. Assisted conception has enabled many people to have children who would otherwise not be parents. However, these medical developments have raised very important questions about the nature of parentage and childhood in Western society. They have outstripped society's existing moral discourses, making ethical reasoning profoundly difficult. For example, resources in the UK are limited; not all health authorities will pay for treatment and many people have to obtain treatment privately, thus ensuring that in some parts of the country, only those with enough money will have the opportunity to try to become parents. This raises further questions about the nature of families and whether potential parents ever have a right to a child.

In a study of first-time motherhood in the UK (Thomson et al., 2011), the experience of surrogacy is explored through Cathy's account of becoming a mother. Cathy (aged 38) responded to an advertisement placed on a disability website looking for first-time mothers-to-be. She defined herself as disabled, and explained that she has a congenital heart defect which has caused a stroke on her left-hand side. Cathy's route to motherhood is through partial surrogacy in which the surrogate mother, Emma, provided the egg but Cathy's husband Ian provided the sperm. They met through membership of a surrogacy organisation which provided a support network and a way of matching intended parents with surrogate mothers. The process was carried out via self-insemination, and Emma conceived on the third attempt following one miscarriage.

Unlike other mothers, Cathy did not have the physical experience of pregnancy and birth. The implied consequences of embodying pregnancy as the preparatory state for motherhood is challenged in situations where women become mothers without going through pregnancy. Adoption and surrogacy provide examples of different routes to creating a family, raising questions that may challenge the status and identity claims of maternal subjects: how do women become mothers without going through pregnancy? What counts as your 'own' child and how are these meanings established? What are the impacts of this on children? Cathy experienced pregnancy as both intimate and estranged when she became a mother through surrogacy. Employing a woman to carry and give birth to her baby involved Cathy in establishing bonds of connection that were both emotional and legally binding. A contract with a surrogate mother prompted Cathy to consider her claim to motherhood through the eyes of others. Cathy's main concern was captured by the idea of 'passing', a racialised term referring to black people whose light skin enables them to pass as white.

In the following extract, Cathy considers disclosing the surrogacy to people on her new course.

CATHY: Well I was thinking shall I do it or not. But then other people were telling all sorts of things that were really personal like you know, like they had been in abusive relationships, one was an ex drug addict so you know really heavy stuff so I just thought you know go on why not, go for it. And the next person said and my child was adopted and I thought, oh, oh! (laughs) That's good! (laughs) I was like oh my goodness. Because they had just adopted a baby boy about a year ago and that was really nice because it made me feel really, like oh my goodness someone is in a similar boat to me. You know because it is, people do have strong, I don't think that they do about adoption so much, but they do have strong views about surrogacy some people think it is a terrible thing to do and there is no way people should do it, you know very anti. For other people that isn't the case. And a lot of the stuff in the press is very anti. You know you tend to hear all these horror stories, you don't hear the happy stories that myself and quite a few of my friends have got.

INTERVIEWER: Yeah. (laughs) I just wonder how you would feel if you hadn't told anyone?

CATHY: I don't think I could. I mean I could get away with it because she looks so much like me. I mean obviously our families know obviously you know, I mean who have I told? People at work know, people at college know because I decided to tell them they wouldn't have known otherwise, immediate neighbours know, I haven't told the bloke upstairs yet because he moved in after she was born so why should I. But the two on either side they have been here years so I told them, they would have to know because they knew I wasn't pregnant. So I mean actually when I told the woman who is above on that side she said ooh you didn't have to tell me, I would have just assumed you had adopted.

… Most people just assume, it is better than assuming we just kidnapped her (laughs) … Where has this child suddenly appeared from (laughs) It was you know it was obvious. No cops arriving. I don't think you can get away with not telling people and at some stage down the line the child would have found out. You know so. I mean I haven't told the girls at the nursery, I don't think, no I

> don't think I will actually. There is no reason to really. The older she gets there is less reason.
>
> (Interview transcript, Thomson et al., 2011)

Harbouring anxious feelings about her ability to pull off the trick of becoming a mother, Cathy wondered what neighbours would say when she appeared with a baby, having never been pregnant. Should she explain the situation? Would she look like a baby snatcher? Could she pass and be accepted as a *real* mother? Once the child was born and legally hers, Cathy gained confidence as a mother, yet the narrative work of establishing corporeal connections continued, involving an ongoing intensive awareness of her connection with her child as seen through the eyes of others.

Similarly, the experiences of children born through these technologies need to be examined. Some campaigners, especially those who were born through artificial insemination, have demanded the right to trace their biological parents, arguing that knowing their biological parent is an intrinsic part of their identity. This led to a change in the law in the UK in 2005. Whether sperm donors have a right to anonymity remains controversial as, in different contexts, these men may be constructed as responsible or irresponsible fathers. In studies carried out on how children of donor insemination feel about the circumstances of their birth, key issues of identity and belonging in families arise:

> I needed to know whose face I was looking at in the mirror – I needed to know who I was and how I came to be – it was a very primal and unrelenting force which propelled the search and it was inescapable and undeniable.
>
> (Rachel, quoted in Turner and Coyle, 2000, p. 2046)

For some children of donor insemination, however, counter-narratives also exist, as the need to locate the absences of biological inheritance may not be as strong as the emotional ties of the present.

Summary of Section 3

As family forms change dramatically, the concept of family has been redefined in terms of a focus on family practices, what families do rather than what they are.

Family practices include stories, images, emotions, memories and embodied experience which leave a trace across generations.

New reproductive technologies challenge normative notions of family and break down the concept of a single biological mother.

The possibilities offered by assisted conception may create ethical dilemmas for parents and their children.

---

4 Home as a material space

In this section, we document the connection between family and home, marked particularly by starting a family. If the idea is assumed of family as created by practices of 'doing', attention may be drawn to the home as the site where family practices are developed and repeated. Home is the location most closely associated with family life. The 'family home' links individuals to the past and future as the place of their childhood and the imagined space for a new generation. Recognising growing up as a place-specific experience, many new parents go to great lengths to realise the dream of a family home that fits with their ideas of a physical space in an environment suitable for child-rearing. This may involve a re-evaluation of lifestyle and priorities: moving from the city to the country, investing in a bigger house, being close to extended family are common considerations in setting up a family home.

The birth of a first child may signal a lifestyle change that places the home at the centre of the transition from being a couple to being a family. Thomson et al. (2011) note how the reorganisation of domestic space is treated as a venture into the future, a space that can be filled with the desires and imaginative projections of becoming new parents. Many women marked the journey through the display of baby things, arranging items in aesthetic ways in a room designated as the nursery. The ultrasound scan becomes the first visible display of family-to-be that commonly exists as a symbolic marker of change, new life and impending motherhood. Women displayed the images generated at antenatal appointments in the home, on the fridge or kitchen noticeboards. One woman, Marion, arranged all her ultrasonic scan images in a line along the mantelpiece like birthday cards, making them the celebratory focal point of the room.

Figure 6   Ultrasound images displayed on a mantelpiece (Source: Thomson et al., 2011)

4.1   Starting a family

Within the minority-world context, Thomson et al. (2011) found that the idea of 'starting a family' created an opportunity to get everything around the house 'sorted', giving the couple a joint project anchored in the family rather than in work. Women spoke of having the kitchen done, putting in radiators and redecorating, as well as preparing the baby's room. Naomi, a 35-year-old professional, summed up this approach by telling us that before the pregnancy they had put up with things being half done and other things not working. Having a baby motivated her and her partner to become 'housey', prioritising their personal lives by making sure that the domestic space was prepared for the arrival of the baby. Informed by pregnancy magazines, baby books and websites, many women chose products with care, and reported putting time and energy into finding the 'right' baby buggy, baby gym or nursery furniture. Taking pleasure in the exercise of consumption in new markets, first-time pregnancy is presented as a time when it is necessary for couples to re-evaluate, change and spend.

Activity 5   Reading B

Allow about 35 minutes

Go to the end of the chapter and read Reading B, 'Making babies and mothers: from nurseries to baby showers', by Alison Clark. This account of maternity and materiality is based on an ethnographic study of mothers living in a particular set of streets in north London.

As you read, consider the following questions:

- How do ideas of family, home and place come together for women in Clark's study?

- Clark describes the nursery as 'a key site of desire and fantasy'. What do you understand by this?

- Decorating the nursery has significance beyond the act of preparing a room. Make a list of the meanings associated with decorating a nursery as outlined in the extract.

Comment

Decorating the nursery highlights parental sensibilities and aspirations; the room itself can become an idealised expression of their tastes and values told through the lens of the environment they choose for their children. As you will see from the discussion that follows, the materiality of family and home is imbued with significance. For Clark, interpreting these practices produces insights into social class, parenting style, investments in child development and fantasies of an ideal childhood. It may be productive to consider how these meanings are generated and where women get these ideas from.

The following feature presents an account found in popular culture. Taken from a pregnancy magazine on decorating a boy's nursery, the narrative style works to give value to particular forms of style and taste. In this example, parents draw on the notion of *good taste* as a form of social status that responds to the gender of their child and the circumstances of his birth.

> After indulging in everything pink and floral for their daughter Isabella-Rose, Grace and Michael Saunders decided to opt for classic French antiques for their second child, Gabriel Sky, adding a nautical theme … Gabriel was born at the peak of a summer heatwave so the aim was to create a room that exudes calm and cool … It retains a masculine feel, with a boat-shaped bookshelf,

roughly-hewn boat ornaments and collection of *Tim at Sea* classic stories …

Classic antique pieces are another important element. Key features include a vast French armoire found at a Paris flea market and a charming turn-of-the-century rocking horse, which Grace and Michael spotted – and bartered for – on Portobello Road. And the finishing touch? A watercolour of flowers painted by Gabriel's grandmother.

(Junior: Pregnancy & Baby magazine, April 2005)

In this example, decorating a child's bedroom extends beyond the intimacy of the family to become an exercise in class cultural distinction that, like other forms of consumption, speaks to wider social formations that point to the link between notions of taste, social class and cultural capital (Bourdieu, 1984). The French antique furniture and vintage seafaring paraphernalia can be seen as an expression of parental aspirations that is for *them* rather than for the child. Interestingly, the tasteful cosmopolitan couple introduce an intergenerational element into their son's nursery as a 'finishing touch' – a reminder of their creative lineage that is present but not integral to the overall design.

4.2   Materiality and the production of family narratives

The creation of a nursery offers the possibility for an elaborate display of motherhood as parents-to-be create a special place within the home for the new baby. Women participating in the *Making Modern Mothers* study (Thomson et al., 2011) presented this space in various states of 'readiness', from bare walls splurged with paint pot colours and decorating mess to pristine and beautifully finished rooms. The new baby's room usually spoke, consciously and unconsciously, to the desires of the maternal as women sought to surround the child with the things that appeared important to them as a new family. While some women took the view that the child is entering the world of the couple, others worked to create a unique environment for their baby. Choosing primary colours or pastels, gender-specific items or neutral pieces, purpose-made nursery furniture or customised pieces all pointed to the significance of the maternal project as an investment in shaping the world of the baby in ways that are imbued with emotional connections.

Hannah, a 26-year-old woman, spoke of decorating the nursery as a way of displaying the things that were important to her and which, she hoped, would become important to her child. Hannah wanted to keep the memory of her dead mother alive and her child to know her mother by creating a presence out of absence. She placed a framed photograph of her mother in the nursery and planned to talk about her routinely, share the activities her mother enjoyed and take her child on regular visits to the grave. Spelled out in magnetic letters on a radiator was the message 'Mummy and Daddy love you'. Working to create family bonds and maintain intergenerational connections became key features in the way Hannah prepared for the birth of her child.

4.3 Young motherhood and single parenthood

For first-time mothers-to-be, preparing for the birth can be both a simple, practical matter of being ready and an elaborate baby audit of imagining, doing and projecting. In all cases, the 'situation' of motherhood comes into sharp focus as personal circumstances, age and family resources shape the contours of the pregnancy and birth experience in consequential ways. In the context of Western trends to delay motherhood in order to gain qualifications and establish careers, young mothers appear out of place. Policy perspectives identify teenage pregnancy as a 'social problem' leading to a cycle of disadvantage for mother and child (Cabinet Office, 1999; House of Commons Health Committee, 2003), while media commentary questions young women's ability to mother. Within a childhood studies framework, teenage pregnancy challenges the idea of childhood as an age-related state of 0–18 and may contradictorily position a young woman as a child having a child. In the *Making Modern Mothers* study (Thomson et al., 2011), the grandmother of a teenage mother expressed concern with the way her 15-year-old granddaughter was preparing for the birth of her baby:

> I went in to Kim's bedroom one day and … she had this big suitcase, from under her bed, and I says to her: 'What are you doing?' And it was full of baby things, 'Oh I'm taking notes on what I've got', and I says, 'Why, is that so you don't duplicate anything?' 'Oh no I just like doing this.' … I just thought it was funny, why would she want to take a note of what was in the suitcase? … I mean she knew what was in there and I always, my interpretation of it was that it was like a child with a doll, and I

think that's what she thought it was going to be, and all of a sudden this baby comes along and, my god, what a responsibility.

(Study field notes, 29 October 2008, Thomson et al., 2011)

Another teenage mother found herself preparing for the birth of her baby in a local authority residential care facility for young mothers. Interviewing her in this setting a few weeks before the birth prompted a mixture of feelings for the researcher and an acute awareness of the teenager's limited resources:

> Sophie meets me and takes me to her unit. It is very small – a kitchen/lounge and one bedroom with just enough room for a single bed, a chest of drawers and nothing else ... I felt that it was compact and had everything she needed but that it was also an infantilising space for a young mother to be. The bedroom in particular seemed to emphasise her youthful status as a child who was expecting a child. It was a girl's room, there was a cartoon motif on her duvet – it's not My Little Pony but it reminds me of that. A moses basket on a stand and a baby relaxer lined the corridor-like space next to the bed ... she had bought a few basics – nappies, sterilising kit, vests and socks.

(Study field notes, 22 August 2005, Thomson et al., 2011)

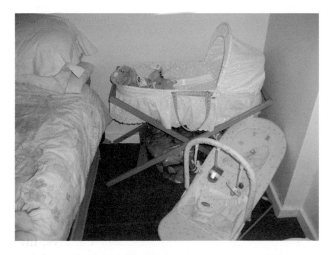

Figure 7   Sophie prepares for the birth of her first child

Across the study as a whole, young mothers, aged 15–18, feature as an identifiable cohort, defined in relation to older first-time mothers and other young women who do not become pregnant. Social class remains embedded within the age category, further defining teenage motherhood as aberrant and out of place. Thomson et al. (2011) conclude that young motherhood can be seen as part of a biographical narrative that gives some women a route into an emergent adult identity that makes sense at the level of the local.

Summary of Section 4

Family and home are strongly connected, since home is the site where family practices are developed and repeated.

'Starting a family' may run in parallel with the material project of establishing a family home.

Material practices, such as decorating the nursery, generate insights into wider social formations.

Personal circumstances, age and access to resources shape the experience of starting a family and engagements with material culture.

---

5 Children's perspectives on home and family

While the terms 'home' and 'family' are sometimes assumed to belong together, this is not always the experience of children and young people. Children may spend a large proportion of their childhood living away from their birth family. Other groups of children may live their childhood with their family but be homeless or move frequently from one temporary home to another. These experiences challenge the idealisation of shared family life within a settled domestic environment. Moving away from home can be a marker of the transition from childhood to adulthood, but this pattern too is challenged by increasing numbers of young adults being financially unable to move out, and by young people who choose to leave while they are still regarded as 'not yet adults'. We look now at children in two contexts in which the link between home and family is disrupted – children in residential care homes and homeless young people – drawing on first-hand accounts of what home and family can mean in these circumstances.

5.1 'Home' away from family

A range of circumstances – of health or social welfare, or legal and personal circumstances – may result in children experiencing institutional care. Medical reasons due to illness or disability may lead to long periods of living in hospital, or in residential school or other long-stay provision. Alison recalls how her father, now in his eighties, remembers his long stay in a TB hospital in the 1930s, only able to see his own father waving once a week from the perimeter fence of the hospital grounds.

Figure 8   Children's ward, Darlington Memorial Hospital, circa 1930

Welfare issues and family circumstances may also result in a placement in a residential care home (or 'residential unit', as they are described in Scotland). A further group of children and young people may be detained in a residential institution as part of the judicial system, while others experience institutional life in boarding school out of parental choice. The values underpinning these different institutions will influence what attempts are made to create a sense of family or establish family-like practices as well as a feeling of home. Holloway makes a similar observation about the social organisation of childcare provision being influenced by ideology as much as by the physical reality of the space (Holloway, 1998, p. 48).

The views and experiences of young people who have lived in residential care have been an under-researched area (Emond, 2003; Stevens, 2006). What can we learn from research to help untangle some of the complex ways of doing and displaying family and home in these institutions? In their study of residential care homes, McIntosh and colleagues (2011) explain that:

> the residential care context ... constitutes a challenge to taken-for-granted understandings of what it means to be a family, a parent and a child.
>
> (McIntosh et al., 2011, p. 181)

Such homes are complicated, as they operate simultaneously as a living space for children, a work environment for adults and an institution. Each of these functions places different and sometimes contradictory expectations across the generations. These expectations are often implicit. McIntosh and colleagues illustrate how this can lead to feelings of ambivalence among staff and children as to how to relate within these shared environments. The research team chose to illustrate this complex negotiation of being a home and possibly ways of 'doing and displaying family' by looking at practices around food and mealtimes.

Activity 6   What does eating together 'like a family' involve?

Allow about 30 minutes

Read the information in the table below, about food routines in three residential care homes. Make notes on the similarities and differences in mealtimes in these different institutional homes, and answer the following questions:

- How do the food routines compare with your own experiences of mealtimes in your childhood and now when you encounter meals with children?
- What sense of 'family-like' practices do you gain from these descriptions of the different homes?
- What differences are there in the expectations of the young people's role in mealtimes?
- What can you learn about the role of adults in these institutions?

Table 1   Food routines in three residential care homes

	Wellton	Highton	Lifton
Age of children	**9–13 years**	**12–16 years**	**14–18 years**
Characteristics			
Ethos	Focus on providing safety and structure; consistent implementation of clear boundaries and routines. Emphasis on children experiencing 'normal' family-like living and learning practical skills	Focus on overcoming institutional characteristic, creating a relaxed environment, recognising diversity, offering choices. Emphasis on maintaining safety and developing independent living skills	Focus on being 'family-like', creating connectedness, and building relationships. Emphasis on creating a sense of belonging rather than developing children's independent skills
Food routines Shared mealtimes around the table	Tea (children make their own lunch supervised by adults)	Lunch and tea	Lunch and tea
Breakfast (some variation at weekend)	Prepared at staggered intervals to avoid clashes and delays	May be in their bedrooms or may take something to eat on the way to school	Individualised routines between particular children and staff
Supper	Supper kept to a minimum: usually just juice in children's bedrooms as a means to settle them for the night	Toast and cheese in the dining or living room. Prepared by children or staff	Tea and toast in the living room. Other snacks if requested. Prepared by staff

(Continued overleaf)

Table 1 continued Food routines in three residential care homes

Characteristics	Wellton	Highton	Lifton
Participation Organisation of meals	Cook prepares tea on weekdays. Care workers prepare meals when the cook is off	Cook prepares lunch and tea at weekends and some weekdays. Assistant managers, domestic and care workers prepare meals when cook is off	Cook prepares lunch and tea on weekdays. Assistant managers, domestic and care workers prepare meals when cook is off
Who participates in the main meal?	Care workers and children	Care workers, cook, assistant managers and children	Care staff, cook, managers, domestic and admin. staff and children
Cleaning tasks	Cleaning rota: each child takes turns doing the dishes. Care workers contribute to cleaning	Children expected to clean their own dishes. Care workers contribute to cleaning	No expectations that children clean their own or others' dishes. Cook and domestic staff mainly responsible for cleaning

(Source: McIntosh et al., 2011, pp. 178–9, Table 10.1)

Comment

Sharing a meal together may be seen as one example of a family-like practice, but what does this involve? The descriptions in the table point to questions about where a meal is taking place – is it in a dining or living room? Perhaps the home that allows children to eat breakfast in their bedrooms or on the way to school is more family-like? The answer may depend on your own experiences and attitudes to family and mealtimes, and to whether informality, sharing or establishing routines are key factors.

The children and young people in these three homes appear to participate, to a greater or lesser extent, in the food routines, although none of these groups appears to play a key role in the preparation of food. There appear to be differences in priority given to developing independent living skills. In Lifton, this is contrasted with creating a sense of belonging and connectedness so that the children are not expected to prepare or clear away the food. This is one example of where an understanding of what being 'family-like' means has translated into the routines and relationships established between children and adults. This may differ from your own interpretation of what 'doing family' means.

Similarly, the roles of the adults in these homes differ in terms of the expectations of what type of environment is being created – is it one that prioritises nurture and safety or one that emphasises developing independence?

Ideas about family impacted on the culture and everyday routines in the residential homes in this Scottish study. The institutional interpretations of what it meant to be a 'home' did not always agree with the views of the children and young people involved. For some, sharing mealtimes was a positive experience; for others, any attempt to be family-like was not welcome:

> I just *feel* like they're more like a mum and dad, well like a family, to me than my mum and dad will ever be. [...] All the staff are caring and willing to help you, but if you muck stuff up in Lifton they'll be like, they'll give you the chance to help. (Adam, young person, interview, Lifton)
>
> *(Quoted in McIntosh et al., 2011, p. 182)*

> Aye, I know Scott's cooking's nice, but once you've been in your own family home for quite a bit and you're used to a family home, and you're used to your family's cooking, when you get brought away from that it's just like basically sitting eating at your mate's house and that's fucking rancid. (Malcolm, young person, interview, Highton)
>
> *(Quoted in McIntosh et al., 2011, p. 182)*

In the same way that mealtimes in domestic settings are more than just preparing, eating and clearing away, the importance of mealtimes in these residential settings was not only about eating together, but had a wider social significance. This involved the general atmosphere created, and the possibility to relax and chat together and talk over the day.

food - some
~ sense of tension

Interviews with staff revealed how the desire to create such an atmosphere was, in some cases, driven by a belief that this was what a 'normal' family should do, thus linking to an idealisation of notions of family. This was one of the complex factors at play in the practice of creating a Christmas buffet – an activity that represented an extra effort by staff to go beyond their scheduled duties to provide a feast. McIntosh and colleagues describe how this could be seen as a way of 'displaying family' to both the resident young people and also to the visitors who were invited to take part. This links to Finch's (2007) notion that the audience for the family-like practices can be an important part of the process.

However, just as family mealtimes can be a source of tension, so sharing food in these residential homes also created sources of tension:

Nika: How about in here? Do you think it's [food] bringing people together in here?

Callum: Nah.

Nika: But people are sitting together, does that not count?

Callum: Nuh.

Nika: Why not?

Callum: 'Cause it has to be family and stuff.

Nika: It has to be family?

Callum: And friends. (Callum, young person, interview, Wellton)

(McIntosh et al., 2011, p. 188)

Callum's perspective points to the significance of the relationships involved rather than the activity itself. The residential home could set out to follow family-like practices, but it was not those of *his* family or friends.

5.2   Family away from 'home'?

We have been discussing circumstances in which home and family are separated. We will now look at experiences of youth homelessness to continue to explore some of these complex connections between childhood, home and family. The term 'youth homelessness' can cover a range of circumstances in which young people find themselves without a permanent roof over their heads and living apart from family. In their longitudinal study of homeless youth in Melbourne, Australia, Mallett et al. (2010) emphasise how being homeless is more than being without a roof:

> For young people home does not only mean a physical place; it is understood as a place where one feels connected, wanted and supported. Young people emphasized similar definitions of homelessness. Most understood it as much more than an absence of shelter: to be homeless is also an absence of caring, love and belonging.
>
> (Crane and Braddock, 1996, cited by Mallett et al., 2010, p. 2)

Sometimes this absence of belonging is filled by strong support from other homeless peers. Ben, one of the young people in Mallett and colleagues' study who chose to leave home, describes how his friends became his family:

> Basically we support each other and sort of, most of us are in the same predicament or, you know, got similar kind of life struggles. So we just support each other, 'cause there's no one else … yeah and we support each other just with relationships and things like that, sorting out family problems that we are having and stuff.
>
> (Quoted in Mallett et al., 2010, p. 90)

Peer support and tensions among peers were two of the factors emerging from Tom Hall's (2003) detailed ethnographic study of homeless young people living in England. His study is based on a year's fieldwork in which he lived in bedsit and hostel accommodation.

Activity 7   Reading C

Allow about 30 minutes

Go to the end of the chapter and read Reading C, 'Southerton, England, the local young and homeless', by Tom Hall. This is an extract from an article by Hall, recounting the experiences of young people who were unemployed, homeless and living away from their families.

As you read, make notes in response to the following questions:

- What details do you see of the transitory nature of the homelessness described?
- What do Samantha's and Tony's accounts reveal about the links between relationship breakdown and their homelessness?
- What networks are described which might replace support from families?

Comment

Hall describes how the homeless young people he met, all in their mid to late teens, were constantly moving between different types of informal housing arrangements, bedsits and short periods in an emergency hostel as well as, for some, periods living on the streets. For the majority of the time, it was not so much a question of being 'roofless' as not having one place to call home.

The accounts by Samantha and Tony both reveal how underlying tensions with family members were involved in the circumstances that led to their homelessness. Attempts to repair these relationships resulted in periods of moving back home before ending up homeless again.

Hall describes a particularly strong network existing among the young people who found a temporary home in bedsits:

> This collection of young, unsettled tenants and hangers on was more than a little fuzzy at the edges, but it had a coherence of sorts as a loose network of friends, associates and occasional contacts. The network was sparse and constantly reconfiguring in places, but extraordinarily dense elsewhere, stringing together clusters of close association.
>
> *(Hall, 2006, p. 147)*

Thus the living arrangements away from home could provide alternative networks of 'support', but were not necessarily seen as providing positive role models for returning to a settled life that those working for official channels of support would have preferred.

One of the questions raised in the two longitudinal studies of youth homelessness in England and in Australia referred to in this section is whether youth homelessness marks an automatic transition to adulthood. The practical decisions necessary to survive without living with family can cause young people to enter a world in which they need to act older than their peers in settled accommodation. This is illustrated by this exchange between Danny and a hostel worker, Ann:

> 'Danny,' says Ann. 'You've got to understand, you're being catapulted into adulthood. You're going to have to behave like twenty when you are only 16. That starts with not flicking your cigs on the floor.'

> *(Hall, 2006, p. 153)*

In this section we have examined two contexts in which the link between family and home is disrupted. The examples of homeless young people and those in residential care raise questions about what constitutes being a family, and highlights the importance of shared everyday routines in creating a sense of belonging wherever 'home' is found.

Summary of Section 5

There are diverse ways of 'doing' family away from home.

Everyday practices, such as mealtimes, form one avenue for making institutional life more home-like for children.

Being homeless is more than about bricks and mortar, and can involve feelings of isolation and lack of belonging for young people.

New informal networks can sometimes create a sense of belonging in place of family support.

---

6 Conclusion

In this chapter, we have focused on how childhood is shaped within the context of family and home. Children live in many sorts of family and recognise a variety of people as their kin. Family forms change over time, and the nature of parenting and the relationship to children is constantly in flux, changing through both social transformation and technological advances. The chapter has discussed various ways of looking at family and home, and how these ideas are contested, controversial and deeply personal. Sociologists view the family as a key site of socialisation, a process that inducts children into the society in which they live. We elaborate on the idea of family socialisation by also considering the home as a material space for 'starting' and 'doing' family. In this respect, family and home can be seen as spatially bound concepts for social practices that provide the context for children's experience.

The chapter began by discussing the highly charged terrain of who is family: a question that reveals the diversity of family forms and the strong feelings they generate. In recent sociological research, the family has been conceptualised in terms of what families do rather than what they are. The chapter took up this perspective, seeing the family as constituted through the 'doing' of repeated practices, including display. Throughout the chapter, we illustrated the heightened significance of family and home as emotional markers that are compellingly reproduced in different ways. This can be seen most clearly in the illustrative examples profiling efforts to recreate versions of home and family in adverse conditions. The examples from the East End of London, Sri Lanka, and Melbourne and Sydney in Australia, and postcolonial patterns of migration from Jamaica, all provide testimony to an enduring commitment to family and home in contrasting circumstances.

Finally, the chapter explored the way in which children and young people themselves take an active part in forming their families. While some claim kin and others reconfigure familial relations through peers, children's experiences of family and non-family life are as variable as the forms of family and types of home in which children live.

References

Bourdieu, P. (1984) *Distinction: A Social Critique of the Judgement of Taste* (trans. R. Nice), London, Routledge.

Cabinet Office (1999) *Teenage Pregnancy*, report by the Social Exclusion Unit (Cm 4342), London, The Stationery Office.

Children of Men (2006) film, directed by Alfonso Cuarón, Universal Pictures.

Crane, P. and Braddock, J. (1996) *Homelessness among Young People in Australia: Early Intervention and Prevention*, report to the National Youth

Affairs Research Scheme, Hobart, National Clearinghouse for Youth Studies.

Dench, G., Gavron, K. and Young, M. (2006) *The New East End: Kinship, Race and Conflict*, London, Profile.

Emond, R. (2003) 'Putting the care into residential care: the role of young people', *Journal of Social Work*, vol. 3, no. 3, pp. 321–7.

Finch, J. (2007) 'Displaying families', *Sociology*, vol. 41, no. 1, pp. 65–81.

Giddens, A. (1998) *Sociology*, Cambridge, Polity Press.

Hall, T. (2003) *Better Times than This: Youth Homelessness in Britain*, London, Pluto Press.

Hall, T. (2006) 'Out of work and house and home: contested youth in an English homeless hostel', *Ethnos: Journal of Anthropology*, vol. 71, no. 2, pp. 143 63.

Holloway, S. L. (1998) 'Geographies of justice: preschool-childcare provision and the conceptualisation of social justice', *Environment and Planning C: Government and Policy*, vol. 16, pp. 85–104.

House of Commons Health Committee (2003) *Sexual Health*, third report of Session 2002/2003, vol. 1, London: The Stationery Office.

Mallett, S., Rosenthal, D., Keys, D. and Averill, R. (2010) *Moving Out, Moving On: Young People's Pathways in and through Homelessness*, London, Routledge.

McIntosh, I., Dorrer, N., Punch, S. and Emond, R. (2011) '"I know we can't be family, but as close as you can get": displaying families within an institutional context', in Dermott, E. and Seymour, J. (eds) *Displaying Families: A New Concept for the Sociology of Family Life*, Basingstoke, Palgrave Macmillan.

Morgan, D. H. J. (1996) *Family Connections: An Introduction to Family Studies*, Cambridge, Polity Press.

Morrow, V. (1998) 'My animals and other family: children's perspectives on their relationships with companion animals', *Anthrozoos*, vol. 11, no. 4, pp. 218–26.

Ondaatje, M. (1982) *Running in the Family*, London, Faber.

Plummer, K. (1995) *Telling Sexual Stories: Power, Change and Social Worlds*, London, Routledge.

Smart, C. (2007) *Personal Life: New Directions in Sociological Thinking*, Cambridge, Polity Press.

Stark, R. (1985) *Sociology*, Belmont, CA, Wadsworth.

Stevens, I. (2006) 'Consulting youth about residential care environments in Scotland', *Children, Youth and Environments*, vol. 16, no. 2, pp. 51–74.

Thomson, R., Kehily, M. J., Hadfield, L. and Sharpe, S. (2011) *Making Modern Mothers*, Bristol, Policy Press.

Tufnell, C. (2012) 'A new family – the fun and hard work of building a stepfamily', *Care for the Family* [online], http://www.careforthefamily.org.uk/article/?article=91 (Accessed 30 May 2012).

Turner, A. J. and Coyle, A. (2000) 'What does it mean to be a donor offspring? The identity experiences of adults conceived by donor insemination and the implications for counselling and therapy', *Human Reproduction*, vol. 15, no. 9, pp. 2041–51.

Williams, R. (1960) *Border Country*, London, Chatto and Windus.

Williams, R. (1964) *Second Generation*, London, Chatto and Windus.

Young, M. and Willmott, P. (1957) *Family and Kinship in East London*, Harmondsworth, Penguin.

Reading A
Jamaican transnational families

Elaine Bauer and Paul Thompson

Source: *Jamaican Hands across the Atlantic*, 2006, Kingston, Jamaica, Ian Randle.

Donetta Macfarlane has lived for over 30 years in Toronto, where she works as a hospital food supervisor, but she lives as part of a much wider family web. Donetta grew up with her parents in Jamaica on a small farm, but she now describes herself as a 'Jamaican Canadian'. This complexity in identity resulting from migration goes back at least to her parents' generation, for her mother was born to a migrant Jamaican family in Panama, only coming to Jamaica as a small child, and to the end of her life was proud to be able to count in Spanish. In Donetta's generation her sisters and brother were to cross the Atlantic in diverse directions. She was the youngest of seven children, of whom only one has remained in Jamaica throughout. The eldest and the third sister went to England, and although they have now returned to Jamaica their children remain in London. But Donetta, her brother, her two other sisters and also her mother all migrated to Canada rather than England. Another close relative, her mother's sister's daughter Joyce Leroy, migrated first to England and then moved on to New York. Yet despite the vast distances separating them, Donetta's relatives remain in close contact, whether in Britain, North America or Jamaica.

It is this kind of family, maintaining close relationships across national boundaries, with members often holding more than one citizenship, which we call a 'transnational family', that has inspired our project (Goulbourne, 2002). We wanted to understand how far grandparents and parents, brothers and sisters, could still operate as families despite being split up by migration, and whether the family patterns and sense of identity remained simply Jamaican after migration, or new forms are emerging.

Firstly, for these Jamaican families whom we interviewed transnationalism is not a figment of the researcher's imagination, but a reality both in the mind and in practice. Obviously the continual fracturing, both in terms of migration and of multiple partnering, means that contacts are often lost, and there are often gaps in people's knowledge. In any case it is only practicable to keep in active touch with a limited number of kin over such distances. Nevertheless people

maintaining close
family relationships
long distance

were certainly always aware of their Jamaican, British and North American relatives and usually in touch with some of them.

These families are rarely easy to delineate, particularly because it has long been so common in Jamaican families for either fathers or mothers or both to have children with more than one partner. Such multiple partnering is so widespread that very many families become complex structures. Thus the starting point of one of our first families was four half-sisters by the same mother, each with different fathers who had other children. The fathers of two of them had altogether some 30 children from at least ten different mothers. It is impossible to compress this kind of family into the narrow spaces of a conventional Anglo-American family tree. And often it may require a long discussion to unravel precisely how two people are related. Selvin Green recalls how as a child in Jamaica he went to school with 'many, many cousins by my mother's side ... Some of them I can't even remember their names, there's so many of them'. Quite often because of distance or breaches the whole kin network cannot be known. Thus Yolande Woods grew up in Britain believing that she belonged to an unusually small Jamaican family, and only as an adult discovered she had a 'mega-family' of relatives in rural Jamaica. This means that there is always the possibility of unfinished business in setting out these kin patterns: someone unexpected who may suddenly be discovered, or come 'knocking at her door'. These are kin systems which more than most are continually on the move. The sheer difficulties of comprehending such kin links may be one possible reason why Jamaicans tend to simplify. Typically, they do not distinguish half from full siblings, or indeed use these terms, and they call aunts cousins or vice versa with little concern. But when one looks more closely, it becomes apparent that this imprecision is in fact a distinctive structural feature of the Jamaican kinship system.

It is particularly striking that in the Jamaican countryside this broad concept of family has been paralleled in practice by a traditional usage of 'family land' on which any member of the family has a right to come and live – thus creating both a bond and also sometimes a source of conflict. Family land is freehold land owned in common by the family, most of which was acquired by former slaves in the post-emancipation period (Besson, 2002). It is usually transmitted by custom rather than formal law, and all recognized descendants through both sexes of its original owners have accepted rights to use it and to build a house on it. The land should be transmitted undivided, so that the co-heirs have

At School Am Many Cousins

joint rights to the whole rather than actual pieces of it. It is also traditionally regarded as inalienable. This reluctance to sell is strengthened by the fact that in many cases family members are buried there, so that their graves give an element of sacredness to the family land. Often children were also linked to the family land through the planting of 'navel trees', as Dick Woodward remembered:

> It's an Ashanti practice in West Africa, that the umbilical cord, when you're born, is cut off, and a piece of it is kept in the room until you're old enough to understand, and then it's buried in the ground and the tree is planted on it. That is your link with this spot, … your link to the place, as your family, your responsibility.

In practice, however, priority is given to those family members who are most in need, and those who occupy and cultivate particular bits of the family land, especially over more than one generation, may come to be seen as owners of it. On the other hand, those who have migrated or otherwise done better are expected to suspend their claims. Nevertheless these absent members are recognized as having a latent right to return to use the land for example on retirement. 'Thus is the *entitlement* to freehold land which is the crucial aspect of family land, rather than the *activation* of such rights' (Besson and Momsen, 1987, p. 15). In short, in terms of land, 'family' is seen as encompassing all those descended from the same ancestors, with no formal or gender distinctions accepted between them in terms of rights, but prioritization based on individual need and circumstance.

This concept closely matches the working of the overall kin system in other ways. For example, in terms of the mutual aid which is such a strong feature of these families, such as helping with migration or caring for the children or for the old, two features are striking. The first is that help sometimes comes from or is given to quite distant kin in the complex wider family structure, including kin by marriage. But this inclusiveness is countered by the second feature, selectivity. Thus while most migrants feel an obligation to send regular money and gifts home, they are likely to focus on those they feel are most in need. For example, one New York Jamaican explained how he sends remittances not to his mother, but the younger sister: 'Of all the family members, she is the one who is struggling most to make ends meet'. We view this combination of complexity with pragmatic selectivity not as a sign of weakness in the kin system, but as a positive characteristic, which enables its resilience in supporting family members. The flexibility of Jamaican kin relationships is empowered by their pragmatism and informality.

Remembering points of pain

It is worth exploring a little more deeply how emotional loss is handled, both because it is a central issue for migrants, but also because it highlights the workings of the Jamaican kin system.

There is, firstly, certainly a kind of grief intrinsic in migration itself, even when made in a spirit of hope for betterment. Some migrants for years continued to feel a general sense of loss, which they expressed in terms of feeling socially isolated.

… These feelings of loss were much more acute when they concerned separations between parents and children. When she was 17 Verity Houghton's mother left for Canada, preparing the way for the rest of the family, but to Verity 'It felt like someone – someone had died.' Isabelle Woods' mother left London for New York when she was under 5, but she still remembers her distress: 'I was bitter towards that. I didn't see the need for her to leave.' Roy Cripps did not see or hear his mother for five years after she migrated ahead to England: 'My mother – I miss my mother dearly, dearly, I really did.'

The other most notable points of pain sprang from the widespread practice, both in migrant families and in Jamaican families generally, of children being brought up by substitute parents, typically grandmothers or other older kin. It is clear that in most instances these older caregivers proved more than adequate substitutes for mothers. Selvin Green stands for many others when he says, 'I was pretty close to [my mother], although I was closer to my grandmother.' Connie Dixon calls her grandmother 'a saint'. But because of their greater age grandmothers were more likely to die than mothers, and for Connie the day her grandmother died was 'the first time I've ever felt my heart ache, and it was literally, my heart was aching'.

There is, on the other hand, rarely any emphasis on pain through absent or missing fathers. In general, when a father is absent but 'owns up' to being a parent, exchanges photographs and sends occasional money and gifts to his children, his behaviour is regarded as acceptable. The contact and gifts are seen not only as helpful but as important symbols of caring. Thus Selvin Green described how he sustained contact in this way with children he had left behind through migrating to England: 'So

it's continuous communication with barrels and letters and money …
You just keep communicating. You can't lose track of them.'

References

Besson, J. (2002) *Martha Brae's Two Histories: European Expansion and Caribbean Culture-Building in Jamaica,* Chapel Hill, NC, University of North Carolina Press.

Besson, J. and Momsen, J. (1987) *Land and Development in the Caribbean,* London, Macmillan.

Goulbourne, H. (2002) 'Questions of theory, definition, purpose', in *Caribbean Transnational Experience,* London, Pluto Press.

Reading B
Making babies and mothers: from nurseries to baby showers

Alison Clark

Source: 'Maternity and materiality: becoming a mother in consumer culture', in Taylor, J. S., Layne, L. L. and Wozniak, D. F. (eds), 2004, *Consuming Motherhood*, New Brunswick, NJ, Rutgers University Press, pp. 55–71.

Young families living on a single street in North London referred to here as Jay Road engage in a range of infant-related consumptive activities, from the decoration of nurseries to the exchanging of secondhand babies' clothes. The examples presented here are representative of a range of practices associated with the provisioning of infants and, in particular, the ways in which these activities related to a localized meaning of mothering and class. …

The informants featured in this study are not necessarily defined as middle class in terms of formal definitions of education and income (Marshall et al., 1988). Jay Road has no discernible 'community' or class-specific demographic as such. Rather, social class arises as a definition through the actual practices of provisioning, which, in terms of the construction of mothering, lends the neighbourhood a particularly significant cultural geographic meaning.

Many residents with small children, or those planning a family, identified the greenness, easy access to parks, and associated amenities as an attractive feature of the area. For Jay Road is equidistant from an overtly white, middle-class, cosmopolitan area (Ibis Pond) and a more urban, ethnically mixed and predominantly working-class area (Wood Green). The polarization of these areas becomes a pronounced means by which, in the process of conceiving of motherhood, women construct a class disposition toward place and practice. The safety and intimacy of Ibis Pond, with its green, village-like atmosphere, is often contrasted with the harsh urbanism of Wood Green. In the following excerpt, taken from a conversation with Sally, who moved to Jay Road several months prior to the birth of her son, the harsh urbanism of Wood Green was encapsulated by a seemingly portentous shopping trip for the baby-to-be: 'The first time we went to Wood Green [High Street] was the week before he was born, and I went with my mother-in-law to look for a cot. We were walking under the car park area and got hit by a flying bottle. We got cut, so I've not had good associations with Wood Green, not my sort of place.' Middle-class dispositions in and around Jay Road are not a priori reflections of economic and cultural privilege. Rather, many inhabitants on the street are less stable in their class positions. This may transpire in the use of oppositional geographical locations such as Ibis Pond and Wood Green. In this sense Miller (1998), discussing this locality of North London, describes a process of 'shopping for class' as people 'try on' different class positions; 'The problem of job insecurity combined with better possibilities of class switching is not somehow less "authentic" or more superficial than a consistent identification with a particular cluster of values. Many people inhabit not one or other site, but encompass the relationship itself and the field of difference' (Miller, 1998, pp. 157–8). Class here, then, is understood as a social practice rather than as a static identity.

In Sally's description of her ill-fated shopping trip, the idyllic innocence of a baby's cot, and the social process of provisioning the nursery is contrasted with the anarchic alienation of the working-class urban area. Sally uses the symbolism invoked by the incident to mark the end of any potential relationship with Wood Green and, by association, any of the urban 'messiness' it denotes. But this is not merely a straight enactment of a class disposition (Sally herself was brought up in a working-class area of a major city); rather, it is the intersection with a new and burgeoning social identity as a mother that makes this encounter specifically poignant. It also marks the beginning of imagined and enacted trajectories around provisioning and its values, which are inextricably linked to the social making of infants.

The nursery, a room given over to the nurturing of infants and the housing of their related material culture, has evolved as a key site of desire and fantasy in the context of mothering in contemporary consumer culture. While women, such as Sally, might have the space and resources to go shopping for their nursery, even mothers on Jay Road precluded from physically making a nursery often fantasized about their 'ideal' baby room. Popular childcare consumer magazines, recommending nursery styles ranging from the Scandinavian 'natural look' to the cheery primary-colored 'modern look', promote the idea that a major project of pregnancy is the construction of this child-centered space. While fantasizing around this space offered some women pleasure, for others, making sense of the multitude of styles and objects associated with its construction was an onerous task.

Nursery

Provisioning an unborn infant requires choices and expertise in an unfamiliar arena where the stakes could not be higher – for every object and every style has attached to it some notion of a 'type' of mothering or an expression of a desired mother/infant relationship.

Historically, the nursery itself has evolved as a morally pertinent domestic space. In Britain, from the mid-nineteenth century onward, it emerged as a discrete domestic space within middle-class housing, coinciding with the proliferation of child-rearing advice literature aimed at mothering as an increasingly ideologized arena (Hardyment, 1983). The nursery was seen as an essential space for the correct instruction of infants, and its hygienic, thoughtful decoration was viewed as an instrumental part of this endeavor. Although nannies and other child-related servants may have used the space, the middle-class mother was expected to oversee its decoration and provisioning.

By the turn of the century the nursery was seen as such an integral part of 'proper' child rearing that popular advice literature pleaded with mothers to turn their drawing rooms over to their children if they had no other rooms available. Books such as *Nursery Management* (1914) stressed the importance of modern decoration and recommended nonmorbid decorative subjects, creamy yellow walls, a sunny disposition, short neat curtains, and simple stained floors with removable rugs (Hardyment, 1983, pp. 141–2).

With a new emphasis on development rather than nurturance, by the mid-twentieth century the nursery became more commonly referred to as the 'play-room'. With its new nomenclature came new understandings of the nursery's role in the development of the independent child. However small the space, pleaded one contemporary advice source, its existence was essential in maintaining a healthy separation of infant and mother, for 'if in hearing distance of mummy [the infant] will constantly call out to her' (Page, 1953, p. 101).

In the context of North London homes, nurseries and playrooms have taken on a meaning more indicative of an idealized, child-centric culture described by contemporary scholars of childhood (James and Prout, 1997; James et al., 1998). In practical terms, a *nursery* generally refers to an infant's bedroom and the *playroom* denotes an area of daytime use and toy storage. But ideologically, these areas have become a key means of valorizing the otherwise ostensibly mundane and utilitarian aspects of caring. Although such areas are not formally designed into any of the informants' homes, the conjuring up of the nursery, if only metaphorically, is a key means of imagining the physical presence of an infant-to-be and its objects.

Gemma lives with her husband, Anthony, in a two-bedroom Victorian terrace house (on one of the less expensive streets adjacent to Jay Road), and she decided to convert a guest bedroom into a nursery. In the latter stages of her pregnancy, Gemma gave up work as a part-time salesperson in a natural health food store to spend more time at home preparing for the birth of her son. The couple depend on the single income generated by the husband's position as a visiting lecturer in a London art school and so are fully aware that a new child will drastically change their relaxed attitude toward household budgeting. In this case, Gemma's extensive redecoration and refurbishment of a customized nursery relies solely on homemade and customized goods rather than brand new, shop-bought models of furniture and equipment. Gemma and her husband did not originally own their home together. Once Anthony's bachelor home, the house has been gradually transformed into a family home through the joint purchase of secondhand furniture and collected artifacts. For Gemma, however, the creation of a themed nursery, a project initiated prior to the birth of her son and extended several months after, is not shared with her husband. Rather, it is the major focus of her time spent at home alone with her unborn and now her new infant son: 'I've got all the furniture in his room, Charlie's room at the moment I'm going to paint, I'm going to stencil on little cowboy motifs and stuff to make it look all "Westerny", so I've got a constant running list of what I'm going to do; it's just having the time. I've … taken a very long time to do it. And it's not like nursery rhyme [themed], it's like cowboys and stuff, it's a bit more grown up than a typical nursery, which drives me mad.' Although Gemma insists the nursery is incomplete (she intends, for example, to make three-dimensional cacti from vivid green felted fabric), upon entering six month-old Charlie's room, one is stunned by the minute attention paid to detail in the decor, from the embroidered cowboy hats on the bed linen to the tasseled 'poncho' lampshade. Provisioning for Charlie's room is an integral part of Gemma's present mind-set as, like the majority of nonworking mothers on the street, she spends a large proportion of her time alone with her child in the home. But in Gemma's case, her enthusiasm for home crafts and design generates a type of motivation and sociality that carries beyond the domestic sphere. She visits local furniture auctions and charity shops, for example, with her baby, looking for cheap items to renovate and paint. Because Gemma left her country of origin (the United States) twelve years prior to her marriage in England, she does not have direct contact with any extended family, and her new role of mother is largely self-taught. Although she has had contact with middle-class mothering organizations in the area, such as the National Childbirth Trust (NCT), she remains peripheral to this social network and disassociates herself from what she views as typically British middle-class mothers' concerns. She is less purist, for example, in her critique of consumerism, gleefully telling of how she combined her trip home to America with a massive shopping spree in which she managed to fit out Charlie with a wardrobe of branded clothing half the price of that available in Britain. Similarly, she happily receives gifts of branded toys unavailable in the United Kingdom from relatives and friends in the United States.

Unlike the core of middle-class mothers on Jay Road, previously sociable women who self-sacrificially deny themselves a social life with the birth of their new child … Gemma makes concerted efforts, within weeks of her child's birth, to visit pubs with friends and generally regain her social self. In this sense, Gemma's nursery project melds the knowledge and skills of a previous identity with those of a new mother to create a revalorized role expressed in her concerted effort to use an atypical nursery motif indicative of her and her son's perceived individuality.

References

Hardyment, C. (1983) *Dream Babies: Childcare from Locke to Spock*, London, Jonathan Cape.

James, A., Jenks, C. and Prout, A. (eds) (1998) *Theorizing Childhood*, New York, Teachers College Press.

James, A. and Prout, A. (1997) *Constructing and Reconstructing Childhood*, London, Falmer Press.

Marshall, G., Newby, H., Rose, D. and Vogler, C. (eds) (1988) *Social Class in Modern Britain*, London, Hutchinson.

Miller, D. (1998) 'John Lewis and the cheapjack: a study of class and identity', in Miller, D., Jackson, P., Thrift, N., Holbrook, B. and Rowlands, M. (eds) *Shopping, Place and Identity*, London, Routledge.

Page, H. (1953) *Playtime in the First Five Years*, London, Allen & Unwin.

Reading C
Southerton, England: the local young and homeless

Tom Hall

Source: 'Out of work and house and home: contested youth in an English homeless hostel', 2006, *Ethnos: Journal of Anthropology*, vol. 71, no. 2, pp. 143–63.

In the remainder of this article I draw on fieldwork and arguments developed more fully elsewhere (see Hall, 2003; also 2001). The fieldwork requires some introduction. In the early 1990s I spent a year in southeast of England in a town I will call Southerton: a busily provincial place, that was part of a larger and expanding conurbation, not too far from London. Throughout my time there I lived in bed-sit and hostel accommodation together with a shifting collection of young people in their mid-to-late teens, all of whom were homeless when I first met them and many of whom remained so, off and on, throughout the twelve months that I was in contact with them – estranged from their parents, sometimes roofless, and otherwise stringing together a succession of stays in stop-gap, emergency and locally rented, run-down bed-sit accommodation. They were also jobless: out of work, with little if any experience of employment, and struggling to get by on the very periphery of the welfare system, slipping through the benefits net altogether from time to time. Britain was in economic recession at the time and youth employment opportunities were slim. Fewer than one in ten 16-year-olds were leaving school and entering employment (Roberts, 1995, p. 7).

Of the one hundred or so young people that I got to know during fieldwork, almost all had at one time or other stayed at Southerton's only direct-access hostel for the young homeless, the Lime Street hostel, a voluntary sector project offering short-stay accommodation for young people in acute housing difficulties. At the time of writing, the hostel is still open and continues to provide emergency accommodation for local young people with nowhere else to stay (upwards of 120 young people in the last year).

The hostel, a three-storied terraced property close to the town centre and train station, has overnight rooms and beds for up to ten young people. It is a 'direct access' project, taking on (almost) any young person in need of accommodation, at face value and without third-party referral. Most of those coming to stay arrive in the wake of some or other family dispute. Some ring the bell, late at night, angry and upset, having 'walked out' of home only hours ago. Others turn up, bedraggled, after a couple of days spent making do – staying with friends and/or sleeping rough. Still others have been away from home and living independently for some time but have run into difficulties, lost their accommodation and do not see returning to their parents as an option. Samantha was one such teenager. Aged sixteen, she arrived on Lime Street with an eventful and involved housing history already behind her:

SAMANTHA: I was just fed up with the rules and that. My dad was quite strict with me really and I'd just had enough. I didn't get on with them at all when I was at home, so I just, like, up and left. We had a big row and fighting and that first of all … I stayed at my friend Sue's place up the road for the weekend until I got somewhere sorted. Then I went and stayed with my nan, but I got into a bit of trouble there … then I moved back home. I don't know why. My mum wanted me to, and in a way I did [too] … but we had another big row and my mum said to get the hell out, so I did. But the police picked me up … they put me into emergency accommodation … [and] in the end I moved in with this guy called Jim. We was really good mates and that, and if I didn't have any money he'd help me out and he was always there, sort of thing. But everything went wrong … I phoned my social worker but she wouldn't re-house me cos I'd done so many bunks before … I tried a couple of places, but they didn't have no accommodation for me so I come here.

Still others have no family home to speak of. Like most projects for the young homeless, the Lime Street hostel sees its share of 'looked after' young people from local authority care.

The hostel is open all year round and generally operates at, or very close to, its full complement of ten residents. But the turnover is brisk. Some young people stay for no more than a single night before moving back home or in with a friend or somewhere else again. Most stay longer, a few days at least and perhaps up to eight weeks, which is the maximum residency on offer. There is no bar to the number of times a

[handwritten margin note: rules / Same / dad strict.]

young person can stay and a good few of those who pass through the hostel are back again in a matter of weeks, sometimes days. Tony was one such 'regular' on Lime Street during my fieldwork.

TONY: … [the first time that I stayed at the hostel] they found me a bed-sit. I was there for about four and a half weeks and then I got kicked out. The landlord was a bit of a wanker. He kicked all the under-eighteens out for no reason. So I went back to the hostel … I stayed for about a month and then I found another place, but I didn't like it there either cos I didn't get on with any of the residents. I was 17 when I moved in there. People were always fighting and the landlord wouldn't do nothing about it and I just got hacked off with it. Then I moved back again and the staff found me a place on a training scheme. I was at the hostel two months that time, until just before Easter. Then over Easter I went home cos I was talking to my mum again. But my mum can only stand me for so long, and I can only stand her for so long, so … I moved back to the hostel.

Tony's story is his own, but not out of keeping with other residents'. The same goes for Samantha. This is the sort of thing – family arguments, evictions, further complications, unspecified injustices, sudden reversals and upsets – that workers with the young homeless hear day in, day out.

These were Southerton's young homeless then. Young people in various difficulties, away from home and out of work and moving through an assortment of short-lived, insecure and unsatisfactory living arrangements – friends' floors, hostel beds, and substandard rented rooms. A few of these young people make cameo appearances in this [reading], with little by way of introduction or biographical context, which is much the same way they 'appeared' at the hostel – arriving suddenly and without much explanation.

Bed-sit rooms and 'DSS' tenants

There was, during my time there, a definite 'scene' in Southerton, associated with a dozen or so notorious rented bed-sit properties clustered together in and around the town centre. Owned by some of Southerton's less esteemed landlords, these properties constituted something like an informal sector of the local housing market, let by the room and by casual agreement on a no-questions-asked basis and without written tenure or legal agreement. Poorly maintained and managed with indifference (and occasional intimidation), a very few of these properties were simply decrepit and unfit to live in. The rest were passable, if drear and cramped. All were disreputable: cheap, shabby and a locally recognised hub for drug use and general misbehaviour. The occupancy was always mixed, but predominantly young people, mostly teenagers living away from home and on benefits. Tenancy in these properties was a precarious affair. Turnover was extremely high and evictions commonplace. On any given day there would be an indeterminate number of young people 'in residence': those only just arrived, those due out by the weekend, those staying with friends (sleeping on floors and sofas), and those stuck in the same room for weeks now but looking to move out and on.

This collection of young, unsettled tenants and hangers on was more than a little fuzzy at the edges, but it had a coherence of sorts as a loose network of friends, associates and occasional contacts. The network was sparse and constantly reconfiguring in places, but extraordinarily dense elsewhere, stringing together clusters of close association. This included a handful of more established, longer-term occupants – who had been around and 'in the bed-sits' for some time (if not in any one property for much more than a month or two) – around whom a good deal of life in the bed-sits revolved.

These were the bed-sits, then. The grubby end of Southerton's rented housing market, home to assorted 'DSS'* tenants, teenagers and trouble makers. During my fieldwork, and still today, a good share of the young people coming to stay at the Lime Street hostel arrived having first stayed, and then run into difficulties and out of options, in rooms like these. Many more, most in fact, moved (back) there when they left Lime Street, having nowhere much else to go.

Note

* The acronym DSS stands, or rather stood, for Department of Social Security ... this was the government department responsible for the management and payment of social security – benefit – claims, albeit through an executive agency called the Benefits Agency. For young people like Samantha and Tony, DSS stood as a catch-all, shorthand term for a number of things: the benefits they received (*I've been on DSS since I left home*), the offices they dealt with in the pursuit of their claims (*I've been down the DSS all morning trying to get things sorted*), and the status of being 'in receipt of benefits' (*I'm DSS, aren't I? Like everyone else round*

here). ... There is no longer a Department of Social Security, although the acronym DSS is still widely understood.

References

Hall, T. (2001) 'Caught not taught: ethnographic research at a young people's accommodation project', in Shaw, I. and Gould, N. (eds) *Qualitative Research in Social Work*, London, Sage.

Hall, T. (2003) *Better Times than This: Youth Homelessness in Britain*, London, Pluto Press.

Roberts, K. (1995) *Youth and Employment in Modern Britain*, Oxford, Oxford University Press.

Chapter 3

Public spaces

Peter Kraftl

Contents

In this chapter, you will:

- consider debates about 'public space' and contrasting meanings of this term
- explore how young people in public space are represented as both threatened and a threat
- investigate a range of sites designed for children in public spaces
- gain an understanding of how young people use and inhabit public spaces in diverse ways, and explore examples of the responses that these actions evoke in 'adult' society.

1 Introduction

The focus of this chapter is on how children and young people can seem 'out of place' in public. You were introduced, in Chapter 1, to the concepts of space and place, and you explored how these concepts can be used to understand children's experiences and contemporary ideas about childhood. In this chapter, we continue the discussions begun in the introduction to this book, about the spatial contexts of children and young people, and about how they appear 'out of place' in locations where the environment is made and defined by adults. Building on the perspective developed in Chapter 1, we will consider further the way in which children inhabit space and the contested nature of their relationship to the public. Young people are represented through various configurations of risk – as being 'risky' or threatening, and as being 'at risk' or threatened in public space – and their presence in public spaces can reflect how young people are (or are not) viewed as members of society. We will relate these representations to the idea of 'the public' and how – as with the idea of 'the private' – it is being defined, redefined and contested in contemporary society. We will discuss how recent urban design and young people's participation in it reflect new modes of governance in society. In addition, we will explore how young people engage in perhaps surprisingly diverse elements of life in public spaces, which, in turn, can challenge assumptions about what is official and unofficial use, who can join in and whose rules apply.

2 Setting the boundaries

2.1 Youth as threat and children 'at risk': the politics of public space

In October 2009, the BBC reported that police in Gipton, a suburb of Leeds (England), had been granted 'a dispersal order to tackle anti-social behaviour among young people' – that is, the power to move groups of people deemed to be causing 'trouble' away from a defined geographical area. These powers have been granted to several police forces across the UK, and tend to single out groups of young people (although sometimes to protect other young people from them). The same news item noted that 'the order also bans under 16s from entering certain public spaces within the zone between 2100 GMT and 0600 GMT' (BBC, 2009). A local police inspector was quoted as saying, 'Members of the public, local businesses and visitors to the area have the right to enjoy this part of Leeds without being unduly affected or intimidated by groups of young people' (BBC, 2009). His comment could be interpreted as implying that young people are in a separate category from those who have a right to inhabit a particular public space.

bans on under 16's entering certain public spaces

A different approach to preventing young people from loitering is represented by the 'Mosquito'. This device emits a high-pitched noise which, since hearing range naturally reduces during the ageing process, can typically only be heard by young people under the age of 25. The sound is irritating enough to force those affected to move on. The United Nations Convention on the Rights of the Child (UNCRC), the Children's Commissioner Sir Al Aynsley-Green and human rights groups such as Liberty have all criticised its unregulated use by shops, councils, businesses and even private homes in the UK. Such use, they argue, breaches young people's human rights; the noise can be painful, there is little research into its impact on health, and it also affects babies and children who are present with their parents or on their own (Akiyama, 2010). These responses have, in turn, drawn the ire of advocates of the device. In February 2008, the *Daily Mail* ran a story under the headline 'Buzz off!', highlighting how it had stopped racist attacks by 'gangs of yobs' on an Indian restaurant owner, and quoting a Tory MP as saying, 'The good professor [Aynsley-Green] needs to come down from his ivory tower and see what it's like living in the real world'

(Hickley, 2008). In a further twist, it has been reported that some young people have recorded the Mosquito noise on their mobile phones to play back in school, disrupting classes without the teacher being able to understand why – an example of technology being used to subvert the purpose for which it was developed and, depending on your view of the matter, of young people's creativity or endless capacity to cause trouble (Morgan, 2006).

The battle lines here are familiar: many adults – and indeed many young people – are intimidated by groups of young people, sometimes for good reason. Meanwhile, young people in the UK may argue that they have nowhere else to go when they want to be with peers and away from parents, particularly in urban or low-income areas where housing is overcrowded and/or badly sound-proofed and gardens are small or non-existent. But children are also often perceived as being 'at risk' in public spaces, or 'exposed' to an adult world which they are too young to understand and which is beset by multiple dangers. Cases of child abduction, though rare, receive huge media and public attention, as have more recent proposals to restrict advertising containing 'sexualised' imagery from being sited near to schools.

groups of youths intimidating

Risks to children in public spaces

Figure 1   Young children in a busy street

It is not just the nature of public space, but also of how children and youth are viewed, which is at stake here. For example, in London in 2010, when police deployed the 'kettle' against young people protesting about government cuts to education funding, some parents responded by setting up a group called 'Stop Kettling Our Kids'. Moreover, in the left-of-centre magazine *New Statesman*, journalist Laurie Penny wrote

Kettling is a tactic in which large numbers of police cordon demonstrators in a specific area, sometimes denying toilet facilities or permission to leave for long periods.

that she 'didn't understand quite how bad things had become in this country' until she saw 'armoured cops being deployed against schoolchildren in the middle of Whitehall' (Penny, 2010). Describing protesters as 'schoolchildren' emphasises their vulnerability; if this term was transposed with that used in relation to the Mosquito device mentioned earlier ('gangs of yobs'), it would create quite a different effect.

These examples show how the geography of childhood is constructed across time and place, such that young people can be constructed as 'children' in one locality and context but as 'yobs' and 'youth' in another (Nayak, 2003). In Chapter 1, Clark and Gallacher discussed the argument that 'childhood … is that status of personhood which is by definition often in the wrong place' (Jenks, 2005, p. 73). This suggests that the 'problem' with young people is where they are – on the street, outside shops and restaurants or (as with the Mods and Rockers in Brighton during the 1960s) congregating on the seafront. It highlights the central significance of spatial processes in contextualising childhood and youth, and our ambivalent responses not only to young people's presence in public spaces but to those places themselves. As Nayak argues, we need to acknowledge 'the contradictory practices of children and see … their activities as situated responses, continually reworked by landscape, peers and social situation' if we are to move beyond binaries of innocent/evil, risky/at-risk (Nayak, 2003, p. 311).

2.2   Defining public space

Before we continue, it is useful to explore some key dimensions of 'public space' as we discuss it in this chapter. The term 'public' can be used in contradictory ways – for example, when private fee-paying educational institutions are described as 'public schools'. In addition, ideas about 'public sector', 'public sphere' or 'public service' are highly contested and politicised.

Public space as democratic space or public sphere

'Public space' often invokes ideas of democracy, which we enter as 'citizens'. The 'Athenian model' of direct democracy involved public assemblies (in the 'agora' or marketplace) which all citizens could attend and vote at. While this is rather remote from our own model of representative democracy, it resonates with notions of public open spaces as a place for free (political) expression, where we have the 'right' to protest about issues of the day. Speakers' Corner in Hyde Park, Tiananmen Square in China and, more recently, Tahrir Square in

Egypt and Syntagma (Constitution) Square in Greece have all been the sites of popular gatherings and democratic protest. More generally, public spaces – including public parks, streets, urban squares, libraries, mass transit systems, and so on – may be seen as democratic insofar as they are for everyone, open, common and shared with 'all walks of life', even providing a place for interaction across social hierarchies. And, figuratively, 'the public sphere' refers to an arena of debate by an informed electorate which ensures that democracy is 'healthy' and elected representatives do not abuse their power. The place of young people in these definitions is partly a question of how far, or even whether, they are seen as citizens with the right to express political views, particularly given that they are not allowed to vote until they are aged 18.

However, 'the public' is an ambivalent concept. A thesaurus could suggest alternatives such as 'riffraff', 'rabble', 'mob', 'multitude' or 'the great unwashed': that is, the term 'public' can connote the chaotic coming together of undesirable elements, the insistent presence of the poor and working class, and whatever infringes on the desire for privacy. Likewise, in the UK 'the public sector' can be seen either negatively or positively. Advocates argue that public sector institutions like the BBC, libraries, the NHS and the Office of National Statistics make a crucial contribution to the democratic public sphere, because being publically funded but independent of both government and market enables them to provide information free from undue political or commercial bias. However, and particularly since the 1980s, the advocates of market forces have depicted the public sector as elite, unwieldy, unresponsive and slow to innovate, and have demanded that public ownership be reconsidered.

Public as opposed to private space

The public sphere can also signify the realm of paid work and public institutions as well as politics – a realm distinct from 'the private sphere', involving domestic family relations, 'personal life' or that which falls outside the purview of the state. In liberal philosophy, the private sphere is seen both as a place of refuge and as apolitical in the sense that individuals within it are free to make their own decisions. Feminists, among others, however, have taken a less sanguine view, arguing that various kinds of oppression and even abuse experienced in the home are political and not personal issues, just as the political sphere is also personal.

The private sphere is also usually considered the appropriate site for sexual intimacy, as the humorous comment directed at amorous couples in public, 'Get a room!', acknowledges. However, it is often the heterosexual/adult/married couple that is privileged. Young people, whether gay or straight, may have no choice but to conduct their sexual and emotional lives in public. In other respects too, young people may have less freedom in private space than adults, since they may have to obey parental rules, share rooms with siblings, limit their socialising, and so on.

Public as opposed to 'privatised' (commercialised) space

As noted earlier, issues of public funding and ownership have become complex and disputed in recent years. In the UK, land and buildings that were previously owned by government or local authorities – including many schools, leisure and sporting facilities – have been sold to private companies to develop and run. Out-of-town retail developments and shopping malls have continued to grow alongside the emergence of 'gated communities', the widespread adoption of technological surveillance devices such as CCTV (closed-circuit television), and the increasing monopoly of large supermarket chains and other corporate brands across the country. Some commentators have described this as the 'privatisation' of what was formerly 'public' space, in doing so associating the latter with democratic accountability and the former with powerful, unelected multinational corporations. These commentators point out that decisions about access to many of these spaces and the activities that go on there are, to some extent, in the hands of private security officers and their management or landlords. However, privatisation, where private companies rather than the public sector own and/or provide services and facilities, has an ambiguous relationship to 'the public', especially where education or health are concerned (Buckingham, 2011).

Public space has long been 'commercialised', in the sense of being used for the display of advertising. Billboards carrying promotional messages are now such a pervasive feature of the landscape as to be largely unremarked, except when people object to particular advertisements or to finding them in, say, the vicinity of schools. It has been argued that private management rescues the public realm from neglect and underuse; that cash-strapped councils cannot make use of land even where they own it, whereas private developers will have a stake in attracting people to mixed use (retail, leisure and/or housing) developments – for example, by funding public art and events. In other words, private ownership does not in itself mean that 'democratic', vital and publicly accessible space is immediately lost, although it may have other more long-term and insidious consequences, as we will discuss later.

Finally, some commentators draw attention to 'marketisation' – that is, how market practices and ways of thinking (e.g. in terms of profit and loss, customers or clients, consumer satisfaction and consultation) have permeated all areas of life, including education, health and even the conduct of personal intimate relationships, thus extending across any public–private divide. As we continue through this chapter, we will use the term 'commercialisation' rather than 'privatisation' to capture these complex developments (Buckingham, 2011) and to question their consequences for children, young people and public space.

Access and mobilities

In relation to each of these definitions, questions can be raised about access and how it is differentiated according to gender, class, age, sexuality and ethnicity. Participation in the agora was, after all, confined to Athenian-born, free, land-owning males and, historically, men have been able to move freely between public and private spaces while women and children have been confined within the private. The term 'streetwalker' for a sex worker reveals deeply ingrained cultural beliefs that 'decent' women somehow do not belong on the streets. Meanwhile, feminist campaigns have always involved claims to visibility in public spaces (Tonkiss, 2005).

Some scholars have argued that the growth of consumer society has enabled women to gain new access to public space – for example, as key consumers and shop-workers in the urban department store during the nineteenth century (Bowlby, 1985; Wilson, 1991). Other writers have observed how the anonymity of a big city can offer many social groups the pleasure, as well as the fear, of going unnoticed. Yet the freedom to move in public – how far one is deemed 'out of place', as discussed in Chapter 1 – continues to be differentiated according to ethnicity, gender, age and class. For example, police powers of 'stop and search' are used predominately against young minority ethnic people, and against young men more than young women. Arguably, children have the least freedom to access public space independently, and these limitations are primarily age- rather than status-related. Children are trained in how to move around and use this space; they are most likely to have to seek permission to do so; they are most likely to be escorted by adults; and adults often assume the right to define what spaces are safe and appropriate for them.

A second key issue is that of mobilities – how one travels between different kinds of spaces, which relates, in turn, to how one comes to know and define one's local environment. Forms of transport are saturated with powerful but contradictory meanings, such that a car can signify individual liberation or selfish gas-guzzling, while taking the bus can represent social solidarity or (in words often attributed to the former Prime Minister Margaret Thatcher) that 'a man who ... finds himself on a bus can count himself as a failure in life'. In recent years, young people's independent mobility, like their access to public space, is considered to have declined in many minority-world countries, and parents who let their children out unaccompanied are even deemed irresponsible. For example, in 2010, the case of parents who let their 5- and 8-year-old children cycle unaccompanied to their school a mile away was hotly debated in the media and online parenting forums (see Wilkes, 2010).

Environmental researcher and campaigner Mayer Hillman (2002) makes an analogy between children and prisoners: both, he argues, have a roof over their heads, regular meals and licensed entertainment, but spend most of their waking hours under surveillance and are not allowed out on their own; yet children have not committed any crime. The removal of their basic freedoms is done in the name of protecting them, primarily from the risks posed by motor vehicles. Reductions in traffic casualties do not necessarily mean that streets are safer, he notes; these reductions may in fact be due to fewer children being allowed out as the street has become increasingly defined as a place for cars. Hillman argues that adults too have withdrawn from the street, with the result that its potential as a site for children's play and informal learning, with supervision or occasional intervention from adults if necessary, is disappearing. He uses the term 'battery-reared' to describe today's children, as does 'toxic childhood' campaigner Sue Palmer (2006). We will return to some of these issues later.

Activity 1   Recalling public spaces
Allow about 20 minutes

Think back to when you were 10 years old. How did you get around your local surroundings and to and from school? At what age were you allowed out unaccompanied? What kind of distances did you travel? (You might consult a map or an online topographical program to get an estimate of distances.) Where did you spend your leisure time – in your bedroom, in a garden, on the streets, in shopping centres, fields or other unsupervised areas? How does this compare with your observations of children of the same age in your neighbourhood today?

Comment

The perception often prevails that children in the past had greater independence than today's children. However, the task of recalling your childhood relies to an extent on the vagaries of memory. Our childhood memories are often influenced by nostalgia, strong emotions (both positive and negative), shared processes of storytelling among and between generations, and our own imagination (Jones, 2003).

These comparisons will also depend on the geographical context. In some areas, children may be scarcely visible; in others, children may be playing out in the street or front gardens. In densely populated urban areas or housing estates with small gardens, young people may be more visible on street corners, green spaces or playing fields. Some retail outlets, such as fast-food outlets, may attract children and young people. And the picture may be quite different at night. In some parts of the world, public places are the context for children working in informal trades, blurring the boundaries between home, play and work, as we will discuss later.

Summary of Section 2

The issue of children and young people's 'place' in public space is contentious, as they are often deemed to be both risky and/or at risk.

'Public space' has many meanings: it is often associated with accessibility and democracy; new forms of commercialisation are giving rise to anxieties.

Whether or not we deem a public space to be 'for' young people depends very much on how we view young people as members of the public and, indeed, as citizens. However, it is important to recognise the complexity and geographical specificity of these debates.

playparks
- no standard on quality

suggestion of discrimination

no - commercialised play areas mere parks

3 Public spaces for young people

3.1 Commercialised spaces

Although most local authorities provide public play-parks for children, their quality is variable. At the time of writing, there are no nationally agreed standards for the quantity and quality of open-space provision in the UK. It also appears that the earlier consensus that such facilities are publicly funded, and therefore free to access, may be faltering. For example, a storm of protest greeted Wandsworth Borough Council's proposal, in May 2011, to introduce a £2.50 weekend charge for its Battersea Park Adventure Playground. The council argued that the charge would be appropriate because most of the children using it came from outside the borough. The idea that taxpayers' responsibility and care should not be towards children collectively but only to particular children, in a delimited area, might itself indicate a shift towards more individualised, or even 'privatised', notions of childhood.

Instead, public spaces for children are increasingly commercialised and consumer-oriented spaces. They are, as cultural historian Dan Cook notes, inherently paradoxical: they are not made or owned by children, but we recognise their 'iconography' – for example, 'the primary colors, the blocked, angled or backward letters, the scribble-writing effect, the chalkboard motif' – and understand that it demarcates what is for children or what belongs to children from other items in 'the visual–spatial landscape of commerce' (Cook, 2003, p. 147). These public commercialised spaces combine consumption, education and entertainment (or 'edutainment'), as David Buckingham (2011) has noted. Theme parks, for example, are now a major leisure destination for families with children. Since they first opened in 1955, Disneyland theme parks, with entertainment and rides based entirely around the company's products, have persuaded many families that childhoods are incomplete without experiencing their 'enchantment' – so successfully that even some charities bankroll the Disneyland magic by funding trips for terminally ill children. Companies and brands increasingly sponsor rides in other theme parks, as well as exhibits in settings such as museums, zoos and 'heritage industry' attractions. Besides promising entertainment, they generally also include information about conservation, wildlife, the environment, and so on, as if to convince parents of the value-added nature of the experience (see Buckingham, 2011).

Figure 2   Families enjoying the Chinese New Year holiday in a theme park at Sungkai, Perak, Malaysia

McKendrick et al. (2000) discuss the expansion, in the UK, of commercialised children's play spaces that provide soft-play areas, 'ball parks', climbing frames and safe surfaces. Corporate providers such as Tumble Tots and Wacky Warehouse have identified a gap in the market for challenging forms of play in a regulated environment. They assure parents that they are offering 'carefully structured' physical activities on 'unique equipment' run by 'specially trained' staff to develop 'confidence and self-esteem' (Tumble Tots, 2012). They also appeal to parents by providing widescreen TV and on-site cafés or bars, or by being located in shopping centres. The latter feature entertainment alongside consumption: in the Westfield shopping centre in London, for example, provision for children includes a free soft-play area, 'kiddy cars' for hire, 'safe shopping' wristbands and family rooms. Stores such as the Early Learning Centre welcome children by providing play areas in which they can sample toys and games.

These examples seem to suggest that the commercial market can indeed provide opportunities for leisure and play. However, Buckingham (2011) points out that most of these opportunities are more readily available to children from families with cash to spare. This may mean that poorer children are more likely to be confined to the home, bearing out Hillman's image of the 'battery-reared' child. Alternatively, poorer children may opt to play outside, but come under greater surveillance because they are not confined to the 'official' spaces designated for their

Cook (2003)
Not modern /
1910's - playareas in
shops

[for parents
benefit.

Children's spaces
easily recognisable
bright colours
patterns

use. This, in turn, makes it more likely that they are deemed a trouble and a nuisance – 'youth' and 'yobs', indeed.

Cook's (2003) history of children's consumer culture in the USA shows that these are not entirely new developments. Even in the 1910s, department stores and some hotels offered play areas where mothers could 'check in' their children while they went shopping. Often child-scale toilet facilities and other services such as hairdressing were also on offer. Nonetheless, scholars have been sharply critical of these commercialised spaces. McKendrick et al. (2000) argue that children's needs and interests may be of less significance than those of parents. Stuart Aitken (2001) interprets these spaces as a direct reaction to the 'spectacles of fear' about dangerous streets, and sees them as 'kid corrals' where children can be 'sequestered' away not only from the streets but also from other children, who might play too rough. Cook (2003, p. 151) reflects that 'commercialized play, for Aitken, is part of a larger self-sequestering of the middle-class away from inner city moral pollution into gated, private communities'.

Whether or not one accepts these criticisms, Cook argues that they ignore how children are addressed and constituted by these spaces. He shows that, as a market developed for specific children's clothing departments in the 1920s and 1930s, stores increasingly addressed the child directly, respecting and legitimating the 'child's perspective'. However, they catered for children's assumed views and concerns in ways that were sharply differentiated by gender and age. Departmental floor-plans constructed what Cook calls 'something of a gendered, spatial biography of commercialized childhood, designating an appropriate path to follow requisite for specific age ranges' (Cook, 2003, p. 156). Teenagers, for example, were not obliged to walk through 'baby' sections, and were offered vistas on to other departments that hinted at their future selves and identities (for girls, from sportswear on to the millinery and style sections). However, younger children could glimpse these as they shopped, so that they might aspire to be more like the older age group, thus building future markets. In other words, stores enacted 'the *idea* and *practice* of progressive, age-graded desire and consumption' (Cook, 2003, p. 157).

Similarly, in today's commercial outlets, children recognise 'children's spaces' because they are greeted with the images, sounds and characters familiar from their media worlds. Children's stores remain gender-segregated and careful to ensure that younger children are not 'contaminated' by the sections for older children while, at the same time, encouraging 'aspirational' consumption and play. Such practices encourage children to understand themselves and others through the meanings of retail space. Ironically, Cook argues, while this could be seen as a 'commodification' of childhood, commercial interests are not so much manipulating children as respecting them and taking them seriously.

3.2 Public space: better by design?

Previously, many UK towns and cities were designed around the needs of motorists, with attention focused on facilitating traffic flow and parking provision. As a result, they could be difficult to negotiate, particularly on foot, and public spaces encouraged movement through them rather than 'hanging about'. This may have intensified negative responses to young people in public space, since, rather than using it for instrumental purposes (going to work, going shopping), many groups of young people choose to 'hang out'. They are seemingly doing nothing while perhaps talking, laughing, listening to music or draping themselves on benches or steps.

However, you may have noticed some changes in the design of public spaces in recent years, and may be aware that members of the public, including young people, are increasingly being invited to participate in designing them. We now go on to contemplate the reasons for these shifts and some of their ambivalent effects, and to consider how far some features of design, including participatory processes, can be seen as new modes of governing conduct and behaviour in public spaces.

3.3 'Live-able' neighbourhoods: the case of Home Zones

We will start with an example of a project that attempts to acknowledge the needs of young people in urban design: Home Zones, an initiative to make streets and neighbourhoods more 'live-able'. 'Home Zones' are streets or small areas of a district where priority is given to those (pedestrians) who live in and use those streets rather than to those who travel through them. Their most obvious characteristic is an attempt to slow, interrupt or even divert the flow of vehicular traffic, generally through a mixture of signage, traffic-calming measures and street design. The idea is to make streets more 'live-able' places for residents, so that roads become places to walk, meet and talk. Residents can sit on benches; and children can play games or impromptu team sports and meet friends, without having to look over their shoulder or be confined to a playground or park. As Gill (1997) puts it, this measure is

[handwritten margin note: Change in the public space planning — children now involved]

not 'anti-car'; rather, it is a matter of redressing a balance that has emphasised the needs of car drivers over those of pedestrians.

In the Netherlands and Denmark, Home Zones (or their equivalents) have existed since the 1960s. Karsten and van Vliet (2006) argue that Home Zones in these contexts provide positive steps in creating what they call 'child-streets', even though they are designed as places for all age groups. Focusing on the Netherlands, they suggest that Home Zones could begin to address some of the fears about children's safety and health that were mentioned earlier in this chapter. Dutch Home Zones have several features:

- They are small-scale, often comprising an individual street or part thereof, and are therefore key to promoting spaces that are physically accessible to younger residents.

- They include green spaces and dedicated play spaces to address children's desire for local places to play; they use traffic calming to reduce through traffic and increase the visibility of local residents in the streetscape, promoting relations between children and adults.

- They do not simply include playgrounds as play spaces: rather, local residents want 'a broader range of spaces that are not exclusively meant for child play: roof terraces, courtyard gardens, the sidewalk in front of the home' (Karsten and van Vliet, 2006, p. 159) in which children can play but which have other possible and simultaneous uses.

In the UK, the New Labour government (1997–2010) introduced legislation that would encourage Home Zones, with the first 14 pilot projects starting in 1999. Research in the UK context has provided important evidence about the viability of Home Zones as officially sanctioned places for children's play. Clayden et al. (2006) showed that, in one of their case-study Home Zones in Sheffield, 65 per cent of respondents thought that children were playing and using the street more frequently, while 50 per cent felt safer, demonstrating that the increased presence of children in public spaces need not necessarily lead to perceptions of increased danger. However, in their other case study, adults responded far more negatively, noting that the Home Zone had increased 'youth nuisance, vandalism … reckless riding of motorcycles and motor scooters, noise and verbal abuse' (Clayden et al., 2006, p. 63).

Figure 3   A Home Zone in Manchester, UK

It seems that, in their attempts to integrate young people into public spaces rather than segregate them into playgrounds, some adults still perceive that young people 'threaten' the use of public space by its somehow more 'legitimate' users. Admittedly, Home Zones demonstrate a profound age bias when it comes to planning for young people's play: as with playgrounds, they tend to have younger children (under 10) rather than teenagers in mind. Clearly, more work is required if attempts to make public spaces more 'live-able' are to better integrate the play and leisure needs of diverse groups of young people.

3.4   Redesigning public space, redesigning publics

Activity 2   Neighbourhood design and use

Allow about 20 minutes

Think about how public space in your local neighbourhood is designed. What effect might these features have on how it is used, including by children and young people. For example, are all kerbs dropped to allow those with buggies, wheelchair users or children on scooters or bicycles to negotiate them with ease? At crossroads, can pedestrians take the most direct route that they want? What kind of seating is available and where is it located? In parks, are there areas hidden from public view? What measures have been taken to slow traffic in residential areas?

Comment

Depending on where you live, you may have noticed some changes in the design of public spaces in recent years, echoing the developments referred to above in relation to Home Zones. In many urban centres, roads are being pedestrianised, traffic-calmed or made available for shared use with grants from government or the EU. Kerb-sides are being dropped to allow easier movement. When the weather permits it, cafés, bars and restaurants encourage punters to sit outside. Official sites are being provided for street entertainers and buskers. Local parks are being used for diverse purposes: fitness boot-camp training, running, Tai Chi, local arts, music, crafts and gay-pride festivals. These developments aim to enhance the environment for a range of social groups, and to encourage modes of being in public space that are convivial as well as consumption-oriented. Games makers are even using cities as settings for entertainment experiences: an example is '2.8 Hours Later' by Bristol-based company Slingshot (the title references Danny Boyle's zombie-horror film, *28 Days Later*, of 2002). The game involves 250 players across a city who must find survivors while evading the 'zombie hordes'.

Alternatively, you may not even recognise such measures in your own neighbourhood – perhaps because it is too rural, too suburban, too isolated, rundown, based primarily around housing rather than retail, and so on. You may also have noticed other developments instead of or alongside these, such as gated communities or the increased use of CCTV.

The approaches noted above are often described as emulating Continental traditions of urban design, and are child- and youth-friendly in that they reflect young people's tendency to use public space for socialising and recreation (as we discuss in later sections). However, they should also be understood as reflecting a particular approach to dealing with social problems. Seating in many places (such as bus stops) is now designed to prevent anyone lying down on it, thus ensuring that it is not occupied by homeless people sleeping rough. Public spaces hidden from view often attract illegal or semi-legal activities, such as drug dealing and youth alcohol consumption or sex. Opening them up – for example, by clearing foliage or creating new pathways across them – attempts to discourage these activities and to encourage 'pro-social' usages instead. We see a shift here from controlling public spaces through rules and policing, to a 'pedagogy' of design that encourages particular kinds of conduct and self-regulation. To some, such approaches represent creative and non-authoritarian responses to social problems; others have criticised them for relocating problems rather than addressing their causes or even the genuine needs they represent (such as the need for more housing for those on low incomes, or social venues for young people). Areas outside city centres may find that similar problems increase in their locality, but may lack the high-profile or political clout necessary to ensure that these problems are dealt with.

In addition, these developments respond to and promote a consumption-oriented economy and new spatial and temporal uses of public space. Many town centres now operate contrasting diurnal and nocturnal economics, welcoming diverse populations during the day, but at night effectively becoming 'no-go' zones for older age groups as young people fill commercial bars and nightclubs. Similarly, many cities have developed gay-friendly districts as part of a regeneration strategy for rundown industrialised areas. Residents and local councils often accept or even welcome such strategies as a necessity for economic survival.

However, there are costs as well as benefits. Youth drunkenness, for example, might be set in the context of commercial strategies by breweries and bars to sell more alcohol by not providing seating, by offering 2-for-1 and 'happy hour' deals, and by targeting a narrow age range of clientele rather than a cross-generational one that might exert 'natural' checks on certain forms of behaviour. Other long-term effects of this commercial reorientation are, to some extent, unknown: for example, will it become increasingly difficult to occupy public space without spending money, as provision of seating and toilet facilities falls to businesses which reserve them for customers? While non-corporate consumer endeavours (such as farmers' and craft markets) can be accommodated, will those who challenge consumerism (whether politically, as protestors, or by circumstance, such as homeless people) be excluded? And what about the many areas that are excluded altogether from this 'renaissance' in public space?

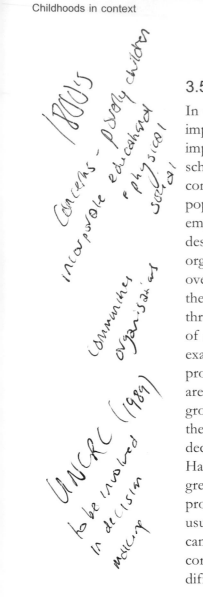

1800's

Concerns - poorly children
incorporate educational
& physical
social

communities
organisations

UNCRC (1989)
to be involved
in decision
making

3.5   Young people participating in urban design

In the nineteenth century, much concern was expressed about the impoverished youth who spent their time on city streets. Planned improvements to urban spaces often incorporated social and educational schemes aimed at young people. However, these should be seen in the context of more general attempts to gather knowledge about populations in order to develop them as a resource in nation and empire building (Gagen, 2004). Contemporary discussions of urban design emphasise 'participation', meaning that groups – communities, organisations, segments of society – should have some kind of control over matters that affect their lives. This may mean that a group can set the agenda – define their own interests and demand resources to follow through a plan – or 'have a say' over a predefined issue, in the manner of a local consultation over the building of a new school or park, for example. For Ward (2007, p. 701), participation is a process that provides an 'empowering or facilitating role' to groups whose interests are usually under-represented. Young people are one of these key groups and, following the United Nations Convention on the Rights of the Child (1989), the right of even young children to participate in decision making has been enshrined in many geographical contexts. As Hart (1992) argues, the level of young people's participation can vary greatly, from a tokenistic questionnaire that is practically ignored, to a project in which children raise an issue, research it and take action on it, usually with support from adults. A very wide range of agencies – campaigning bodies, charities, schools, quangos, think tanks, corporations and more – have got involved in realising and promoting different kinds of participation.

We now go on to discuss some examples of young people's participation in issues related to public space. Besides giving a flavour of what is involved, we will consider how these projects (re)imagine citizenship, young people and/or the public realm, partly by asking why and how they challenge existing practices or ways of doing things.

Concerned for Working Children, an Indian NGO (non-governmental organisation), works at the level of a 'panchayat' (a local cluster of villages) to enable young people who are engaged in paid work to define and research concerns that affect their everyday lives and labour. Typically, the young people carry out research exploring the exploitation of their labour and their positioning in relation to adults in the public realm. Using this information, the young people in each panchayat have set up a local government that mirrors the adult version. They elect

Children's Participation

Figure 4   Children in a parade demonstration to support ecology, in Cusco, Peru

members and manage their own affairs, setting up task forces to deal with particular issues. They have support from adults, who facilitate meetings and ensure that the young people and adult governments meet, and provide resources and personnel for their task forces. It is reported that since Concerned for Working Children began, this participatory process has reduced the exploitation of child labour.

If we view this initiative as an intervention into existing relationships in the public sphere of work and governance, we can see that it successfully 'problematised' child labour – that is, it made it visible in new ways and challenged exploitation. However, it was not a top-down measure in the way that legislation is, for example: while laws are important, they must be implemented, enforced and monitored to effect real change. Instead, the NGO worked from the bottom up to achieve its aims: its participatory processes mobilised the capacities of young people themselves to force adults to rethink how things were done, exerting an effective moral pressure rather than a legal one.

A second example of young people's participation comes from Vietnam. In 2007, an exhibition called 'Hanoi 5000 Hoan Kiem Lakes' was staged in the city of Hanoi (Drummond, 2007). The six artists who produced the exhibition used two methods to involve children in attempts to image the 'urban futures' of the city. First, they interviewed 250 young people (some on camera), using their voices as part of the exhibition. They then organised a workshop in which young people were invited to reflect on the use of art for imagining urban futures. The artistic outputs included collaborative paintings, models and installations, some inspired by young people's voices from the interviews, others the result of direct collaboration between the artists and young people. Drummond (2007) argues that a key point of the exhibition was to valorise the very voices that are usually derided as 'childish' when it comes to future designs for a city. Indeed, while the direct impacts of young people's participation in this case were unclear (in terms of city planning), the exhibition did at least provide a forum for young people to discuss and air their aspirations.

In other instances related to the design of public space, young people have often been involved in contributing ideas for 'youth-specific' issues, recognising that they have different perspectives and knowledge of their local area derived from their experience and status: for example, many projects aim to improve a local area through murals and other art forms. The extent to which these areas subsequently remain free from graffiti, vandalism or fly-posting may be taken as evidence of whether or not participation was genuine and led to community 'ownership' and protection of the sites.

However, some researchers have argued that adult 'teenaphobia' can outweigh youth expertise. For example, a study in Western Australia suggested that, despite consultation findings, skateboard parks are often unsuitably located in remote sites due to adult opposition to, or fear of, a more visible public youth presence (Taylor and Khan, 2011). Like the Hanoi example, this highlights a significant point of debate about young people's participation: although it may offer a forum for young people to express their views, this does not necessarily mean that their participation has any impact on their everyday lives or leads to changes in policy making in relation to the public spaces in which young people often feel so marginalised. This may be why participation is often framed in terms of rather vague and individual benefits such as 'raising self-esteem'. Critics have charged that participation can be used as a 'box-ticking' exercise to justify an existing policy, often initiated by adults who hold the key to resources and define political agendas; or that it recruits young people to police other youth, or devolves responsibility to them without providing adequate resources for them to act fully on that responsibility. The notion of 'taking responsibility' may seem uncontroversial in some respects, particularly in relation to according young people 'rights'. Yet, as Purdy (1992) argued, young people – indeed, adults – are not sovereign agents who can do as they please, but live in relation to others – family, peers, teachers, and local and national governments. The problem is that, in many ways, young people have been asked to become responsible for their individual lives without being provided the financial, social or educational means to do so (Mizen, 2003).

Another example related to skateboard-park provision perceptively suggests how participation can reimagine citizenship in less than 'empowering' ways. Ocean Howell (2008) found that although over 2000 new skateparks were built in the USA between 1997 and 2006, many cities assume no liability for injuries while expecting skateboarders to secure private funding, police surrounding areas and be entrepreneurial (e.g. in hiring out the space for filming). Previously, however, cities fully financed playgrounds, supervised them and organised programmes of activities. Howell argues that the comparison shows how the citizen- state relationship is changing, 'away from entitlement and toward contractualism' (Howell, 2008, p. 477). Table 1 summarises some of the advantages and disadvantages of children's participation.

Table 1   Some advantages and disadvantages of children's participation

Advantages of children's participation	Disadvantages of children's participation
Participation may provide access to knowledge and experiences of an under-represented group in society	Participation is often initiated by adults, and often by adults in power, who hold the key to resources and define political agendas
Children often have intimate knowledge of local places which adults ignore or bypass	Some groups of children (e.g. disadvantaged children) have been under-represented in some participation processes
Children may express different needs from adults (e.g. around education and play)	Participation can be used as a 'box-ticking' exercise to simply justify an existing policy
Children may express needs that also affect adults (e.g. around intergenerational tensions in public space) but from a different viewpoint	

(Continued overleaf)

Table 1 continued   Some advantages and disadvantages of children's participation

Participation may help combat social exclusion among young people, and raise self-esteem Participation can be part of young people's broader learning (i.e. education beyond school) Young people may feel a greater sense of ownership and belonging in their local community	Participation may represent a way for adults in power to devolve responsibility to young people without providing adequate resources for young people to take on that responsibility fully Participation may produce several 'facts' about children's lives, but have little direct impact on policy making or planning Participation is often limited – either happening at the small scale or for a short time period Participation can actually reinforce, rather than overcome, power relations between adults and children (adults 'give' opportunities to participate)

Summary of Section 3

Public places designed for young people are increasingly commercialised or consumer-oriented spaces, such as theme parks, shopping malls and stores, and urban centres.

Many changes in the design of public space represent new modes of governance or attempts to affect conduct by means other than overt rules and regulations.

Young people's participation in decision making has been a popular way of asserting their (partial) rights to citizenship, often with respect to public spaces; but the exact form of this citizenship is also being reimagined.

4 Young people using public space: home, play and work

4.1   Youth cultural practices and public spaces

Fran Tonkiss (2005) asks us to 'think of the delights that small children will find in the most common-place spaces, the endless play of crawling backwards down stairs, balancing on the edge of walls, disappearing behind corners'. She argues that 'we do not entirely lose this pleasurable relation to ordinary spaces, … [for] making yourself at home in the routine passages of everyday life, producing your own version of the city' (Tonkiss, 2005, p. 139). While she includes us all in her argument, she notes that many scholars of the urban have celebrated youth as particularly creative and subversive in how they negotiate, navigate and make use of public spaces – in the process, she remarks, often romanticising them and overstating their novelty. Nonetheless, youth cultural practices such as skateboarding and graffiti can be seen as 'different ways of reading, writing and speaking urban space' (Tonkiss, 2005, p. 137), in contrast to its 'official' regulation by bye-laws and rules requiring us to keep 'off the grass' or 'dogs on leashes', avoid 'ball games' and 'alcohol consumption', 'pick up litter', 'leave quietly', 'close the gate behind you' or 'be considerate'.

Figure 5   Young skateboarder in action

In the UK, young people in a study by Matthews et al. (2000) argued that spaces constructed for young people, like youth clubs, were often boring, static spaces where it was difficult to express oneself. They thought that some youth clubs offered very limited, structured activities, had outdated facilities (because of limited resources) and were too well supervised by adults to offer them the freedom they desired. They therefore used the street as a livelier space for displaying their identities:

> It's [the street] where everybody comes … to meet … It's where everybody hangs out, sits on walls, smokes cigarettes, chats. It's … a place where you're likely to meet up with lots of other people … Where you meet your mates … try to figure out what your next move is going to be. (16-year-old-boy)
>
> (Quoted in Matthews et al., 2000, p. 58)

This suggests that young people use public spaces for activities that might resemble playing: they are having fun, perhaps playing cards or impromptu games of football. But they are also engaged in the search for meaning, both in terms of their personal or collective identities, and in terms of testing out their roles as they become adult under changing social and economic circumstances.

Some writers have used the term 'liminal spaces' to describe streets and various suburban or commercial spaces where identities and rules of behaviour are not settled (Matthews, 2003). Shopping malls have been the focus for considerable debate because rules about appropriate behaviour, dress and comportment are changeable, often seem arbitrary, and are enforced by private security firms against whose authority there is little redress. Some evidence suggests that security personnel often target young people and, specifically, groups of young black men (Davis, 1990), particularly if they are seen to interfere with the business of consumption. However, young people still use shopping malls. While spending money is sometimes a focus, malls are also desirable because they are warm and sheltered, with plenty of points of interest for hanging out, strolling around and playing games.

Activity 3   Reading A

Allow about 45 minutes

Go to the end of the chapter and read Reading A, 'Redefining public space in the shopping mall', by Hugh Matthews, Mark Taylor, Barry Percy-Smith and Melanie Limb. In the reading, Matthews and colleagues examine how young people follow, resist and subvert adult-imposed rules in shopping malls.

When you read the extract, look for the following four key themes:

Figure 6   Shopping mall in Chongqing, China

- young people's frequent use of the shopping mall, where they see it (ironically) as an inclusive space where they can meet friends
- examples of young people being moved on by security guards, even when those young people feel they are 'doing nothing' but hanging around
- a broad feeling among young people that they are 'under surveillance' all or most of the time
- a series of strategies used by young people to subvert, resist or parody adults who ask them to move on.

Comment

This study highlights the way in which many public spaces – shopping malls, airports, parks and urban streets – are being regulated through CCTV, security patrols and even biometric testing. It also discusses how young people negotiate the idea that their presence in public space is a threat, and how they assert their own agency and work around some of the rules that seemingly govern shopping malls.

As we noted earlier, young people often challenge the distinctions between activities in the public and private sphere, sometimes as a form of resistance, sometimes through lack of choice. Bull (2000) shows how, when it first arrived, the seemingly mundane use of the personal stereo stirred significant debate about the proper use of public spaces. He argues that television had also privatised forms of entertainment that had previously been public and communal affairs (like going to the cinema or theatre), but the television at least reinforced the sanctified divide between public and private. The personal stereo, however, represented a form of private consumption that was taking place in public spaces. People could, ostensibly, shut themselves off from the world while moving through a city. Bull claims that many people deemed this a challenge to the assumed rules of public space. In terms that we considered earlier, the personal stereo was a technology that was 'out of place', but was made doubly transgressive through its association with young people, who are, of course, also 'out of place'.

Figure 7 Skateboard ramp and walls covered with graffiti

Parkour is the movement around an environment by incorporating obstacles.

Graffiti, skateboarding, parkour and other practices are also predominately associated with youth, and it is probably fair to say that public opinion on them has changed considerably in recent years. Although they are often designated 'destructive' and 'antisocial behaviour', and policed in terms of trespass, public order and criminal damage, or even (in the case of graffiti) classified along with assault and battery, they have also found their way into art galleries, films and music videos, and been appropriated by a range of institutions, including big corporations that want to borrow their patina of urban cool. Increasingly, graffiti are given public 'official' sites by local authorities, hoping to prevent their spread elsewhere.

Nancy Macdonald's (2001) study of graffiti subcultures argues that graffiti style is highly rule-bound, typically progressing from 'tags' to 'dubs' or 'throw-ups' (initials filled in with black or silver/gold, respectively), to highly creative 'pieces' (or 'masterpieces' when using more than two colours). Tags are a writer's first step into a graffiti apprenticeship. They are part of how a writer (who is usually young and male) builds a unique identity, how he gets seen and develops a reputation. According to where they are placed in relation to others, tags can signify a greeting, respect, acknowledgement, challenge or insult. Macdonald argues that graffiti can be seen as a 'moral career', as it is a structured, hierarchical world in which, through hard work and learning, one can progress from 'toy', or amateur, to recognised 'king', often for no material reward and at considerable personal risk.

Tonkiss (2005) reflects on the diverse 'stories' that graffiti tell, what they reveal about the social and political geography of urban space. Political uses of graffiti deal in slogans and signs – 'smash the state', 'eat the rich' – but even in these compressed forms, graffiti offer 'an assertion of something, a criticism of public reality', according to the cultural critic Susan Sontag (2001, p. 148). Feminist graffiti 'disrupts' sexist advertising and, in so doing, disrupts the established power relations of space (such as the commercial 'right' to display women's bodies). Racist and sectarian graffiti, by contrast, 'aim to convert space into territory', to claim entitlement and belonging, and to deny it to others. In some respects, Tonkiss suggests, these graffiti actually highlight that this is a doomed enterprise, but they may also be read as 'calling-cards of other forms of violence, signatures of more effective modes of exclusion … [meanwhile] the use of tags, throw-ups and bombing as the marks of individual writers or of crews' are an assertion of 'presence', stating 'I was here' (Tonkiss, 2005, p. 141). This can be read, variously, as a challenge to urban anonymity; as a refusal to accept that any spaces can be off-limits or are uninhabitable; as the voice of the powerless; as a sign of ownership that serves to alienate other users.

4.2   Public space as home and work: street children

Public space is the arena in which some groups of young people (whom we will call 'street children' for shorthand) live all or most of their lives, using this space for working, sleeping and much else besides. Van Blerk draws attention to the under-researched area of the spatial dimensions to street children's lives:

> Street children, by their defining terminology, are prominently
> located in urban public space: the alliance of 'children' with the

'street', referring to all urban public spaces, disclosing much about their lives ... Therefore, spatial processes cannot be excluded from any interpretations of how street children create and develop their identities. Despite this, the particular geographies of homeless street children have only recently received attention.

(Van Blerk, 2005, p. 5)

Activity 4   Street children in public spaces

Allow about 20 minutes

Make notes on your responses to the following questions:

- In what kinds of activities are street children engaged? How do these activities relate to the use of public space?

- What do you think are the principal challenges and opportunities that present themselves to street children?

Comment

The term 'street trades' tends to refer to engagement in informal economic activities such as selling, shoe-shining, cleaning and sex work. Street children's use of public spaces tends to be more diverse and even more contested than that of children who live in a private home. When Bromley and Mackie (2009) undertook research with over 100 street children engaged in street trades in Cusco, Peru, they found that street trades are a key way in which street children forge strategies for survival, especially (but not only) in poorer countries in the majority global south. Their first finding confirmed that 89 per cent of their respondents traded because they had to, to pay for food and education (Bromley and Mackie, 2009). Street trades also afforded young people limited forms of empowerment, enabling them greater opportunities for play – for example, in pay-entry public parks or internet cafés. Boys (94 per cent) displayed a much stronger desire to earn their own money than girls (39 per cent).

Bromley and Mackie went on to explore negative outcomes from street trades, which included the danger of accidents, theft and abuse, lack of time for playing, and interruption of schooling. However, positive outcomes included enjoyment from work, socialisation and learning skills, economic empowerment, increased self-esteem and confidence, and improved spatial awareness of Cusco's public spaces, gained from learning the best sites for trading. Bromley and Mackie (2009) argue that national and international policies universally condemn and prohibit child street work, drawing implicitly on the construction of children as 'innocent angels' who require protection. They suggest that this inflexible assumption could actually be quite damaging for street children like those in Cusco; rather, a more flexible approach would recognise the benefits of 'lighter forms of child work' (such as market-trading) and reorient 'international policy from condemnation of child work to supportive protection' that mitigates against some of the preventable, negative outcomes listed above (Bromley and Mackie, 2009, p. 155).

Jen Couch's (2010) work with street children in Delhi focuses on the rights that street children perceive they should be afforded. Couch identifies four 'rights' that children in Delhi wanted, the first (as in Cusco) being the right to choose to work. They also wanted the right to participation – for example, 'the right to play in the park as the rich children can do, but we must behave in the park and not pick flowers' (unnamed child, cited in Couch, 2010, p. 159). They wanted the right of assembly, since many street children in Delhi had been badly beaten and victimised by the police, especially around the city's railway stations. As in Langevang's (2008) work in Accra, street children associated in groups to overcome this victimisation and to afford senses of self-esteem and confidence. Children differentiated between 'acceptable' and 'unacceptable' work. Often, so-called 'middle-men' exploit children by moving them to factories with intolerable working conditions. Thus, many children prefer working on the streets of Delhi but with protection provided by NGOs. In work with street-based child sex workers in New Zealand, Abel and Fitzgerald (2008) identified that support was crucial as those young people made transitions to adulthood. Without support, those transitions were characterised by high levels of risk and limited future opportunities for work outside the sex trade.

A final, notable aspect of research with street children is how they perceive and make 'home' in public spaces. In Ugandan cities, van Blerk (2005, p. 14) argues, children displayed forms of 'multi-belonging': they moved between various locations – within a particular city, between their family home and the street, between different cities, and between cities and rural areas. In some cases, if they were moved on by the authorities, young people used movement as an escape mechanism and had to exhibit flexible forms of belonging that could be adapted to new places. Van Blerk's work is particularly notable for two reasons. First, it undermines the assumption that place-based forms of belonging must be tied to one place (particularly the home). Ursin (2011) makes a similar point in the case of street children in Salvador, Brazil: rather than being 'home-less', she finds that they actually regard public places as being a better place than domestic environments for acquiring essential aspects of feeling at home, such as autonomy, safety and belonging. Secondly, van Blerk's work undermines the idea that street children are confined to public spaces in particular cities; rather, some children may only live on the streets part-time (actually spending some time at home); and some may spend time moving between cities or living in rural areas, dependent, for example, on seasonal patterns of work. This blurring of boundaries mirrors some of the experiences expressed by homeless young people, which you read about in Chapter 2.

4.3   Gender and public space

Perceptions of safety and danger in public space are gendered, in that women are specifically afraid of sexual violence. Women's fear is also spatialised: it affects how they use and move through space, as well as the meanings different spaces have at certain times of day (shopping precincts seen as 'safe' during the day may empty at night, for example) (Valentine, 1989, 1991). Langevang (2008) showed how young men in Accra, Ghana, appropriate street spaces in order to produce a sense of collective, male identity. In a context of mass youth unemployment, urban restructuring and the marginalisation of young men, groups of young men are often seen as 'signs of unemployment and idleness' (Langevang, 2008, p. 239). Hanging out is seen as a danger or threat to society, and there are conflicts between claims to space by those who are hanging out, those who are working, and those who are moving through public spaces. In Accra, groups of young men hang out, sitting and talking in 'bases' (such as street corners) for many hours every day. But, Langevang argues, bases are significant spaces where 'young men create personal bonds, socialize, and discuss and practise masculine identities … they produce a space through which they endeavour to satisfy their social and material needs and to find meaning in a changing urban environment' (Langevang, 2008, p. 239).

Research by Mikkelsen and Christensen (2009) in Copenhagen, Denmark, has explored how young people are mobile in public spaces. They argue that much research has privileged the notion of children's 'independent mobility', partly out of nostalgic yearning for more 'authentic' kinds of outdoor play that may or may not ever have existed in the past. Their methods enable them to present a more nuanced picture of why and how young people move through public spaces. Rather than stress the presence or absence of adults, they note that young people's mobility is 'primarily social', and that companionship of different kinds – including pets, friends and relatives of different ages – is fundamental to it. Young people also displayed an array of concerns that were not simply about playing or hanging out: ways of 'feeling safe', instrumental concerns (getting to a friend's house or school), and preferences among girls rather than boys for moving in groups, both for safety and for socialisation.

Activity 5   Reading B

Allow about 20 minutes

Go to the end of the chapter and read Reading B, 'Gender in public space: "shining" masculinity and "demure modern" femininity', by Ritty Lukose.

When you read the extract, look for examples of the following observations:

- young people's experience of public spaces is shaped by gender
- youth culture in Kerala reveals the influence of local and global factors.

Comment

Lukose's research is set in Kerala, a southern Indian state which has for many years been held up as an example of positive development policies, since a left-wing government funded health care, education and other services, leading to high levels of literacy. It is now, however, facing a less certain future. Lukose – who was born in Kerala but now lives in the USA – based her research in a 'backwater' town and college, showing how young people make sense of themselves and their lives in relation to ideas about consumption and globalisation. In this reading, she discusses how consumption has produced new forms of masculinity and femininity in public space.

Lukose evocatively conjures up the experience of being young in Kerala. It is an experience that is strongly shaped by gender, space and style. Young men and women have a shared understanding of masculinity and femininity, and the norms and values that apply to each. For young men, there is a desire to inhabit an aspirational masculine identity compressed into the term *chethu*. Imbued with this notion of being, young men have adopted a style of hanging out, doing nothing and looking cool which can be seen as an 'in-the-moment' performance and an entitlement to space. For young women, claims on space have remained more circumspect and contoured by notions of reputation; this has had an impact on what women do, where they go and how they look. Appearing in public entails forms of self-monitoring in order to perfect and perform an enactment of youthful femininity that walks the line between being demure and being modern.

In keeping with youth cultures in other locations, dress and attitude become signifiers that carry meaning for young people as they draw on features of the local and the global to fashion a unique style. Lukose's study speaks back to commentators who suggest that processes of globalisation have produced sameness out of diversity. Young people in Kerala demonstrate an awareness of global products and an agility in drawing their own meanings out of the confluence of local and global flows.

Summary of Section 4

Young people who 'hang out' in public spaces are seen as 'out of place', but these practices can be key to the production of young people's identities and ways of coping with socio-economic changes.

There are many ways of interpreting youth cultural practices such as graffiti, but they should be seen as more than simple 'vandalism' or invasion of 'proper' public space.

Street children are engaged in diverse economic activities that go beyond the overwhelming concern with 'play' in much research on children and public space; boundaries between 'home', play and work may be blurred.

Consumption has produced new forms of masculinity and femininity in public space.

5 Conclusion

Debates about young people in public spaces are geographically and historically specific, complex and contradictory. Debates about public space, whether in Gipton or Accra, frequently draw on the idea that children are 'out of place' there. These contradictions are apparent because of the contradictory ways in which both public spaces and childhood are defined. In most contexts, the majority of children do not have the power to overturn the regulation of their use of public space, but they negotiate public spaces with a mixture of satire, creativity and a sense of simply 'getting on with life'.

References

Abel, G. and Fitzgerald, L. (2008) 'On a fast-track into adulthood: an exploration of transitions into adulthood for street-based sex workers in New Zealand', *Journal of Youth Studies*, vol. 11, no. 4, pp. 361–76.

Aitken, S. (2001) *Geographies of Young People: The Morally Contested Spaces of Identity*, London, Routledge.

Akiyama, M. (2010) 'Silent alarm: the mosquito youth deterrent and the politics of frequency', *Canadian Journal of Communication*, vol. 35, no. 3, pp. 455–71.

Bowlby, R. (1985) *Just Looking: Consumer Culture in Dreiser, Gissing and Zola*, New York, Methuen.

British Broadcasting Corporation (BBC) (2009) 'Police are given dispersal order', *BBC News*, 25 October [online], http://news.bbc.co.uk/1/hi/england/west_yorkshire/8324967.stm (Accessed 3 June 2011).

Bromley, R. and Mackie, P. (2009) 'Child experiences as street traders in Peru: contributing to a reappraisal for working children', *Children's Geographies*, vol. 7, no. 2, pp. 141–58.

Buckingham, D. (2011) *The Material Child: Growing up in Consumer Culture*, Cambridge, Polity Press.

Bull, M. (2000) *Sounding Out the City: Personal Stereos and the Management of Everyday Life*, Oxford, Berg.

Clayden, A., Mckoy, K. and Wild, A. (2006) 'Improving residential liveability in the UK: home zones and alternative approaches', *Journal of Urban Design*, vol. 11, no. 11, pp. 55–71.

Cook, D. T. (2003) 'Spatial biographies of children's consumption: market places and spaces of childhood in the 1930s and beyond', *Journal of Consumer Culture*, vol. 3, no. 2, pp. 147–69.

Couch, J. (2010) 'Our lives, our say: street and working children talk about their rights in Delhi', *Journal of Social Inclusion*, vol. 1, no. 2, pp. 151–65.

Davis, M. (1990) *City of Quartz: Excavating the Future in Los Angeles*, London, Vintage.

Drummond, L. (2007) 'Hanoi 5000 Hoan Kiem Lakes: using art to involve young people in urban futures', *Children's Geographies*, vol. 5, no. 4, pp. 479–88.

Gagen, E. (2004) 'Making America flesh: physicality and nationhood in early twentieth-century physical education reform', *Cultural Geographies*, vol. 11, no. 4, pp. 417–42.

Gill, T. (1997) 'Policy review: Home Zones', *Children and Society*, vol. 11, no. 4, pp. 268–70.

Hart, R. (1992) *Children's Participation: From Tokenism to Citizenship*, Florence, UNICEF Innocenti Research Centre.

Hickley, M. (2008) 'Buzz off! Outcry as Children's Tsar says ultrasonic "mosquito" device is a breach of teenagers' human rights', *Mail Online News*, 13 February [online], http://www.dailymail.co.uk/news/article-513822/Buzz-Outcry-Childrens-Tsar-says-ultrasonic-mosquito-device-breach-teenagers-human-rights.html (Accessed 15 March 2012).

Hillman, M. (2002) 'Are we developing battery-reared or free-range children?', blog post, 14 March [online], http://www.mayerhillman.com/Articles/EntryId/57/Are-we-developing-battery-reared-or-free-range-children.aspx (Accessed 9 June 2012).

Howell, O. (2008) 'Skatepark as neoliberal playground: urban governance, recreation space, and the cultivation of personal responsibility', *Space and Culture*, vol. 11, no. 4, pp. 475–96.

Jenks, C. (2005) *Childhood* (2nd edn), London, Routledge.

Jones, O. (2003) '"Endlessly revisited and forever gone": on memory, reverie and emotional imagination in doing children's geographies', *Children's Geographies*, vol. 1, no. 1, pp. 25–36.

Karsten, L. and van Vliet, W. (2006) 'Children in the city: reclaiming the street', *Children, Youth and Environments*, vol. 16, no. 1, pp. 151–67.

Langevang, T. (2008) 'Claiming place: the production of young men's street meeting places in Accra, Ghana', *Geografiska Annaler: Series B, Human Geography*, vol. 90, no. 3, pp. 227–42.

Macdonald, N. (2001) *The Graffiti Subculture: Youth, Masculinity and Identity in London and New York*, Basingstoke, Palgrave.

Matthews, H. (2003) 'The street as a liminal space: the barbed spaces of childhood', in Christensen, P. and O'Brien, M. (eds) *Children in the City: Home, Neighbourhood and Community*, London, Routlege Falmer.

Matthews, H., Limb, M. and Taylor, M. (2000) 'The "street as thirdspace"', in Holloway, S. L. and Valentine, G. (eds) *Children's Geographies: Playing, Living, Learning*, London, Routledge.

McKendrick, J. H., Bradford, M. G. and Fielder, A. V. (2000) 'Kid customer? Commercialization of playspace and the commodification of childhood', *Childhood*, vol. 7, no. 3, pp. 295–314.

Mikkelsen, M. R. and Christensen, P. H. (2009) 'Is children's independent mobility really independent? A study of children's mobility combining ethnography and GPS/mobile phone technologies', *Mobilities*, vol. 4, no. 1, pp. 37–58.

Mizen, P. (2003) 'The best days of your life? Youth, policy and Blair's New Labour', *Critical Social Policy*, vol. 23, no. 4, pp. 453–76.

Morgan, G. (2006) '"Teen buzz" is the new classroom weapon', *Security News*, Compound Security Systems, 23 May [online], http://www.compoundsecurity.co.uk/security-news/teen-buzz-new-classroom-weapon (Accessed 15 March 2012).

Nayak, A. (2003) '"Through children's eyes": childhood, place and the fear of crime', *Geoforum*, vol. 34, no. 3, pp. 303–15.

Palmer, S. (2006) *Toxic Childhood: How the Modern World is Damaging our Children and What We Can Do About It*, London, Orion.

Penny, L. (2010) 'Inside the Whitehall kettle. Police violence against children', *New Statesman*, 25 November [online], http://www.newstatesman.com (Accessed 7 June 2012).

Purdy, L. (1992) *In Their Best Interest? The Case Against Equal Rights for Children*, Ithaca, NY, Cornell University Press.

Sontag, S. (2001 [1987]) *Where the Stress Falls*, New York, Farrar, Straus & Giroux.

Taylor, M. and Khan, U. (2011) 'Skate-park builds, teenaphobia and the adolescent need for hang-out spaces: the social utility and functionality of urban skate parks', *Journal of Urban Design*, vol. 16, no. 4, pp. 489–510.

Tonkiss, F. (2005) *Space, the City and Social Theory: Social Relations and Urban Forms*, Cambridge, Polity Press.

Tumble Tots (2012) Programmes overview [online], http://www.tumbletots.com/our-programmes.php (Accessed 9 June 2012).

28 Days Later (2002) film, directed by Danny Boyle, 20th Century Fox.

Ursin, M. (2011) '"Wherever I lay my head is home" – young people's experience of home in the Brazilian street environment', *Children's Geographies*, vol. 9, no. 2, pp. 221–34.

Valentine, G. (1989) 'The geography of women's fear', *Area*, vol. 21, no. 4, pp. 385–90.

Valentine, G. (1991) 'Women's fear and the design of public space', *Built Environment*, vol. 18, no. 4, pp. 288–303.

Van Blerk, L. (2005) 'Negotiating spatial identities: mobile perspectives on street life in Uganda', *Children's Geographies*, vol. 3, no. 1, pp. 5–21.

Ward, K. (2007) 'Geography and public policy: activist, participatory, and policy geographies', *Progress in Human Geography*, vol. 31, no. 5, pp. 695–705.

Wilkes, D. (2010) 'Boris backs couple threatened by social services for letting their children cycle to school', *Mail Online*, http://www.dailymail.co.uk/news/article-1291970/Couple-threatened-social-services-children-ride-bikes-school.html (Accessed 8 June 2012).

Wilson, E. (1991) *The Sphinx in the City: Urban Life, the Control of Disorder, and Women*, London, Virago.

Reading A
Redefining public space in the shopping mall

Hugh Matthews, Mark Taylor, Barry Percy-Smith and Melanie Limb

Source: 'The unacceptable flaneur: the shopping mall as a teenage hangout', 2000, *Childhood*, vol. 7, no. 3, pp. 279–94.

Within late modernity, boundaries between adults and children have become even more contested. Children, today, are 'less subsumed within an adult world of discipline and control', partly because adults are more likely to recognize them 'as able, willing and reliable contributors within their own significant social contexts', albeit home and school, and partly because children themselves are more likely to think in terms of competencies and capabilities rather than subordination (Wyness, 2000, p. 1). Hengst (1987, p. 74), in a slightly different vein, suggests that childhood is gradually becoming liquidated because 'society' is invading all those areas in which formerly children had been trained to meet the qualitatively different demands of adulthood. A consequence is that the gap between generations is constantly narrowing and 'the processes of upbringing … increasingly lose their effectiveness'. In essence, children are becoming less child-like, as links with parents have weakened, and through actions that contest parental control and responsibility.

For many adults, however, social ambiguity of this kind provides contexts with which they find difficulty in coming to terms, especially beyond the home and school, for it fundamentally challenges what the Stainton-Rogers have termed the 'masonry of the mature' (Stainton-Rogers and Stainton-Rogers, 1992, p. 146). Wyness (2000, p. 2) describes how this conception rests on 'the notion of a child as a fixed material object with little or no social status'. From this viewpoint the child is invisible and 'childhood is a transitional phase which is only complete once children enter adulthood'. In effect, children are little more than adults-in-waiting or less-than-adult (Matthews and Limb, 1999) and 'not part of the social world that counts' (Wyness, 2000, p. 24). As adulthood is approached, so children become progressively more visible and more adult-like, and a process of social integration begins. However, with the 'alleged loss of authority and abdication of responsibility within families', children are being propelled into situations where their presence is uncomfortable for many adults (Murray, 1990) and where they are perceived to be less than ready. Wyness (2000, p. 24) colourfully suggests that here 'we are presented with the image of the man-child, the demonic precocious deviant who has become all too readily visible. 'Visibility'… signifies a problem for society.' Discomfort is all the more acute given the way that children are still positioned on (or rather 'off') the political and social policy agenda. Despite the proclamations of the United Nations Convention on the Rights of the Child (1989) and the Children Act (1989), children form a structurally disenfranchised group within society, especially so given that 'institutions and politicians are by and large not accountable to children' (Wyness, 2000, p. 25). Accordingly, children are rarely provided with opportunities to make their voice heard and they are not expected to have a claim within the public realm (Matthews and Limb, 1998; Matthews et al., 1998, 1999).

While the new sociology focuses on how these boundary disputes are contested in social space (James et al., 1998; Jenks, 1996), geographers have begun to explore their spatial outpourings, Valentine (1996a, 1996b, 1999), for example, considers how managing children's use of places is a constant 'headache' for most parents. While parents are torn between wanting to protect their children from danger and wishing to give them increasing independence, children are seemingly becoming keener to claim their autonomy, especially in the face of peer pressure 'to "play" outside the home, further, longer and later' (Valentine, 1999, p. 137). Sibley (1995) observes how the way in which space is organised is deeply invested with cultural values. He suggests that the regulation of space by adults is closely associated with the social production of identities in young people. By defining limits and drawing boundaries based upon age-related assumptions, adults attempt to shape and command the process of growing up. Where it is acceptable to be and what is meant by 'out-of-bounds' are socially constructed. Massey (1998) notes that this spatiality of childhood is mapped by differing rationales. Some age lines are drawn for control, so playgrounds are perceived as acceptable and safe places for toddlers at particular times of the day but deemed as unacceptable places for teenagers, especially during the evening when unregulated by the adult gaze (Matthews, 1995; Sibley, 1995). Others are drawn for (moral) protection, such as the age limits that define entry into places serving alcohol and showing certain sorts of films. Whether for protection or control, Qvortrup et al. (1994) suggest that young people are increasingly becoming confined to acceptable 'islands' by adults and so are spatially outlawed within society. In effect, adults have (re)defined the public domain as their own private space (Valentine, 1996a), where children have no right of presence. It is when they are out and about that young people are frequently defined as a problem. Their visibility in public places is often seen as discrepant and undesirable. Young people, here, are a polluting presence, because by congregating together they are seen to be challenging the hegemony of adult ownership of public space. Children have no place on the landscape. …

In this [reading], we consider young people's use of a particular type of street site where boundary disputes between adults and children are common, the shopping mall. We suggest that these temples of mass consumption constitute an important cultural space for young people that defines a kind of thirdspace. We recognise, however, that the mall is a special kind of 'street' setting, a delimited, overseen and regulated place that is far removed from the anarchic voids that comprise many outdoor environments. The implicit nature of the mall, with its effect of panoptic surveillance, defines a 'safeness' that is seldom experienced elsewhere when young people are out and about. First, we briefly examine the findings from a number of studies that have considered how young people use these places and then discuss the results from a detailed survey of young people 'hanging around' in five shopping malls in the East Midlands (UK). In so doing, we draw heavily upon the views and expressions of the young people themselves in order to get as close as possible to their worlds of experience. …

Methodology

The study was undertaken in five shopping malls in the East Midlands of the UK. In each case self-completed questionnaires and taped discussions were carried out with groups of young people seen to be hanging out in the mall. All of the interviewers were registered outreach youth workers. We targeted young people aged 9–16 years and more than 400 respondents took part in the survey (Table 1). In the largest mall, the Grosvenor Centre, we carried out informal interviews with another 32 young people (Table 2). While it was not possible to gain parental consent from the young people prior to participation, we asked each person if we could write to their parents informing them about the project. If the parents had objected to their child's participation it would have been possible to withdraw that child's contribution. No parents did object, but we did find that not all of the young people (about 7 percent) wanted us to inform their parents and we respected their feelings in this matter.

Tables 1 and 2 reveal a skewed age and sex distribution. The majority of those taking part were aged 12–16 years and largely comprise groups of young girls. While the overrepresentation of 12- to 16-year-olds provides a reasonably accurate reflection of the age groups most seen to be hanging out in the mall, the gender imbalance was an outcome of a higher refusal rate among boys when invited to take part in the survey.

In presenting the results we draw attention to three recurrent themes: the mall as a teenage hangout; the mall as a zone of conflict; and the mall as a cultural boundary zone. Our work is grounded upon a conviction that there is no such thing as 'the child', nor is there a universal experience that can be termed 'childhood'. We emphasize the importance of difference and diversity among young people and the multiple realities that define how each person encounters place and space (Matthews and Limb, 1999). As such, our results provide a mere glimpse into the social complexities of mall life and many more studies are needed if a clearer representation is to emerge.

Table 1 Age and sex distribution: self-complete questionnaires (frequencies)

Age	Male	Female	Total frequency	Percentage
9	1	7	8	2
10	4	7	11	3
11	10	24	34	8
12	27	32	59	15
13	27	36	63	16
14	20	64	84	21
15	22	38	60	15
16	28	27	55	14
Missing values	18	12	30	6
Total			404	–
Percentage	38	62	–	100

Table 2 Age and sex distribution: informal interviews (frequencies)

Age	Male	Female
12	1	3
13	3	6
14	2	6
15	3	4
16	–	4

Results

The mall as a zone of conflict

Shopping malls have been identified as an important site for young people to mix socially and to develop their own identities. They are also places where the values of consumerism define the mainstream. For young people with limited resources malls are often contradictory places. On the one hand, they represent the images and consumption to which many young people aspire; on the other, much of what is available is out of reach and underlines their marginality within society. When young people gather in shopping malls their presence is often deemed to be unacceptable, partly because these places are commonly interpreted to be an extension of the public realm of adults (in which young people have no place when adults are around) and partly because their behaviour is perceived to be at odds with the norm. The hiring of private security guards and the use of surveillance cameras ensures a moral regulation of public space that controls both access and behaviour and those who do not belong are moved on (Fyfe and Bannister, 1996). Rose (1991) and Breitbart (1998) suggest that the continual growth of privately managed public spaces of this kind is symptomatic of a trend that attempts to remove all young people from the street, 'delimit their geography and enforce their invisibility' (Breitbart, 1998, p. 307).

Through attempts by adults to define and regulate the mall for their own purposes, collisions and conflicts with young people are commonplace. From our survey, nearly half (46 percent) of those interviewed had at some time been asked to move on. The proportion was higher for boys (57 percent) than for girls (39 percent). Regulation of this kind was mostly carried out by security guards (89 percent), but also included shopkeepers (30 percent), police (20 percent) and vigilant adults (14 percent).

Most instances of being moved on occurred when young people were hanging out in those places that were perceived to be for movement and flux, even though design afforded opportunity and space for small groups to gather.

> We were moved the other day … just chatting and that, looking over the balcony over there … we were told that we can't stand there as we were blocking the way, yet there was plenty of space for people to pass. (Girl aged 15, Grosvenor Centre)

I'd only just turned up ... I saw me mates sitting outside HMV ... went across and this security geezer come up and tells us we got to go ... we weren't doing anything ... having a fag ... we says why? He says just get going. (Boy aged 15, Grosvenor Centre)

On other occasions, young people were moved on when their behaviour was seen to be out of keeping with the purpose of the particular setting. For example, we observed in one of the malls a group of teenagers being moved when sitting on the wall of an indoor fountain. Around the fountain there were several benches, but elderly adults had taken these. We asked members of the group what had just happened:

He says that we can only sit on the benches, what a tw(!) ... but we can't sit there with those grannies there. (Girls aged 14, Newlands)

Even when not being asked to move on, many young people felt that they were under constant surveillance (70 percent). This feeling was common among boys (73 percent) and girls (69 percent). When asked why they were being watched, answers highlighted feelings of social exclusion and of being outsiders within the public realms. Reasons ranged across 'they think we'll steal something/are shoplifters (30 percent), 'we're young (14 percent), 'to make sure we behave' (10 percent), 'they think we're bad', 'they think we're loud' and 'they suspect us'. It is not surprising that young people's reactions included feelings of being 'angry, bad, not trusted, like a criminal, stupid, dodgy, paranoid, judged, guilty, insecure and victimized'. Two accounts distil some of these negative perceptions and experiences.

When we enter a shop they think we're shoplifters ... I was trying on some clothes in T.S. when one of the assistants comes up all high and mighty like and asks me have I got any money and if so, to prove it ... what a b(!) nerve ... it is as if they are forcing you to buy something. (Girl aged 14, Grosvenor Centre)

They make you feel that you do not belong, that you should be outside. (Boy aged 14, Newlands)

The mall as a cultural boundary zone

In this section we discuss why, despite hassle and confrontation, young people continue to assert their right of presence in the mall. We use the concept of thirdspace to make sense of young people's place use. According to Soja (1996), those 'who are territorially subjugated by the workings of hegemonic power have two inherent choices: either accept their imposed differentiation and division, making the best of it; or mobilise … and struggle against this power-filled imposition' (Soja, 1996, p. 87). Both of these choices are inherently spatial and inevitably result in 'division, containment and struggle'. Foucault (1982) had earlier suggested that cultural politics of this kind can be both oppressive and enabling, 'filled not only with authoritarian perils but also with possibilities for community, resistance and emancipatory change' (Soja, 1996, p. 87). As subalterns within adult society, young people have responded in both of these ways to their sociospatial marginalization. On the one hand, their withdrawal to the street after dark and to other backstage places without adults can be interpreted as a spatial concretization of their lack of choice. Here, young people are pushed into settings that have been abandoned by adults and their presence further labels them as 'outsiders'. On the other hand, young people's occupancy of some settings, such as the mall, can be interpreted as counterhegemonic or a manifestation of a cultural politic that challenges their marginality. From this perspective the mall becomes a symbolic site of contest and resistance, a place infused through and through with the cultural trappings of thirdspace. When there, young people are asserting the right of the 'hybrid', no longer child but not quite adult, to be active agents in the spatiality of place. By stubbornly hanging on, so these young people begin to test the borders of identity.

The ideas of bel hooks (1989, 1990) further add to others' observations. Her essays on the cultural politics of difference and identity examine the ways in which cultural groupings (notably African-Americans) choose to develop and envelop symbolic spaces where they can begin a process of 'revision', that both contests their marginality and disputes, disorders, and disrupts the boundaries of power. hooks (1990) examines how these journeys into thirdspace are routed along paths that push against the borders of oppression and domination and define a 'profound edge' (hooks, 1990, p. 149) of resistance along the margin. From this perspective the shopping mall becomes both a site of defiance and of 'openness and opportunity', a radical location where young people can attempt to redefine their position in both cultural and geographical space. Hanging out together in the shopping mall can thus be interpreted as the spatiality of inclusion not of exclusion, a behaviour that connects and combines young people into 'polycentric communities of identity and resistance' (Soja, 1996, p. 99).

In this vein, our survey uncovered a range of strategies that were used by young people when faced with the demand to move on. The most common strategy was to move to a different part of the mall (45 percent) or to leave then return after a short period (31 percent). Only a small minority (9 percent) felt sufficiently intimidated not to return.

> See that geezer [a security guard] he picks on us. What a prat! We don't go though. If he says get going or something, then we smooch around a bit until we find somewhere else where he can't see us ... we won't leave until we wants to go. (Boy aged 15, Grosvenor Centre).

Young people found it difficult to rationalize why they were being targeted in this way. We noted a strong sense of injustice and incredulity as to why they were being excluded matched by an insistence on their right to these spaces.

> Why pick on us? It's not fair; we're not doing any harm ... not troublemakers. Why can't we meet here? Look at them there ... they're standing and talking [pointing to two adult couples] ... why don't they get picked on? We have a right to be here like anyone else. (Girl aged 14, Newlands)

> Why should we go? ... We're human too. (Girl aged 16, Grosvenor Centre)

Lieberg (1995) provides an additional insight into young people's tenacious occupancy of these sites. For him the mall is symbolic of a space outside place. 'While one is in a place in a physical sense, the ... spatial construction and organisation refers to other places and other worlds' (Lieberg, 1995, p. 737). Through the intense commercialization of the mall, teenagers have access to cultures and values that supersede the parochial. The mall symbolizes the modern and the exciting and by hanging out there teenagers are demonstrating an awareness of an international (youth) culture that (re)invigorates their attempts to be counted as visible and full members of society.

In their responses too, there was a strong sense of wanting to belong. When asked about how they would change a shopping mall, suggestions included providing more places where young people could hang out without fear of being moved on (40 percent) and encouraging shopkeepers to be more tolerant of their presence (27 percent). Only 3 percent suggested removing or reducing the number of security guards, the vast majority valuing the policing of place. For these young people, moral regulation and control was seen to be an acceptable part of that society to which they sought access and membership.

By valuing the security afforded by the mall, these young people are perhaps hinting at a larger issue, one that relates to their underlying relationship with and continued dependence on adults. From this perspective the panopticon of the adult gaze provides a safety net that enables young people to develop their identity, individuality and even promulgate acts of rebellion, without real danger. In so doing, the mall becomes the liminal space of the hybrid, a place where young people can safely challenge the 'oppressors' (adults) while casting aside the trappings of niceness, servility and politeness that define the myth of the 'proper' child as envisaged by many adults.

Conclusion

In this [reading] we have considered the importance of the shopping mall to a group of young people living in the East Midlands of the UK. We have shown that for many young people the mall provides a convenient meeting place where they can hang out together, within a 'bright' and safe environment. Yet their occupancy of this setting is not unproblematic. Like the *flaneur* of history, many adults, for example, perceive the public and visible presence of young people, especially in a site that is beyond the home and school, as uncomfortable and inappropriate. Despite constant attempts to move them on, however, young people stubbornly remain within the mall asserting a right of presence.

In order to (re)interpret these behaviours (both that of teenager and adult) we have drawn upon the new literature of the cultural politics of difference and identity. We suggest that through their various attempts to assert a right of presence, both 'backstage' and 'on stage', young people assume the mantle of the hybrid. Here, young people are no longer child, living within the safe haven of the home, nor quite adult, with powers to move freely and unassailably within the public domain. By locating themselves in the settings that transgress and so question the spatial hegemony of adulthood, young people journey into the interstitial territory of thirdspace. From this perspective the mall assumes a cultural importance over and above its functional form. In this scenario the mall is both a 'real and imagined space' (Soja, 1996), a lived place where young people, through their shared subjectivities, contest and challenge their marginality. Like hooks (1990) in her observations on people of colour, we contend that through their collective action of being together young people within the mall are often engaged in a process of 'counter-hegemonic cultural production' that both challenges and revises what is meant by being 'out of place' (hooks, 1990, pp. 1–2). By not giving way, young people carve out a cultural space that both redefines their position within society and continues to reposition the boundaries between adults and children.

References

Breitbart, M. (1998) '"Dana" mystical tunnel: young people's designs for survival and change in the city', in Skelton, T. and Valentine, G. (eds) *Cool Places: Geographies of Youth Cultures*, London, Routledge.

Foucault, M. (1982) 'Afterword: the subject and power', in Dreyfus, H. and Rainbow, P. (eds) *Michel Foucault: Beyond Structuralism and Hermeneutics*, Chicago, IL, University of Chicago Press.

Fyfe, N. and Bannister, J. (1996) 'City watching: closed circuit television surveillance in public spaces', *Area*, vol. 28, no. 1, pp. 37–46.

Hengst, H. (1987) 'The liquidation of childhood: an objective tendency', *International Journal of Sociology*, vol. 17, pp. 58–80.

hooks, b. (1989) *Outlaw Culture: Resisting Representations*, New York, Routledge.

hooks, b. (1990) *Yearning: Race, Gender and Cultural Politics*, Boston, MA, South End Press.

James, A., Jenks, C. and Prout, A. (1998) *Theorizing Childhood*, Cambridge, Polity Press.

Jenks, C. (1996) *Childhood*, London, Routledge.

Lieberg, M. (1995) 'Teenagers and public space', *Communication Research*, vol. 22, no. 6, pp. 720–44.

Massey, D. (1998) 'The spatial construction of youth cultures', in Skelton, T. and Valentine, G. (eds) *Cool Places: Geographies of Youth Cultures*, London, Routledge.

Matthews, H. (1995) 'Living on the edge: children as outsiders', *Tijdschrift voor Economische et Sociale Geografie*, vol. 89, pp. 123–202.

Matthews, H. and Limb, M. (1998) 'The right to say: the development of youth councils/forums in the UK', *Area*, vol. 30, pp. 66–78.

Matthews, H. and Limb, M. (1999) 'Defining an agenda for the geography of children', *Progress in Human Geography*, vol. 23, no. 1, pp. 61–90.

Matthews, H., Limb, M., Harrison, L. and Taylor, M. (1998) 'Local places and the political engagement of young people', *Youth and Policy*, vol. 62, no. 4, pp. 16–30.

Matthews, H., Limb, M. and Taylor, M. (1999) 'Young people's participation and representation in society', *Geoforum*, vol. 30, pp. 135–44.

Murray, C. (1990) *The Emerging British Underclass*, London, Institute of Education Affairs.

Qvortrup, J., Bardy, M., Sgritta, G. and Wintersberger, H. (eds) (1994) *Childhood Matters: Social Theory, Practice and Politics*, Aldershot, Avebury.

Rose, T. (1991) 'Fear of a black planet: rap music and black cultural politics in the 1990s', *Journal of Negro Education*, vol. 60, no. 3, pp. 276–90.

Sibley, D. (1995) *Geographies of Exclusion*, London, Routledge.

Soja, E. (1996) *Thirdspace: Journeys to Los Angeles and Other Real-and-Imagined Places*, Oxford, Basil Blackwell.

Stainton-Rogers, W. and Stainton-Rogers, R. (1992) *Stories of Childhood*, London, Harvester Wheatsheaf.

Valentine, G. (1996a) 'Children should be seen and not heard? The production and transgression of adults' public space', *Urban Geography*, vol. 17, no. 2, pp. 202–20.

Valentine, G. (1996b) 'Angels and devils: moral landscapes of childhood', *Environment and Planning D: Society and Space*, vol. 14, pp. 581–99.

Valentine, G. (1999) '"Oh please, Mum. Oh please, Dad". Negotiating children's spatial boundaries', in McKie, L., Bowlby, S. and Gregory, S. (eds) *Gender, Power and the Household*, Basingstoke, Macmillan.

Wyness, M. (2000) *Contesting Childhood*, London, Falmer Press.

Reading B
Gender in public space: 'shining' masculinity and 'demure modern' femininity

Ritty Lukose

Source: *Liberalization's Children: Gender, Youth, and Consumer Citizenship in Globalizing India*, 2009, Durham, NC, Duke University Press.

Masculine anxieties

An important concept for understanding the association between youth, masculinity, and new forms of consumption in the Malayalam language is derived from a slang word, *chethu* ... figuratively it means 'sharp,' 'cool,' 'hip,' or 'shiny,' something like 'cutting-edge.' ...

Devan told me that you needed to be *chethu* in order to matter in his college: 'It's the *chethu* style: jeans, a Yamaha bike [he had only a bicycle]. You need to have six or seven jeans, Killer jeans [a brand name]. You need four or five cotton shirts, three to four T-shirts, a well-groomed, *chethu*, smart look. A bike. You must have a bike.' ...

> ... a life that is in the *chethu* way, you enjoy life ... A Yamaha bike, money in the hand, a *line* [slang for a relationship with a girl], that's it, in between you go to a beer parlor and you sip two beers, you have plenty of friends, you enjoy life. ... You don't care about what has happened yesterday. You don't care what will happen tomorrow. You are always happy. That is *chethu*. ...

An important component of the *chethu* style is the consumption of public space itself ... Devan insisted that you needed to have money in your hand. When I asked him why, he said it was to *karangan*. *Karanguga* can be glossed as 'to wander about,' 'to gallivant.' One needs money in order to consume in public. But it implies more than the material ability to participate in spaces of public consumption. Key to this notion is the aimless quality of this mobility – aimless in terms of not having a specific place to go to and also not having a specific goal to accomplish. It implies an ephemerality with respect to both space and time. As he stated, part of having a certain kind of *chethu* style was an attitude oriented toward the present, not the past or future. When folded into the idea of 'wandering about,' it implies a kind of aimlessness with regard to not only the past and future but space as well. Therefore, whether the space was the actual college campus, or a beer parlor, movie theater, park, beach, restaurant, ice cream parlor, or bus stand, it was fodder for wandering about. And what was the reason for going to any of those places? The answer would invariably be *chumma* – for 'no reason.' ...

[Devan's narrative reveals aspiration and anxiety.] He most immediately aspires to the pleasures of consumption, marked by ephemerality and fun. This present is marked by the pleasures of self-fashioning and the consumption and traversal of public space. While trying to hold past and future at bay, he is plagued by the enormous task of having to turn his educated and aspiring self into a model of middle-class stability, respectability, and consumption in the future that is his imagined adulthood. ...

The masculinity of *chethu* is an assertive and aspiring lower-caste, lower-class masculinity that lays claim to the public through consumption. It is marked by precariousness and vulnerability, both in terms of its lower caste and class social location and the wider world of acute unemployment in Kerala. In the broader consumer culture of Kerala during the 1990s, this masculinity sits at the intersection between the developmental state that educates students like Devan and globalization that structures his consumer-oriented visions of the good life.

Feminine resolutions?

... The wearing of the *churidar* [or *salwar kameez*, comprising trousers worn with a long top that usually goes to the knees] among young unmarried women, and now increasingly younger girls as well as recently married women, has increased dramatically in the last fifteen years. ...

For young women today, wearing the *churidar*, as opposed to the *pavada*, is a matter of adorning themselves in the clothing of an 'Indian' public – one that takes them out of a *pavada*-clad *nadu* and yet protects them from the rampant sexualization of a 'western'-identified, skirt-clad modernity. ... The contemporary wearing of the *churidar* is an embodiment of ... notions of modesty in the fashioning of a modern femininity – one that enables and yet circumscribes women's participation in the public. However, the modern public at stake here is a specific, nationally inflected one, an often bemoaned fact within popular discourses about the increasing popularity of the *churidar*. In discussions of the perceived threat to Kerala's regional identity, the displacement of the *pavada* by the *churidar* is a key indicator that

North Indian hegemony is spreading through Hindi movies and Hindi-language satellite television. Students at the college revealed to me the demure modernity of the *churidar* during the early days of my stay in the hostel …

Dressed in a *churidar*, I would walk with my fellow hostelmates to college. After several days, one of my friends came up and informed me that I had to learn how to walk correctly. When I told her I did not understand what she meant, she went on to explain that I walked in an 'open' (*thuranna*) way: I would look around and peer at people walking by and at things on the road. Sternly, she told me that this might be acceptable in Chicago, but not in that town. She told me that it would invite *comment adi* – the pervasive practice of men 'hitting' women with sexual comments as they walk or ride by on roads, at bus stops and train stations, on buses and in trains. She said I should walk straight, I should not look around so much, I should look ahead of me and slightly down, and I should carry my bag and books close to my body. In short, I should walk in an *oudhukam* way. The Malayalam term *oudhukam* can mean 'contained' or 'closed.' I gloss the term here as 'demure.' I had to learn to properly traverse the public in a demure manner. In public spaces, I would have to be responsible for my own containment.

There is no simple correspondence between the wearing of the *churidar* and being demure, as I found out. However, the force of the 'demure modern' is that it is both demure and modern. A young woman wearing a *pavada* could certainly walk in an *oudhukam* manner but could not claim modernity in the same way. Likewise, a woman in a skirt could walk as demurely as she wanted, but she would still be 'modern' in a way that would leave her inescapably vulnerable to aggressive male behavior. …

While the present tense of *chethu* is rooted in an aimless kind of wandering – a restless mobility in search of fun that might or might not lead to a secure future of middle-class respectability and consumption – the present tense of the demure modern is rooted in the body and its containment as it traverses public space. This becomes clear as Devan discusses his idea of the perfect [demure] girl [as] 'one who won't go around for no reason. For no reason, just wandering about. She won't wander about for no reason.'

The demure female body enables a young woman to enter the public, but in ways that circumscribe her movements. She must be goal-oriented and contained as she traverses a public that is also occupied by young men, whose movements and trajectories are different – aimless and wandering. In a sense, this idea of the demure entails carrying the private, 'essential' self into the public. Masculinity 'shines' (*chethu*) in public, whereas the demure is contained. … This 'demure modern' style is both inscribed and performed, one that can be identified, talked about, and contested.

Chapter 4

Making schools: spaces, objects and relationships

Alison Clark

Contents

In this chapter, you will:

- explore how children's experiences of being in school can be examined through the material culture – the relationships between objects, people and places

- analyse how everyday practices in school, such as school dinners, link to theoretical perspectives about children and childhood

- consider how learning is an embodied activity that involves children's minds, bodies, senses and feelings

- critically reflect on the relationships between official and informal narratives about school.

1 Introduction

In this chapter, we will continue to focus on the context of childhood through looking more closely at children and school. Rather than place the curriculum centre stage, we will focus on how school is experienced through the material culture: the relationships between objects, people and places. Learning is not a detached abstract activity; rather, it is an embodied activity which involves children's minds, bodies, senses and feelings, and which is influenced by the context in which the learning takes place. In using the term 'school', we include learning environments for young children in early childhood institutions alongside formal educational provision for children and young people. The emphasis, in this chapter, will be on institutional settings designed for learning, while acknowledging that learning is not restricted to these formal environments. Despite the dominance of institutions for learning in many children's lives, the spaces and places that house the learning have received less academic attention than studies of the teaching practices within them.

The historian Catherine Burke (2005a) points out the value of placing school buildings centre stage:

> Rather than being viewed as a neutral or passive 'container', if recognized at all, the school building, its various rooms and spaces, the walls, windows, doors and furniture together with outdoor 'nooks and crannies', gardens and open spaces are considered here to be active in shaping the experience of school and the understanding of education.

(Burke, 2005a, pp. 489–90)

This will be the approach adopted in this chapter. Classrooms and the 'non-teaching spaces' of the corridors, staff-room, toilets and dinner halls are not empty scenery, but play an active part in shaping children's lived experiences of school. Historians Martin Lawn and Ian Grosvenor (2005) draw attention to the material culture or materialities of schooling. They define this as:

> the ways that objects are given meaning, how they are used, and how they are linked into heterogeneous active networks in which people, objects and routines are closely connected.

(Lawn and Grosvenor, 2005, p. 7)

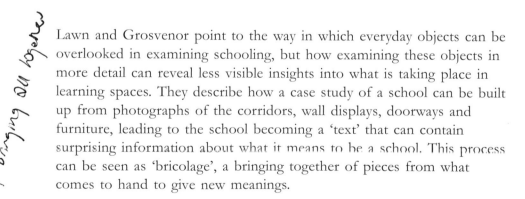

Lawn and Grosvenor point to the way in which everyday objects can be overlooked in examining schooling, but how examining these objects in more detail can reveal less visible insights into what is taking place in learning spaces. They describe how a case study of a school can be built up from photographs of the corridors, wall displays, doorways and furniture, leading to the school becoming a 'text' that can contain surprising information about what it means to be a school. This process can be seen as 'bricolage', a bringing together of pieces from what comes to hand to give new meanings.

We begin by looking at material culture on a large scale through three examples of what have become iconic school designs. The sections that follow continue this theme of looking at school through the physical, material and social environment. First, we begin by exploring three examples of school types that demonstrate the link between design, learning and views of childhood. We then look beyond the walls to focus, at a micro level, on everyday practices within school, using food and eating practices as a means to discover what questions these rule-bound routines can tell us about how childhood is viewed. The final section examines how children and young people may or may not be able to shape their schools by taking part in and disrupting the official narratives of school.

2 Making schools through design

In this section, we explore how school buildings, and the objects and people they contain, can shape children's lived experience of being in school.

2.1   Shaping school through design

Figure 1 A new high-rise school in the mountain region of Mianyang, China

The design of schools is an important factor in what it is like to be a child in school, from the moment of entering the school gate to where children are allowed to sit, how lunchtime is organised and whether there is anywhere to leave belongings during the school day. School design can have a significant impact on children's physical and emotional well-being. For example, can children see out into the playground? Do they have a playground? How far do they have to walk between rooms during the school day? And are there places to be quiet with a few friends as well as be in a crowd? Questions of design may include decisions on both a micro and a macro scale, from the design of pens and furniture, and the installation of technology, to what schools look like from the outside and where they are placed in their communities. Are schools, for example, hidden away on the edges of a community, or are they given status and demanding of attention? The design of schools encodes messages about how children and childhood are viewed, as well as views about the best methods of teaching and learning.

Activity 1   School design from memory

Allow about 30 minutes

Think about the different learning environments you have experienced during your childhood. Choose one environment and draw a plan of the building. Then make notes in response to the following questions:

- What features in the building were the first to come to your mind?
- What impact did the design of the building have on being in this space?
- How were the spaces linked to the events or everyday practices that took place there?

Comment

Author Alison Clark writes:

My school was a newly built first school for 4- to 7-year-olds, built in the early 1960s. It was a low-level construction with access to the outside from every classroom. The school was set next to an estate and surrounded by extensive playing fields. The interior design was child-centred, exemplified by low shelving and drawers in the classrooms and purpose-built, small desks and chairs.

I remember the views out of the classroom. I could sit in the classroom and look out at the school gate and see the way I walked to school with my mother and younger brother. I remember the small library set in a corridor. It had a low glass window and a Picasso print on the wall of a boy with a dove. The reading books were on low shelves for children to be able to go independently into the library and change their own reading books. The hall was where we had school assembly and PE, and where we sat and watched the first man land on the moon. My father came into school once and talked in assembly about his job, and I felt so proud he had come into school to talk to the whole school.

My memories of this school are connected to the practices that took place there. The underpinning philosophy of these postwar schools was based on a child-centred approach to learning which was expressed, for example, through the accessible layout, visibility of the outside world and furniture. The physical and material cultures of the building are also linked to the social relationships taking place within it. Different locations in the school carry particular meanings related to personal events. This is an example of Massey's (1999) concept of 'space-time' which we discussed in Chapter 1; this emphasises how the social and spatial are interconnected.

We will now look at three brief examples of historical and contemporary school designs, chosen for their influential nature. These examples will help us to examine how these school buildings express different views about childhood and learning, and their impact on everyday life in school.

2.2 Board schools

E. R. Robson was the first architect appointed to the London School Board (from 1871 to 1884). Many of the hundreds of London School Board buildings he designed are still operating in the twenty-first century. His key text, *School Architecture* (1877 [1874]) combines meticulous attention to the physical details of design with paying attention to the young users of the buildings.

In the introduction to his thorough text on school architecture, Robson comments on the relative scarcity of reports about the influence of school buildings on children's well-being and learning:

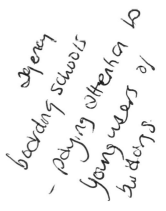

boarding schools, paying attention to the young users of buildings.

The scholastic buildings have not received the same attention. Some of the writers on education give an occasional glance in this direction, but rarely with any serious intention of discussing many of the points of school arrangement. There is no complete handbook on planning and fitting-up school-houses sufficient as a guide to school-founders, school-boards, architects and others, showing the various arrangements which may be considered best for the health, comfort, and effective teaching of children, and setting forth how the different parts of the building should fit together so as to form one harmonious whole. Education itself, being the question of most pressing necessity, has naturally received the first attention. …

If popular education be worth its great price, its homes deserve something more than a passing thought. School-houses are henceforth to take rank as public buildings, and should be planned and built in a manner befitting their new dignity.

(Robson, 1877 [1874], pp. 1–2)

Two aspects of Robson's thinking about school design are apparent from this short extract. He was committed to the link between 'health, comfort and effective teaching' which he documents with examples from his examination of European and American schools. Robson also believed in the status which should be given to school buildings in recognition of the important work taking place there.

The importance attached to the physical well-being of children and adults is demonstrated by Robson's attention to the internal design of school houses, for example in relation to warmth, light and ventilation. Further consideration is given to the often invisible spaces of school – for example, cloakrooms, which seldom appear in official accounts of schools, whether historical or contemporary. Robson provides the following description:

Cloak-rooms. – The common, indeed almost universal, practice of hanging up caps, cloaks and bonnets along the walls of the school-room, would appear (like some other arrangements) to be the result of a cheeseparing economy. Whether from the untidy appearance, the fact that at some seasons of the year many of the articles are wet and send out unpleasant odours, or other reasons, it is a practice not to be encouraged. On the other hand experience in some of the denser and rougher parts of London shows that when an outer corridor or entrance is used as a cloak-room many of the articles are stolen. Hence teachers will frequently be found to favour the use of the school-room for the purpose.

(Robson, 1877 [1874], p. 213)

Figure 2   A board school on Blackheath Road, Greenwich, London; the gabled façade was designed by Edward Robert Robson (1835–1917)

Here we gain an impression of a school room edged in wet coats that added to the unpleasant aroma of the classroom. This is a reminder of school as an embodied experience involving all the senses, the practicalities of which Robson took seriously in his evaluation and recommendations for school architecture.

Robson's most visible legacies to exterior school design were the three-storey, red-brick Queen-Anne-style school buildings, often constructed on constrained urban sites. These schools were described by Conan Doyle's fictional detective Sherlock Holmes as 'beacons of learning'.

The height of the buildings alone, especially since they were constructed at a time when high-rise buildings of this size were unusual, could be symbolic of the status placed on children's learning. However, working-class parents might have seen these monumental buildings as a threatening presence at a time when the London School Board had adopted compulsory education following the Education Act of 1870 (Auerbach, 2009). Embellishments on the external walls, such as grand balconies and ornamental plaques, all added to the sense of importance. The classrooms were constructed with rows of desks, usually screwed to the floor. The classrooms were also planned with an area for general circulation, and some schools accommodated large drill corridors. This belief in the need for movement during the school day was reflected in the design of communal halls in Board schools, and in the importance of playground spaces, whether on the roof, as in some Board schools, or on surrounding land.

This influential school design placed learning firmly within clearly defined boundaries, and strengthened hierarchies within the classroom between teacher and children. These Victorian designs reinforced what the educational theorist John Dewey described as the traditional 'school environment of desks, blackboards, [and] a small schoolyard' (Dewey, 1997 [1938], p. 40). It was also gendered design in which older boys and girls were taught in separate classrooms, and entered and moved around the school through separate entrances and stairs.

2.3 Open-air schools

The open-air school movement has been an influential example of school design underpinned by a strong philosophy about children, childhood, learning and the environment. Here, the link between health and learning expressed by Robson gave rise to an influential range of nurseries and schools in England and across the world. The earliest examples of open-air schools related to the care of weak children, seen to be at risk of tuberculosis and in need of a healthy outdoor environment with access to fresh air. In 1904, an open-air school – called a forest school because it was built in a pine forest – was opened in Charlottenburg near Berlin, Germany (Châtelet, 2011). Rachel McMillan began a Girls' Camp in Deptford, London, which provided girls from impoverished backgrounds with a place to sleep outside, in the belief that encouraging sleep and healthy well-being would improve their ability to learn. In 1914, this provision for older children was extended to include an open-air nursery for young children. Margaret McMillan, Rachel's sister, explained her hopes for the enterprise, which

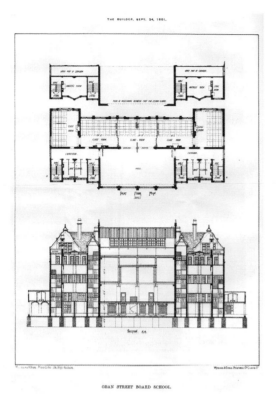

Figure 3   Plan of the first floor and mezzanine of Oban Street Board School, London, designed by Edward Robert Robson

centred on the space that could be offered to young children and their families.

> Our rickety children, our cramped and … deformed children, get
> back to the earth with its magnetic currents, and the free blowing
> wind … To let them live at last and have sight of people planting
> and digging, to let them run and work and experiment, sleep, have
> regular meals, the sights and sounds of winter and spring, autumn
> and summer, birds, and the near presence of mothers – to get
> these things we sacrificed everything else.
>
> (McMillan, 1919, cited in Steedman, 1990, p. 91)

These views about the redeeming qualities of nature were rooted in the
Romantic tradition articulated by the philosopher Jean-Jacques Rousseau
(1712–1778). Rousseau's belief in the garden as a place to educate
children had a profound influence on schools formed by Johan

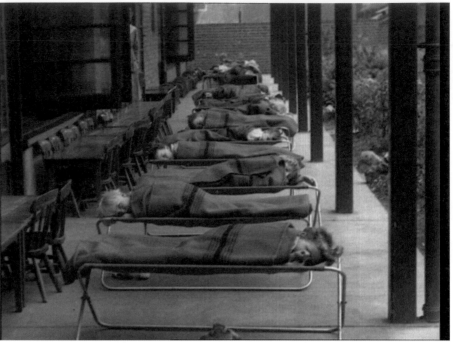

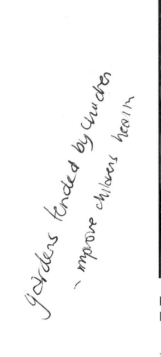

gardens tended by children
~ improve childrens health

Figure 4 Rest time outside the shelter at Rachel MacMillan Nursery School, Deptford, 1939

Pestalozzi, and on the first German kindergartens designed by Friedrich Froebel in which the gardens were tended by children (Herrington, 2001). Drawing on these pedagogical and philosophical traditions and the desire to improve children's health, the McMillans' open-air nursery in Deptford included 'shelters' to foster a positive link between the children's experiences of both their indoor and their outdoor environment. The garden became a vital part of the designed environment, as was the provision of baths in the shelters. Each child was given their own hairbrush, kept on the premises in a special cupboard which still exists in the nursery school (now known as a children's centre) today.

The educational vision for open-air schools was expressed through the design of the spaces and the everyday practices that took place in them. Uffculme Open-Air School in Birmingham, England, was a co-educational school which opened in September 1911 (Châtelet, 2008). The historian Anne-Marie Châtelet describes how classrooms were designed to be open to the elements on three sides. The wood and brick classrooms had folding glass doors and underfloor heating. The only solid wall supported the blackboard. Other key features of the

Good food + rest

provision related to the emphasis on good food and rest. This account by Birmingham's School Medical Officer, from his 1911 report, offers an insight into everyday routines:

> They [the children] receive a breakfast of porridge, milk or cocoa, and bread and butter. It has been found necessary to give some of the children an additional morning meal of hot milk at 11 o'clock. On arrival each child dons a jersey and a pair of clogs, and during the cold weather a knitted cap as well. When sitting at their desks in cold weather the children wrap up their legs and feet in a rug. A two-course meal at 12.30 is followed by one-and-a half hours sleep. At 4.40 pm the children have their third meal and leave for home at 5.30 pm. Each child is provided with a toothbrush, which is used before they leave for home.
>
> (Dr Auden, School Medical Officer, Birmingham, cited in Châtelet, 2008, p. 115)

food & routines 3 meals

Figure 5   A classroom at Uffculme Open-Air School, Birmingham, England

2.4   The preschools of Reggio Emilia

We turn now to a third example of school design, one that is underpinned by a strong philosophy about childhood, learning and the

environment, and which has had a wide impact at an international level. This is a group of municipal preschools in Reggio Emilia, an Italian town in the prosperous Emilia Romagna region of northern Italy. The preschools were first set up in 1967 by Loris Malaguzzi, who was their first Director and the inspiration for the initiative. This early childhood provision has gained international recognition for its approach to working with children under the age of six. Questioning lies at the heart of the Reggio Emilia approach: this is a learning community who are not afraid to ask what it means to be a school. The preschools have strong links with their locality: parents, community members and children are all viewed as active participants in the learning process. Practice is based on an understanding of learning as socially constructed, with children and adults co-constructing meanings (Miller et al., 2003).

The preschools are housed in a range of buildings, not all of which are purpose-built. However, whether or not the building was specifically designed for young children, the physical and material environments play a prominent part in how learning is conceived. Vea Vecchi was one of the first atelieristas to be appointed in the Reggio preschools in 1970. Vecchi articulates the importance of the environment in the pedagogical work in which she has been involved:

> During the course of their long history, the Municipal Infant-toddler Centers and Preschools of Reggio Emilia have dedicated a great deal of attention to the physical environment, and in various moments have carried out specific research on how the school space is inhabited.

> (Vecchi, quoted in ISAFF, 2002, p. 11)

The role of the atelierista comprises that of an educator with an arts background who is based in a learning community and operating from a workshop base, or atelier, within the school. This understanding of the role conveys the sense of an ongoing dialogue between theories of teaching and learning or pedagogy and the design – a dialogue that has at certain moments become the focal point for cross-disciplinary enquiry. In the 1990s, this gave rise to a project called *Children, Spaces, Relations: Metaproject for an Environment for Young Children* (Ceppi and Zini, 1998). The project – a collaboration between educationalists in Reggio (Reggio Children) and architects and designers (the Domus

Academy in Milan) – placed a particular emphasis on learning from the way children engaged with the environment, and on thinking about how design could enhance opportunities for living and learning in these spaces. This project led to the commissioning of a particular range of furnishings for early childhood environments (ISAFF, 2002).

It seems as though this collaborative research provided the opportunity for teasing out some wider theoretical and practical questions about the purpose of education and what it means to be a school:

> It is not an environment that is categorized strictly as a school, nor does it simulate a home or an 18th century village, with all the resulting stereotypes. Instead, it proposes a multifunctional place where children and adults work with both traditional and modern instruments, where they play (with both traditional and contemporary games), where they talk, listen, eat (hopefully good food!) and rest (given that rest is also considered productive). In other words, a place where they live the day, trying to live it with intelligence, care, grace, and with attention to relationships.

> (Vecchi, 2010, p. 12)

Figure 6   The 'piazza', Diana School, Reggio Emilia

What ingredients does Vecchi draw attention to here? The early childhood environment is one that is breaking out of some expected stereotypes. Vecchi questions, for example, the idea of an early childhood space that is aiming solely to emulate a home; and elsewhere, she describes the environment as one that does not seek to be 'babyish', a quality that she associates with adults' nostalgic views of what an early childhood space should look like. Instead, the organisation is an intergenerational one in which both children and adults are engaged together in activities that are centred on living, which includes talking, eating, listening, playing and resting. It is an environment where the traditional and the contemporary meet. Vecchi summarises the vision in this way:

> We believe that daily life is a special teacher and that the environment that hosts this life is fundamental. We are aware that we are talking about a privileged childhood, about schools and environments for only a part of the world. Nevertheless, we are convinced that intelligence, care and attentiveness to childhood are among the most important attitudes for ensuring that what can be defined as privileges actually become rights.
>
> (Vecchi, 2010, p. 12)

This emphasis on 'daily life' as a teacher reveals itself in the building design, in the activities that the children engage in, and in the material resources designed or promoted in the preschools. For example, the building layout of some of the purpose-built preschools contains a central courtyard which is constructed as a meeting place for children of different ages and for adults. These 'piazzas' echo the squares at the heart of towns and cities in Italy, which serve as meeting places for daily interaction.

On a more intimate level, 'daily life' as a teacher can be seen in the incorporation of washrooms, baby-changing areas and sleeping areas as valued parts of the aesthetic and learning environment, with attention paid to the use of materials and the decoration of walls, floors and ceilings. Here, the environment goes beyond simply being an attractive 'container' for young children. Even furniture is viewed as promoting children's active engagement in developing their skills and demonstrating agency. This is seen, for example, in the design of some of the beds for the youngest children, which are shaped like baskets and placed on the floor, out of which young children can crawl unaided when they wake up.

In the next section, we will continue to look at children and school through the everyday practices that take place there.

Summary of Section 2

School buildings and the material environment are not neutral containers for children; they relay messages about views on childhood and learning.

The design of schools, from a macro to micro level, can have an impact on children's daily lives within those spaces, as is shown in historical and contemporary examples of schools.

---

3 Making schools through everyday practices

3.1 Everyday food practices in school

School design is only a part of the story of how schools are made. We now move the focus from buildings to the everyday practices that take place within schools, so that we can look in more detail at how these shape children's lives generally as well as their life in school. These environments are not only institutions for teaching and learning; they are also intergenerational spaces in which adults and children spend many hours of their lives together. Looking at schools through the everyday practices that take place in these institutional spaces can tell us much about the relationships between children and adults.

One such group of everyday practices are those associated with food and eating in school, practices that contain powerful messages about children and childhood. The preparation, transport and consumption of food in school, and the social practices that surround the activity of eating, can be contested sites where power differences are most visible. Questions are raised, such as what food is allowed in school? What food is banned? Where can eating take place? We will look first at examples of children's experiences of eating in school, and the rules and routines that surround food. This will be followed by an exploration of how food is 'governed' in school.

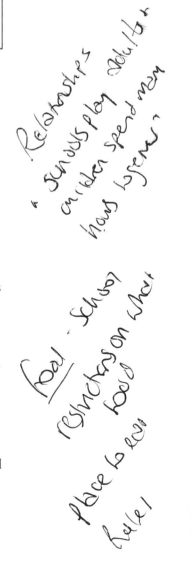

Figure 7 Two schoolgirls eating during the tiffin hours in Taldi, West Bengal, India

School
Smell of food lingers

3.2 Preparing food in school

The preparation of school meals is one starting point for thinking about the everyday practices surrounding food in school. Author Alison Clark, when reflecting on her own memories of her first school, was reminded of the lingering smell of school dinners from the kitchen on the premises, which filled the hall and corridors long after lunchtime was over. The material context of the preparation of food for consumption in school can reveal details about the relationship between food, learning and childhood in a particular setting, as well as wider cultural differences between the school culture and children's home cultures.

Activity 2 Connections to food

Allow about 20 minutes

The following two extracts represent different relationships between the food consumed and the process in which it is made. They are taken from two fieldwork visits undertaken by Alison Clark (2010a): the first was part of a study tour of preschools in Iceland; the second was a return visit to a primary school in England following a longitudinal study of children's involvement in school design.

Read the extracts, then consider the relationship described in each case, between food and the children who consumed the food.

- What similarities and differences might exist between the two?
- What do you consider was the children's likely relationship with the kitchen staff in the two examples? Similarly, what differences might there be between how the kitchen staff viewed children in the two settings?

The preschool was arranged along a wide corridor which was used as a playspace for children as well as a passageway between rooms. At one end there was a large hatch in the wall which was low enough for young children to see into. On the other side of the hatch was a small kitchen where food was prepared for children and staff. During the morning session when I visited the preschool one of the kitchen staff was sitting preparing vegetables, looking out on a block play area where a group of young children were engaged in an intricate construction game. At various points during their play the children came across to talk to the member of staff and then returned to their game.

(Fieldwork notes from a visit to an Icelandic preschool, Reykjavik, 2007)

I arrived at a primary school in London just before lunchtime. A member of the kitchen staff was walking across the school playground from the school kitchen with two large insulated food containers on a trolley. She pushed the trolley into the nursery class where the nursery children were seated, about to have their lunch. The food was then served from the insulated containers onto small plates by the nursery staff and handed out to the seated children.

(Fieldwork notes from a visit to an English primary school, London, 2010)

Comment

Eating in school can hold different meanings for those children who see the food being prepared before eating and for those for whom it is a 'disembodied' activity. Similarly, children may have a different relationship with the adults involved in the preparation of food, especially if this is a part of everyday life in school, open to conversations between children and adults, and a shared experience. It is possible that a member of staff engaged in preparing food in school will feel more connected to the life of the school if children are a visible part of this process and not just the delivery point.

The layout of the learning environments described in these two extracts contributed to the different connections between children and food. In the preschool, the placing of the kitchen next to the play area, together with the low glass doors that opened and the height of the counter, all facilitated the communication between kitchen staff and the children. Similarly, the placing of the nursery class at a distance from the kitchen contributed to the decision to transport the food, ready-made and sealed, across the playground to the nursery class. However, design is only part of the equation here. The different relationships between food and its preparation are also linked to the approaches to food as part of the learning process.

3.3   The dinner hall

Children's experiences of food in school may be closely tied to the physical environment in which lunch takes place. Burke (2005b) reflects on her early memories of school dinners which were closely tied to place:

> One of my earliest memories of school is associated with fear of the school dinner hall. One day, during the school meal, I felt sick and discovered an escape route from the daily hazard of dinner time. I was allowed to lie down on a camp bed inside the reception class room and was left. I found great comfort there with no one to worry me. Somehow I managed to escape each dinner time for a few days as I found myself experiencing the same symptoms as soon as midday approached. A sympathetic teacher led me once more to the little camp bed and I was left alone. Like so many children, it was perhaps the fear of losing control and becoming ill that caused the anxiety and actual symptoms. This may have been magnified by the strange regimentation of large numbers eating together according to rules and orders set down in what was to me, as a newcomer in the autumn of 1962, the alien environment of the English primary school.

(Burke, 2005b, p. 571)

Burke's account shows the close association between the place in which the eating (or avoiding eating) occurs and the feelings this memory induces. The dinner hall held a particular dread for Burke, which, she reflects, may have been the result of the hall's size, and the rules and routines that took place there, as well as the process of eating. Her rescue took the form of 'being ill', which triggered a different response from the adults in charge and resulted in receiving care and comfort in the form of a camp bed in the classroom.

Activity 3   Reading A

Allow about 30 minutes

Go to the end of the chapter and read Reading A, 'Children and food at Prestolee School', by Catherine Burke. This is a further extract from Burke's (2005b) account of the 'edible landscape of school'. The description of Prestolee School describes the headmaster O'Neill's attempts to integrate food and eating into the life of a school.

As you read, make notes about what O'Neill saw as the advantages of raising the status of food and eating within his school community. How were children encouraged to play an active role in the process of enjoying food in school?

Figure 8   Mealtimes at Prestolee School in Lancashire, England, 1944

Comment

From this account, which started in the years between the First and Second World Wars, we can see that school food in this Lancashire elementary school was not regarded as an inconsequential aside to the real business of learning; rather, it was viewed an essential part of being at school and of being nourished. O'Neill, however, was unusual – not in his recognition of the importance of children having sufficient food to learn, but in his vision of a school in which the children were 'learning by doing'. Everyday tasks of living were moved centre stage to form the framework around which learning could take place. This was not a pedagogy that involved presenting children with knowledge, but one in which the views of teaching and learning were developed out of children's active role in creating new understandings based on the things that interested them. The emphasis on doing is symbolised by the replacement of classrooms by workshops. This active approach to learning led to the children's involvement in the construction of the indoor and outdoor environments, including the canteen.

Moving on from this historical account of a school in which food and eating were an integral part of the active learning approach, what evidence is there of children and young people's contemporary perspectives on eating in school? The 'Joinedupdesignforschools' programme, established by John and Frances Sorrell, is a design initiative set up to explore children's priorities for change in school, and to support children and designers working together on possible solutions. Dinner halls and canteens were two of the school areas identified for change, highlighting the link between the spaces, the rules and routines that take place as part of the social process of eating in school.

'The problem with the canteen is that it's horrible.'

'You queue in the rain for most of your lunch break and have to wolf down food you don't like in about 5 minutes.'

'Lunchtime's not a restful time to enjoy good food and company but a rushed stressful event.'

Figure 9   Waiting for lunch: 'the line' (Source: Clark, 2010a, p. 64)

'Five hundred and fifty students need to have their lunch and leave the hall with time to digest it, all inside an hour.'

(Quoted in Sorrell and Sorrell, 2005, pp. 52–5)

These comments show the logistical problems involved in feeding hundreds of children within a short period of time. The queue is a feature of the lunchtimes of many children across the age range from under five to eighteen. In a study of children's involvement in changes to their learning environments (Clark, 2010a), the lunchtime queue was one of the features of being in school pointed to by 5-year-olds. A map made by a group of young children about their existing primary school included a carefully drawn picture of 'the line' (see Figure 9). The drawing shows two adults behind a table each with large spoons; in front of the table is a long line – the queue for lunch. It is not clear just from this illustration whether waiting in line was a positive or negative experience. However, it was an important enough everyday experience to be included by these young children to explain what being in school was like. Waiting was clearly an everyday feature of life at school.

Figure 10 Waiting in line for lunch in Mutoko, Zimbabwe

3.4   The packed lunchbox

The 'packed lunch' and the packed lunchbox represent a particular eating practice in school which is experienced by many children. It crosses the boundary between home and school. As sociologist Allison James has noted:

> The packed lunch in its confusing of two important domains in a child's social experience, is a potentially highly charged and emotive commodity. It represents food from the social context of the home which is eaten within the cultural context of school and in the company of other children.
>
> (James, 1993, p. 144)

The food in a packed lunch has strong connections with the home context in which the food was prepared or purchased, and with the individuals who assembled the pack, whether parents or other family members. Metcalfe and colleagues have focused on the school lunchbox and explored the aspects of private and public lives of which this boundary-crossing object is part (Metcalfe et al., 2008). Their initial research examined three aspects of how the lunchbox can be seen as a container or 'space': first, as a focus for media and government pronouncements on food and healthy or unhealthy eating; secondly, as an object that connects parents and children; and thirdly, as an artefact

MIK – packed lunch combining home + school

(Metcalfe et al.) lunch box

that can be a potent player in children's friendships and negotiations in school (Metcalfe et al., 2008).

In the UK, increasing government and media concern about the rising number of children and young people regarded as obese has led to numerous initiatives and programmes to promote healthy eating both at home and in school. Packed lunches consumed at school have become open to policy scrutiny, as the contents represent a 'window' into eating practices at home. Food contained in the boxes may be open to the gaze of a range of adults, including 'dinner ladies' (or lunchtime supervisors), teachers and researchers:

> Ruby, Phoebe, Robert and Lauren and a few others come and sit with me [AM] in the dining hall. Lauren and Robert are 'on scrapings': they put unwanted food in bins and stack trays and cutlery for washing. Lauren gets me her disposable camera [part of project data collection]. I tell Ruby I'm going to talk to her step dad next week; she seems a little concerned. 'It's OK, I'm not going to check up on you' I say. She says, 'did he say I'm a picky eater, because I am?' I tell her no, I haven't spoken to him yet. She takes out her packed lunch and her mum's forgotten to put anything on the sandwich; it's just bread and butter, so she leaves that and just eats the crisps and chocolate and drinks her drink. I take photos of this and of Phoebe's box: they both have 'Bratz' boxes.
>
> (Fieldnote extracts, December 2006, in Metcalfe et al., 2008, p. 403)

The lunchbox and its contents represent a tangible link between parents and children which 'intrudes' into the school day. As an example, Metcalfe and colleagues highlight the particular cultural importance of bentō (packed lunchboxes) for Japanese children at nursery school (see Allison, 1991). The lovingly prepared food and its presentation are seen as a reflection of maternal affection and 'good mothering'. This suggests that the contents of lunchboxes may form part of wider discussions on what is valued about being a parent and what behaviour is expected from parents.

Children can also use lunchboxes and their contents as bargaining tools to foster or support friendships (Burgess and Morison, 1998; Dryden, et al., 2009). Alison Clark remembers the relative power allotted to her peers at secondary school who had packed lunch rather than enduring the monotony of school dinners. The contents of lunchboxes can become a currency for trading favours and affection.

3.5   Food as a mechanism of control

So far in this section, we have considered the ways in which the everyday practices of eating in school are linked to views about children and childhood, learning and parenting. One emerging theme from this discussion has been that of food used as a mechanism of control. Earlier, we saw how children's accounts of the rituals and routines of 'waiting in line' are one example of the daily performance acted out between adults, who control the eating environment, and children, who take part or disengage. Controlling food and its consumption in school is closely linked to the way in which children and young people's time is governed in school. When they arrive at school, do children know when their next meal will be, who they will be able to sit next to, and how slowly or quickly they will be allowed to eat?

Figure 11   A school canteen with fixed benches and tables

Activity 4   Reading B

Allow about 40 minutes

Go to the end of the chapter and read Reading B, 'Foucault, space and primary school dining', by Jo Pike. This reading brings together questions about power and control in relation to children and food at school, using examples of both the dinner hall and packed lunch. Pike draws on notions of governmentality (for example, Foucault, 1980), to examine how children's (and adults') actions are influenced by the powerful discourse on healthy eating. Make notes on the ways in which the nutritional discourse in the dinner hall maintains its dominance over the social discourse between children and between children and adults. How do the layout of the rooms and the use of the walls and other spatial tactics reinforce the surveillance of the children?

Comment

Pike describes how there are two separate groups of children in the dinner halls that she observed – those who were eating school dinners and those who had a packed lunch. The dominant discourse of healthy eating was promoted through posters on the walls, in the arrangement of the food counter so that everyone had to file past the salad bar, and in the surveillance by the lunch supervisors, which was reinforced in one school by a reward system. There is also evidence of children's self-regulation, as the discussion with the packed-lunch children demonstrates, in which they discuss the high fat content of their chocolate biscuits. This links to Foucault's notion of the self-governing subject.

We can see how food and eating practices in school can provide a way of examining how children are governed in school. It can be seen as one of the means by which decisions made on the macro level of government policy and media interest can impinge on school practices at a micro level, right down to deciding which children are deemed worthy to have a tablecloth. This contrasts with the example from Reading A, in which tablecloths were an important symbol of mealtimes as a shared event for every child.

No voice / (annals of who's eaten, when

Summary of Section 3

The everyday practices surrounding food and eating in school reveal insights into how children and childhood are viewed.

Examining the dinner hall and the packed lunchbox shows how children's experiences of school are influenced by factors from policy at a macro level to parental choice at a micro level.

Food in school can be a mechanism of control in which dominant ideas, such as the importance of healthy eating, can influence how children are allowed to spend their time at lunchtime, who they are with and how they are valued.

---

4 Children's involvement in 'making' schools

4.1 Official, informal and physical narratives of school

The final section of this chapter examines how children and young people can shape their schools by taking part in, as well as disrupting, the official narratives of school. In a cross-national ethnographic study of young people in secondary schools in London and Helsinki, feminist sociologists Gordon et al. (2000) describe three different layers at work in school: the official, the informal and the physical. They identify official school as being how a school is described in the 'documents of the school and the state' (Gordon et al., 2000, p. 53). This is the layer of school that contains curriculum and policy documents, including behaviour policies. It is the school as it is portrayed in a prospectus and on an official school website. In the classroom, it is the school as it is seen through lesson plans and teaching materials, and relates to the formal relationships between teachers and students.

Meanwhile, the informal layer of school is identified as existing in relationship to the official layer, but not just in opposition to it:

> We choose to use the term *informal* rather than create a binary opposition between the official and the unofficial, to indicate that the informal school is different from, and not merely a reaction to, the official school; it has a life and a meaning of its own. Here we expand the analysis of classroom interaction to examine interaction between teachers and students beyond the instructional

relationship, among students in other areas of the school, among teachers, and between teachers, students and other groups in the school (support staff of various types.) School rules are compared with their enactment in practice, informal hierarchies among and between teachers and students compared with formal hierarchies.

(Gordon et al., 2000, p. 53)

Finally, the physical school is seen by these researchers as capable of shaping the lives of children and adults within the spaces, in a similar way to that we have explored so far in this chapter.

Nespor (2002) warns that, in thinking about schools in this way, we need to ask who decides what the official narrative should be, or whether there are many such official ways of making meaning with regard to what is happening in school, which may differ depending on who is providing the definition or carrying out the observations. Nespor also emphasises, as Gordon et al. also point out, how these three layers or narratives of the official, informal and physical are entwined. We will look next at three examples of children shaping/making schools and how these narratives are entangled.

4.2   School uniforms

The issue of school uniform can lie on the fault-line between the official and the informal narratives of school. Rules governing school uniform can be one of the most visible ways in which children's bodies are disciplined in school. However, subverting the rules or establishing different peer-group codes about uniform, can be a tangible example of where the informal culture of school is seen at work.

Activity 5   Uniform codes

Allow about 10 minutes

The lists below are taken from a highly acclaimed academy in the UK which places great importance on maintaining a strict uniform policy. Make notes on what impression you gain about how students are viewed in this school. What differences are there between the expectations for girls and boys? What questions might this raise about the relationship with parents at this school?

Girls	Boys
Academy Blazer	Academy Blazer
Academy Grey Skirt	Academy Grey Trousers
Academy Blouse	Academy Shirt
White Short Socks/Black Opaque Tights	Academy Jumper
Black Outdoor Coat (Plain)	Black Socks
Flat, Black Leather Shoes that can be polished and are not patent or suede	Black Outdoor Coat (Plain)
	Academy Tie
	Black Leather Shoes that can be polished and are not patent or suede

Comment

These lists present what could be regarded as a detailed official narrative of what girls and boys are expected to wear at school. This narrative is differentiated by gender. Both genders are required to wear a formal blazer and formal black shoes, but trousers and ties are only for the boys. The height of girls' shoes is prescribed but not that of the boys'. The items labelled 'Academy' appear to be only available from the academy's uniform suppliers.

There is a strong message here to parents and to students about what is expected in order for children to fit in with the official school. What we cannot tell from these lists is what other requirements there may be regarding students' appearance. What hairstyles (and hair colouring) are acceptable for girls and boys? What jewellery and piercings are permitted or forbidden? What make-up, if any, is allowed? Each of these questions relates to the way in which students' choices about their bodies and appearance are influenced by the official narrative of school.

Gewirtz (2001) chooses school uniforms as one of the factors associated with a market-driven model of education provision. The uniform regulations can also become a visible shorthand for discipline. Gewirtz encountered this view in one of her interviews with the head of a secondary school:

Figure 12   Children in school, Kumrokhali, West Bengal, India

His argument was uniform creates an image of discipline and is therefore attractive to 'aspirant classes' but also that it inculcates a more serious attitude towards school and school work.

(Gewirtz, 2001, p. 33)

The maintaining of this image of discipline can become a time-consuming part of teachers' time in school, as Carrie Paechter (2006) points out:

If the body is simply the negation of mind, and the mind is the focus of education, then the body has to be, in effect, not there. This means that a considerable part of the energy of the schooling system has to go into disciplining and confining the bodies of students, so that they cannot interfere with the main purposes of schooling, which are to do with the mind.

(Paechter, 2006, p. 127)

But uniforms and maintaining appearance in terms of make-up, jewellery and hairstyles can also consume a considerable amount of children and young people's energy in school too. In her ethnographic study of gender and sexual identities in the final year of a primary school, Renold (2005) documents the peer pressure surrounding how to interpret the official uniform. She describes how the 'square girls', who were known for their academic success, did not fit in with the 'girlie culture' that the majority of girls in the classroom followed. This 'girlie culture' included a close attention to high street fashion. Renold observed that the more academic girls were excluded from playground games on account of their 'sad skirts' or official uniform. Gordon et al. (2000) also reported how appearance within the Finnish schools they studied, which didn't have school uniform, and the English schools, which did, was an important part of group membership and individual identity:

> This was particularly marked in the London schools, where some of the girls adjusted their uniforms to enhance their femininity. This gendered display, although contrary to school rules, was not hounded with such devotion to duty by the teachers as in the case of other uniform transgressions.

(Gordon et al., 2000, pp. 190–1)

4.3   School councils

We have been looking in this section at how children and young people can shape their schools by taking part in as well as disrupting the official narratives of school. We turn now to think about school councils as one of a number of ways in which 'pupil voice' may shape schools or be prevented from doing so. Whitty and Wisby (2007) identify a number of different drivers for supporting 'pupil voice': a children's rights agenda; a focus on active citizenship with a future-oriented goal of preparation for citizenship; school improvement linked to school performance and personalisation based on a model of pupils as consumers of education. These different drivers may in turn influence what children and adults expect from school councils. These sometimes conflicting aspirations and expectations can result in school councils being sources of contention in schools. Wyness (2009), in his exploration of decision-making institutions including school councils, identified differences in agenda between some of the teachers and children and young people involved. He illustrates how the children and young people frequently chose topics for discussion which related to the everyday practices of being in school, such as food and eating and toilets which we have discussed in this chapter. These themes are described by various teachers as being 'childish', 'not serious' or 'very safe areas'. These topics are set in opposition to themes relating to the official narrative – the educational agenda within the schools. This raises the question as to what is a 'safe' area for school councils to discuss and who controls this decision. Adults are usually the gatekeepers in school councils who decide what issues are open for debate. It appears that topics which might be seen to relate to the informal and physical narratives of schools, about everyday practices in school which impact on the quality of children's life-worlds, present a risk to adults in authority as they challenge the dominant discourses and threaten to destabilise what is seen to be of value.

Activity 6   Reading C

Allow about 30 minutes

Reading C, 'Teacher concerns about formal mechanisms for "pupil voice"', is taken from a literature review and study of school councils by G. Whitty and E. Wisby (2007). This extract focuses on teachers' concerns about these formal mechanisms for involving children in decision making in schools.

As you read the extract, make notes on the possible barriers preventing teachers' support for provision for pupil voice in schools and the extent to which you agree or disagree with the difficulties raised.

Comment

School councils need to have the respect of students and staff in order to be an effective means by which children and young people can influence the way a school functions. Whitty and Wisby report on some of the concerns expressed by teachers about school councils. Such concerns can be due to a theoretical questioning of whether pupil voice is of value in running a school, as well as practical concerns about timing and organisation. These authors raise the additional issue regarding the extent to which teachers feel themselves to have a role in decision-making processes within school. Teachers who feel that school structures do not allow them to play an active role in shaping what it means to be a school may be less inclined to support ways for students to be proactive. Perceived abilities can also be an issue, whether this leads to an underestimation of what decision making is possible or an overestimation of what students can achieve without training and support.

We end this section by looking at another example of a school council at work, to see if this mechanism can be used to shape the physical and material aspects of school and, in so doing, to challenge notions of whose views count.

Earlier in the chapter, we read about the Living Spaces study (Clark, 2010a, 2010b) in which young children under five were involved in the design and review of learning environments. While this three-year study focused on the views and experiences of the youngest children in the school, at one point in the study the school council was also involved. This was composed of two children, a boy and a girl, from each class in the school, ranging in age from 5 to 11 years old. The group was involved in planned changes to the outdoor playgrounds surrounding the school. As this primary school was in the process of having major changes made to the school building, the play areas were going to be affected by the ongoing work: play areas, including large football pitches, were to be disrupted. The head teacher asked the school council to consider how interim plans could be made to best use the reduced outdoor play space, and what resources could support their plans. The school council began by looking at maps of the school and at photographs, taken by the youngest children in the school, of what they saw as the important places in their school.

> Spending time engaging with material produced by three- and four-year olds in the school community reversed the hierarchy of knowledge which is embedded in most schools. The maps and photographs produced by the nursery and reception class provided the means to cross pedagogical boundaries and enabled children of different ages to co-construct meanings.
>
> (Clark, 2010a, p. 182)

Involving the school council in choosing the physical and material culture of the school presents one way in which the official structures can make room for other narratives about school. Doing so provides real evidence of the value placed on the knowledge generated by the least articulate and least powerful members of a school community.

Summary of Section 4

Schools can be seen as composed of official, informal and physical narratives or layers.

School uniform is one example of where official and informal narratives can overlap.

School councils are part of the official structures and can reveal tensions in terms of how children can shape what schools are like, but they can also be forums for bringing together issues concerning the official, informal and physical.

5 Conclusion

This chapter has looked at the topic of children and school through the lens of material culture in order to explore the different ways in which children and young people are influenced by, and in turn influence, the objects, people and places that they encounter. We began by considering school design and structures before considering everyday practices in these spaces, including those related to food and eating, and to school uniform. Attempts at understanding the complex web of relationships and discourses that exist in schools need to remain open to how official, informal and physical narratives combine. In addition, those seeking different ways of 'making school' may need to remain alert to whose accounts are given currency both within and beyond school walls.

References

Allison, A. (1991) 'Japanese mothers and *obentōs*: the lunch-box as ideological state apparatus', *Anthropological Quarterly*, vol. 64, no. 4, pp. 195–208.

Auerbach, S. (2009) '"Some punishment should be devised": parents, children, and the state in Victorian London', *The Historian*, vol. 71, no. 4, pp. 757–79.

Burgess, R. G. and Morison, M. (1998) 'Chapatis and chips: encountering food use in primary school settings', *British Food Journal*, vol. 3, pp. 141–6.

Burke, C. (2005a) 'Containing the school child: architectures and pedagogies', *Paedagogica Historica: International Journal of the History of Education*, vol. 41, nos. 4 and 5, pp. 489–94.

Burke, C. (2005b) 'Contested desires: the edible landscape of school', *Paedagogica Historica: International Journal of the History of Education*, vol. 41, nos. 4 and 5, pp. 571–87.

Ceppi, G. and Zini, M. (1998) *Children, Spaces, Relations: Metaproject for an Environment for Young Children*, Reggio Emilia, Reggio Children and Domus Academy Research Center.

Châtelet, A-M. (2008) 'A breath of fresh air: open-air schools in Europe', in Gutman, M. and de Coninck-Smith, N. (eds) *Designing Modern Childhoods: History, Space, and the Material Culture of Children*, New Brunswick, NJ, Rutgers University Press.

Châtelet, A-M. (2011) *Le souffle du plein air: histoire d'un projet pédagogique et architectural novateur (1904–1952)*, Geneva, Métis Presses.

Clark, A. (2010a) *Transforming Children's Spaces: Children's and Adults' Participation in Designing Learning Environments*, London, Routledge.

Clark, A. (2010b) 'Young children as protagonists and the role of participatory, visual methods in engaging multiple perspectives', *American Journal of Community Psychology*, vol. 46, nos. 1–2, pp. 115–23.

Dewey, J. (1997 [1938]) *Experience and Education*, New York, Simon & Schuster.

Dryden, C., Metcalfe, A., Owen, J. and Shipton, G. (2009) 'Picturing the lunchbox: children drawing and talking about "dream" and "nightmare" lunchboxes in the primary school setting', in James, A., Kjørholt, A-T. and Tingstad, V. (eds) *Children, Food and Identity in Everyday Life*, London, Palgrave Macmillan.

Foucault, M. (1980) 'On governmentality', in Gordon, C. (ed) *Power/Knowledge*, London, Harvester Press.

Gewirtz, S. (2001) *The Managerial School: Post-welfarism and Social Justice in Education*, London, Routledge.

Gordon, T., Holland, J. and Lahelma, E. (2000) *Making Spaces: Citizenship and Difference in Schools*, Basingstoke, Macmillan.

Herrington, S. (2001) 'Kindergarten: garden pedagogy from Romanticism to Reform', *Landscape Journal*, vol. 20, no. 1, pp. 30–47.

ISAFF (2002) *Atelier 3 Furnishings for Young Children*, Reggio Emilia, Grafitalia/Reggio Emilia.

James, A. (1993) *Childhood Identities: Self and Social Relationships in the Experience of the Child*, Edinburgh, Edinburgh University Press.

Lawn, M. and Grosvenor, I. (eds) (2005) *Materialities of Schooling: Design, Technology, Objects, Routines*, Oxford, Symposium Books.

Massey, D. (1999) 'Space-time, "science" and the relationship between physical geography and human geography', *Transactions of the Institute of British Geographers*, vol. 24, no. 3, pp. 261–76.

Metcalfe, A., Owen, J., Shipton, G. and Dryden, C. (2008) 'Inside and outside the school lunchbox: themes and reflections', *Children's Geographies*, vol. 6, no. 4, pp. 403–12.

Miller, L., Soler, J. and Woodhead, M. (2003) 'Shaping early childhood education', in Maybin, J. and Woodhead, M. (eds) *Childhoods in Context*, Chichester, John Wiley and Sons/Milton Keynes, The Open University.

Nespor, J. (2002) 'Studying the spatialities of schooling', *Pedagogy, Culture and Society*, vol. 10, no. 3, pp. 483–91.

Paechter, C. (2006) 'Reconceptualizing the gendered body: learning and constructing masculinities and femininities in school', *Gender and Education*, vol. 18, no. 20, pp. 121–35.

Renold, E. (2005) *Girls, Boys and Junior Sexualities: Exploring Children's Gender and Sexual Relations in the Primary School*, London, Routledge.

Robson, E. R. (1877 [1874]) *School Architecture: Being Practical Remarks on the Planning, Designing, Building, and Furnishing of School-houses*, London, John Murray.

Sorrell, J. and Sorrell, F. (2005) *Joined Up Design for Schools*, London, Merrell.

Steedman, C. (1990) *Childhood, Culture and Class in Britain: Margaret McMillan, 1860–1931*, London, Virago.

Vecchi, V. (2010) *Art and Creativity in Reggio Emilia: Exploring the Role and Potential of Ateliers in Early Childhood Education*, London, Routledge.

Whitty, G. and Wisby, E. (2007) 'Real decision-making? School councils in action', Department for Children, Schools and Families Research Report DCSF-001, Nottingham, Department for Children, Schools and Families.

Wyness, M. (2009) 'Adult's involvement in children's participation: juggling children's places and spaces', *Children and Society*, vol. 23, no. 6, pp. 395–406.

Reading A
Children and food at Prestolee School

Catherine Burke

Source: 'Contested desires: the edible landscape of school', 2005, *Paedagogica Historica*, vol. 41, nos. 4 and 5, pp. 571–87.

It is clear from the history of the development of the school meal that in England at least, the edible landscape of school has inspired educational experimentation. The combination of fresh air, food and play was characteristic of the development of the kindergarten movement in Europe and the USA as is well illustrated in the work of Margaret and Rachel McMillan ([Moriarty, 1998]). One case in point is found in the example of Prestolee County Elementary School in Lancashire. Here, between 1919 and his retirement in 1953, head teacher Edward Francis O'Neill conducted an extraordinary experiment in harnessing the material, built and living environment to his pedagogical vision of a 'learning by doing' school ([see Burke, 2005]). For O'Neill, the institutional organization of schooling, rooted in hierarchies of power and control, was responsible for failing the majority of children and abandoning them as learners at the cusp of adulthood. A domestication of the school interior and exterior was part of the experiment that saw the replacement of classrooms by workshops, school hall by lounge, and the design and construction of a canteen and milk bar by the children themselves. The milk bar was decorative as well as functional and was positioned with care, as one contemporary 11-year-old child explained:

> There is a milk bar at the top end of the hall where they serve tea ... at eight o'clock every night in the week except Sundays. Before the war we used to have ice-cream sold at the milk bar.

O'Neill considered the edible landscape of children's lives to be fundamental. His was a disadvantaged and poorly nourished school community. He argued that the first requirement for education was nourishment and his inspiration for creating an orchard in the school grounds was his awareness that, for city children, the knowledge of where food came from was totally lacking. The school yard was turned over time into a food and flower adventure garden for play and

pleasure, learning and construction: both beautiful and functional. But inside the school there were rules in the important business of dining:

> There are two dining rooms, the juniors and the seniors ... In the senior room there are nine tables, and fifteen forms. Each form is numbered so that we will know our forms when we see them, this method stops quarrelling and fighting. On the tables there are excellent table cloths and they are kept beautifully clean ... On each table there is a vase with flowers in them: if the flowers are faded you are not allowed to sit down to your dinner until they have been changed into freshly picked ones.

Wartime evacuation of children from cities to rural areas revealed to many temporary hosts the relative malnourishment of urban children. This experience, together with the state's direct control over the diet of the population via rationing, brought about a renewed turn to the importance of school-based nutrition in the immediate aftermath of the war. The 1944 Education Act made the provision of a dining room compulsory in secondary schools and in larger primary schools and the Ministry of Education building regulations laid down the specific number of square feet per child to be allowed. ([Stillman and Castle Cleary, 1949]) The traditional institutional design of dining spaces in schools at this time was challenged by contemporaries who argued for more relaxed, calming and aesthetic spaces.

> If it can be sited so that the outlook is on to the lawn, gardens or trees, full advantage should be taken of this by providing low-silled windows ... the main thing is to try to avoid a dreary institutional character. Nothing is more drab than a large, bleak room, painted in gloomy colours, and with nothing but long parallel refectory tables and benches.
>
> ([Stillman and Castle Cleary, 1949, p. 123])

However, as autobiographical accounts verify, these specifications were seldom considered more important than the regimentation of bodies within restricted time and spaces.

[handwritten margin note: 1944 – Education Act – Compulsory]

References

Burke, C. (2005) '"The school without tears": E. F. O'Neill of Prestolee', *History of Education*, vol. 34, no. 3, pp. 263–75.

Moriarty, V. (1998) *Margaret McMillan: 'I Learn, to Succour the Helpless'*, Nottingham, Educational Heretics Press.

Stillman, C. G. and Castle Cleary, R. (1949) *The Modern School*, London, Architectural Press.

Reading B
Foucault, space and primary school dining

Jo Pike

Source: 'Foucault, space and primary school dining rooms', 2008, *Children's Geographies*, vol. 6, no. 4, pp. 413–22.

Spatial practices

In all four of the dining rooms studied, tables and seating were organised to maximise throughput and minimise the potential for children's social interaction.

The figure above shows a typical dining room in which long tables seating eight children are arranged across the breadth of the room. There is insufficient space for movement between the tables and thus, once children are seated they must remain in this position until they finish their meal. The pillars bisecting the room delineate the packed lunch area to the left from the hot dinner area on the right. This 'corridor' is where children queue to reach the counter and select their meal and consequently where the majority of children's movement occurs in the dining room. Children's travel across the room is necessarily restricted and is permitted only for the purposes of acquiring nutrition rather than for facilitating social interaction with children seated on other tables. Furthermore, the long tables seating four children opposite another four children result in limited potential for social interaction due to the restricted visibility of co-diners.

While denying opportunities for pursuing social interaction, the use of surfaces to display pictures and posters in the dining room signals the acceptance of particular rationalities concerning nutrition. On entering this room there is a 5 A DAY poster illustrating a variety of fruits and vegetables displayed on the glass door. To the left there is another poster also showing vegetables. Above the counter there are attractive pictures of healthy food with the names of the items written underneath and decorating the walls throughout the space are children's posters illustrating 'healthy food'. Additionally, the salad bar is positioned on the left hand side of the room close to the entrance. As a result, all children must walk past the salad bar in order to queue for their main meal and frequently spend extended periods of time standing next to it. Therefore, through the aesthetics and organisation of the space, children are encouraged to adopt eating behaviours which conform to specific nutritional rationalities underpinning school meals and discouraged from pursuing social interactions with peers. Thus, the dominance of the nutritional discourse over the social discourse is maintained through spatial practice.

Space, surveillance and discipline

In *Discipline and Punish*, Foucault suggests 'discipline proceeds from the distribution of individuals in space' (Foucault, 1991, p. 141) and this is particularly applicable to institutional spaces such as school dining rooms.

When transgressions occur within the dining room, separation is employed as a disciplinary tactic and is further pursued outside in the playground where the offending individual's motionless body can be made peculiarly visible among the general hubbub of the playground.

> If it's in the playground we use the line but if they're not nice in the dining hall, if something, well, we separate you know, when there's two parties, they're kept separate anyway, sat on separate tables, so they don't get to each other, and then when they come outside, they're made to stand in the line for five minutes, think

about what they've done, you know, and their behaviour, and then the class teacher is told.

Lunchtime Supervisor School D

This practice is reminiscent of Foucault's notion of the spectacle of the scaffold (Foucault, 1991) where the visibility of the punishment and its association with the offence committed serves as a deterrent for other would-be perpetrators. However, while it is common for separation and segregation to be employed as spatial tactics of discipline, what I pursue here is the notion of these spatial tactics as productive of particular subjective positions, namely in constituting the healthy school dinner eater and the unhealthy packed lunch eater. Foucault suggests that we become self-governing subjects through the construction of normalizing discourses. The dominance of nutritional discourses within the school dining room together with specific spatial practices serves to constitute the school dinner eaters as healthy and the pack up eaters as unhealthy.

In all four of the dining rooms studied, there existed a material or symbolic division between those children who stayed for school dinners under the 'Eat Well Do Well' scheme and those who stayed for packed lunches. In the dining room pictured in the figure above, the queue for school dinners divided the school dinner eaters from the pack up eaters. In another school the waste table where plates are cleaned functioned as a line of demarcation between the two groups. This spatial segregation serves to reinforce differences between school dinner eaters and pack up eaters and facilitates different types of interactions between the adults supervising the space and the children dining within it. For example, as all the meals served under the 'Eat Well Do Well' scheme were deemed to be healthy, adults frequently rewarded the school dinner eaters with positive praise, encouragement and stickers when they ate their lunch. These 'rewards' were not available to pack up eaters whose food was felt to be less healthy.

You see the stuff that they've been packed up with and it's just, like, packets of biscuits and crisps and, and, erm, you know, bars of chocolate and packets of sweets and fizzy drinks and it's everything you can imagine an unhealthy packed lunch to be.

Teacher, School A

In School B, those children eating school dinners that also demonstrated appropriate table manners and other preferred modes of behaviour were selected to dine on a special table at the front of the dining room and with additional privileges, such as juice, tablecloths and flowers. This option was not available to packed lunch eaters who found it more difficult to demonstrate appropriate table manners as they ate the majority of their meal with their hands. Therefore, while it was possible for children seated on one side of the room to access rewards for 'healthy' behaviour, these were denied to children on the other side of the room. Children engaged with these practices in various ways either by taking up, modifying or resisting these subjective positions. Here, children are observed assessing their own 'healthy' subjectivity, which they closely associated with the nutritional quality of their lunch.

> At the pack up table next to me three boys are reading out nutritional information on their chocolate biscuits. 'There's lots of fat in it' one says. 'You're missing football' says one boy as he gets up and leaves the table. 'Are you healthy?' says one of the remaining boys to the other. 'I think salad is nice' he replies. 'There's too much fat in this – it's triple chocolate. Look my pack up is fat!'. 'My pack up is fat' says the other and gets up to leave the table, leaving the last boy eating alone.
>
> Fieldnotes 21-03-07 School C

The segregation of packed lunch eaters from school dinner eaters also enabled different regimes of surveillance to be carried out. While all children were subject to surveillance, those eating packed lunches were subject to normalising judgements around appropriate ways of eating and appropriate types of food.

A.   The dinner ladies do go round looking at the packed lunches of the children, erm, one of mine had, I think it was six quality street chocolates in his lunch. The dinner lady gave them to me and I gave them to his mum.

Q.   Did you have to speak to the mum, then?

A.　I had to speak to the mum. I just said that they're not allowed chocolate.

Teacher, School D

However, those eating school lunches were monitored to ensure that they ate sufficient quantities of food and not just the items that they liked or were familiar with.

> There's a lot that throws a lot away but, you know, if you just took the plate and threw it away for them, they'd be happy for you to do it. If you encourage them, just say, 'just try a bit more, bit more tatie, few more veg' and they do. If you say it they do do it, you know, but you can't force them to eat, but we encourage them to eat, and with that bit of encouragement, they always do it.

Lunchtime supervisor, School C

Here further spatial tactics were also employed to maximise the potential for monitoring the waste food of school dinner eaters as the waste table and bin were generally positioned en route to the exit. Therefore, no child could scrape food into the bin and exit the dining room without being subject to surveillance by the lunchtime supervisor. Packed lunch eaters were generally required to take their waste food home in their lunchbox so that it might be monitored by parents later in the day.

Reference

Foucault, M. (1991) *Discipline and Punish: The Birth of the Prison*, London, Penguin.

Reading C
Teacher concerns about formal mechanisms for 'pupil voice'

G. Whitty and E. Wisby

Source: 'Real decision-making? School councils in action', 2007, Department for Children, Schools and Families Research Report DCSF-001, Nottingham, Department for Children, Schools and Families, pp. 78–80.

Addressing teacher concerns

Findings from both the research literature and the current research suggest that not all school staff are supportive of provision for pupil voice. National organisations in particular felt that for many schools and teachers, perhaps understandably, pupil voice becomes 'just yet another initiative'.

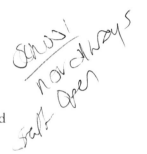

Whether or not as a direct result of this, it is often the case that provision for pupil voice is reliant on one or two members of staff, as was the case at some of the case study schools (see also Estyn 2007). This is problematic for two reasons: firstly, that provision becomes vulnerable should those staff leave the school; secondly, pupil voice usually requires the support of the whole school if it is to function effectively and not fade away. For instance, form tutors can play an important role in providing time for their class to raise issues for the next council meeting.

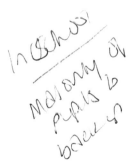

Lack of commitment to pupil voice among staff can be for practical reasons or external pressures. These include, for example, a lack of time or a concern to cover the formal curriculum. Compounding this, a number of the case study schools reported that teachers did not always see pupil voice as a learning opportunity which can feed back into academic work.

Lack of commitment may also stem from reservations about the principle of pupil voice. Davies et al (2006) note that staff can be more concerned about the responsibilities rather than the rights of pupils and that, accordingly, a discourse of rights and political literacy is not always popular in schools. Added to this, as noted earlier, there is the issue of teachers feeling that they themselves do not have a voice in school decision making.

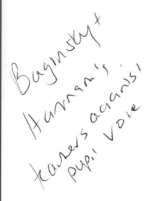

Baginsky + Hannam's teachers against pupil voice

In turn, the research literature suggests that adults' assumptions about children and young people can be limiting. In Baginsky and Hannam's (1999) study, where teachers opposed the introduction of a council in their schools, it was mainly because teachers thought their pupils were too young to participate effectively or that pupils would be unable to adopt a wider perspective than their perceived intermediate concerns (see Grace 1995, and also Wyse 2001).

Equally, though, lack of support can be due to anxieties about the unknown and, as Fielding and Rudduck (2006) put it, the 'rupturing [of] the security of traditional power relations' (p. 225).

Hargreaves (2004) notes the natural suspicions among both pupils and teachers in relation to pupil voice:

> For students, the fear is that staff do not really want to listen, will only hear what they want to hear, and that 'consultation' is yet more empty rhetoric or merely tokenistic if students do not come up with the 'right' message. For staff, the nervousness is that the experience will be an unpleasant one that threatens their authority and control (p. 8).

Related to this, staff could also lack confidence in terms of how best to approach pupil voice activity.

Pupil involvement in teaching and learning matters may be a particular source of concern. But teacher support here is crucial if provision for pupil voice is to move beyond the school facilities/environment issues evident in the literature and the research as hitherto being the main focus of school councils and other provision for pupil voice.

One aspect of pupil voice in relation to teaching and learning that is already relatively well-established in schools, and being supported by the teacher unions, is assessment for learning. The unions that participated in the research recognised the necessity of professional development for teachers if this approach is to yield maximum benefit in terms of improving pupils' learning.

positive assessment for learning

Outside assessment for learning, the involvement of pupils in relation to actual teaching and learning provision was growing among the case study schools. In most cases, though, current involvement took the form of consultation with pupils on matters *linked* to teaching and learning (e.g. having drinking water in lessons or re-arranging classrooms), or surveys on what pupils enjoyed about school. Schools were also taking more care to pass on any ad hoc feedback from pupils to staff. Elsewhere, a small number of the schools were already making use of pupil observation of classes. One school had intentionally used more disengaged pupils as observers, to 'bring them back in'. The school reported that this had been successful for informing teaching and learning, and for improving the engagement and behaviour of the pupils who observed lessons.

But wider research on pupils providing feedback to teachers on their lessons shows mixed responses from staff. Based on evidence from six teachers and their classes, McIntyre et al (2005) reported that teachers found their pupils' suggestions about teaching and learning 'sensible, practical and educationally desirable'. They did, though, differ in what they did in response to those ideas. In the less successful examples, difficulties typically arose where the teacher's expectations of pupils were too high. The study concluded that training and support for both teachers and pupils is necessary if consultation on teaching and learning matters is to be effective. This is certainly an important part of building teacher support for pupil voice.

A further aspect of pupil involvement in decisions around teaching and learning is their participation in the staff appointment process. Three of the case study schools had reservations about pupils' sitting on panels for staff appointments. One saw it as tokenistic, another as undermining to professionals. One primary school felt that younger children's understanding of which candidate would be best may not be robust, feeling that children can get taken in by first impressions. However, even these schools saw the value in pupils' indirect involvement, such as asking them to think about the qualities they welcome in their teachers.

References

Baginsky, M. and Hannam, D. (1999) *School Councils: The Views of Students and Teachers*, London, NSPCC.

Davies, L., Williams C. and Yamashita, H. (2006) *Inspiring Schools – Impact and Outcomes: Taking Up the Challenge of Pupil Participation*, London, Carnegie.

Estyn (2007) *Participation of Children and Young People (3–11 year olds) in Local Decision-making Issues that Affect their Lives*, Cardiff, Estyn.

Fielding, M. and Rudduck, J. (2006) 'Student voice and the perils of popularity', *Educational Review*, vol. 58, no. 2, pp. 219–31.

Grace, G. (1995) *School Leadership*, London, Falmer Press.

Hargreaves, D. (2004) *Personalising Learning – 2: Student Voice and Assessment for Learning*, London, SST.

McIntyre, D., Pedder, D. and Rudduck, J. (2005) 'Pupil voice: comfortable and uncomfortable learnings for teachers', *Research Papers in Education*, vol. 20, no. 2, pp. 149–68.

Wyse, D. (2001) 'Felt tip pens and school councils: children's participation rights in four English schools', *Children and Society*, vol. 15, pp. 209–18.

Chapter 5

Children and work

Lindsay O'Dell, Sarah Crafter and Heather Montgomery

Contents

In this chapter, you will:

- learn about the forms of work that children do and the sites in which they do them
- question why, in the contemporary world, work is sometimes seen as incompatible with childhood
- discuss some of the reasons children continue to work
- evaluate the positive and negative aspects of child work, understanding both the risks and the benefits.

1   Introduction

The issue of 'working children' is an emotive one. The phrase can conjure up images of small children being sent up chimneys in Victorian London or working in sweatshops in Asia, and it is often viewed as an affront to 'civilised' values. A high incidence of child work is often considered either a relic of a distant, less enlightened past, or a sign of contemporary underdevelopment and economic backwardness. Yet the realities are complex, and work and childhood need not be incompatible. This chapter will ask questions about how we can define children's work, whether it is intrinsically bad for children and how children themselves perceive what they do. It will do this by examining some of the various sites where children work, such as the home, the farm, the street, the factory or (more controversially) the school. The chapter ends with a discussion of the various attempts to make judgements about what is appropriate work for children and whether work can ever have benefits for children.

2   Child work and child labour

In academic and policy debates, there is much discussion over terminology and whether to use the phrase 'child labour' or 'child work'. For some, 'child labour' suggests work that is harmful to children, whereas others use the phrase to cover all forms of work, both beneficial and harmful; but there is no agreed standardisation of its meaning. Other commentators prefer the more neutral term 'child work'. They point out that the term 'child labour' is too confusing, with too many different meanings to be useful. In particular, they argue that using the phrase 'child labour' to mean 'harmful work' is problematic since there is no universal agreement about what sort of work is dangerous or damaging to children (this will be discussed in more detail in Section 4). Throughout this chapter, therefore, we use the term 'child work' rather than 'child labour'. Nevertheless, these two phrases are often used interchangeably throughout academic and policy literature, and many authors, including some of the writers discussed in this chapter, continue to use the term 'child labour'. In quoting or summarising them, we will follow their usage, trying only to ensure that this does not cause any confusion.

Activity 1   Defining children's work

Allow about 10 minutes

Think about what exactly the term 'child work' means, and write short notes in response to the following questions:

- How would you define 'child work'?
- What activities would you include as child work, and what would you exclude?

Comment

In many countries, children's work is defined through national and often international legislation, and is seen as an activity that takes place outside the home and for which the child worker gets paid. Our (the chapter authors') list was broader than this, however, and included children working in a factory, delivering newspapers, looking after younger children or working on the family farm. To us, all these activities constitute work, although they are not always counted as such in economic surveys. There are other activities that might not be considered work, such as going to school, helping around the house or doing chores like washing up or tidying a bedroom. However, these distinctions are rather arbitrary: why is a child who washes pots at home regarded as 'helping out', but is viewed as 'working' if he or she does it in a café?

The point of this activity is not to provide right or wrong answers but to show the conceptual difficulty of defining work. Defining work only as 'paid employment' (as many surveys do) is too narrow and excludes some of the most widespread and important of children's activities popularly referred to as 'work', namely those within the house, family business or farm. At the other extreme, some definitions – such as 'any activity to do with shaping one's life and environment' – are simply too broad to be useful. There seems to be very little that this definition would actually exclude. A better definition of work, therefore, might be 'economic activity', which Boyden et al. (1998) define as any activity that contributes to the gross domestic product of a country, as measured by internationally agreed accounting methods. They describe this as work 'in its popular sense', although they acknowledge that it does not correspond to everything that children themselves call work, which sometimes includes 'any assigned task they dislike doing' (Boyden et al., 1998, p. 22).

Finally, it is important to remember that definitions of child work depend heavily on how childhood is conceptualised. Is childhood (or should it be?) a protected space in which children are spared the adult need to work? Alternatively, is childhood a preparation for life in which children must learn responsibility early on, and where a child's income may be the only way of ensuring a family's survival? Are there 'good' forms of child work, therefore, which exist under the watchful and caring eyes of parents, and abusive and violent forms that occur when children work outside the home? These questions rely on an understanding of the context in which child work occurs, and this will be the focus of the rest of the chapter.

Figure 1   Newspaper selling has long been considered a suitable job for children. In this image a 7-year-old boy, James Logullo, sells newspapers in Delaware, USA, in 1910. He told investigators he had been working for three years and earned 50 cents a week

To understand children's work, it would be useful to have a sense of how many children work. However, this is almost impossible to calculate, partly because many children work in domestic or other informal settings and are therefore very hard to research or even count. International organisations have attempted to estimate the number of the world's children who work. For example, the International Labour Organisation (ILO) 'guesstimates' that 215 million children are working (ILO, 2010). Furthermore, it estimates that 115 million of these children do work that is described as 'the worst forms of child labour' (ILO, 2010), which 'by its nature or the circumstances in which it is carried out, it is likely to harm the health, safety or morals of children' (ILO, 2011, p. 4), and which includes all forms of slavery, debt bondage, prostitution and work in pornography, as well as working in illicit activities such as drug production and trafficking (ILO, 2011). None of these figures is completely accurate, however, so they need handling with some caution. Very few countries have reliable statistics for children who work, particularly in the majority world.

Activity 2   Reading A

Allow about 35 minutes

Go to the end of the chapter and read Reading A, 'From useful to useless: moral conflict over child labour', by Viviana Zelizer. This reading is an extract from Zelizer's book *Pricing the Priceless Child*, in which its author looks at debates in the USA, between 1870 and 1930, about child work and whether childhood should be a time of protected innocence or a time of learning how to work. These arguments are not new and have been much debated over the last 150 years.

Zelizer examines how children were once seen as useful and productive members of their family, earning a wage to supplement the family income. But, by the early part of the twentieth century, they had become economically idle and a drain on family resources rather than a boost to them. The child, previously economically valuable, was now sentimentally priceless. Although the reading deals with the last century, the debates it mentions are in many ways very modern and remain pertinent to understanding children's work in the contemporary world.

When you have read the extract, write brief notes in answer to the following questions:

- What conceptualisations of childhood do each of these debates draw on?
- Do you think children should be useful or useless?
- How might these discussions relate to modern debates about child work?

Comment

In the period under discussion, proponents of the argument that the child should be useful deployed a number of reasons as to why this was so. Children's work was, they claimed, an economic necessity that supported the family. Furthermore, it was something that 'everyone' did, and it stopped children being idle and growing up to be 'nonworkers', a drain on their families and, ultimately, the state. They related children's work to the need for mutual support among family members, and positioned childhood as a time of preparation for adulthood and of economic utility. In contrast, those who saw the child as useless emphasised childhood as a condition of dependency and innocence, separated and different from adulthood. In this vision, childhood is a time of economic uselessness, where children are valued for the love and companionship they give their parents, not for the money they bring into the family.

How you react to either of these arguments will depend on your own circumstances and beliefs about what childhood should be like. However, they remain relevant to discussions on child work today. Many international organisations promote the idea of childhood as a protected space, conceptually separate from adulthood. Others, however, argue that work is a necessity for many children and, rather than ban it outright or try to eliminate it, it would be better to regulate the conditions of work and allow children to earn money if it is necessary for their own or their family's support. Such discussions are ongoing and remain unresolved.

In the UK and other European countries, children continue to work but this is strictly regulated, and in few cases is children's income now essential to family earnings. Studies of household income in the UK have shown a progressive decline in contributions from children. For example, in Merseyside in the 1930s, young people aged 14–21 contributed 24 per cent of the family's total income. Even in the 1950s, working youngsters in the same area continued to hand over their entire wage packet to their mothers, receiving spending money in return. Today, working for the family is almost unheard of. In the 1990s, only 1 per cent of young people aged 13–18 claimed that they worked because it was 'essential for making ends meet for my family'

Figure 2 Children working in a Maryland oyster cannery, 1900

(Cunningham, 2000, pp. 423–4). In the UK, almost all children who work do so part time, and most of them combine work with schooling. Estimates of the numbers of working children vary among researchers, as do estimates of the amounts of hours they work, but it is calculated that about a million children aged 13–15 work – roughly 40 per cent of the age group. Of these, about half work up to 5 hours per week, one-third work from 6 to 12 hours and one-sixth over 12 hours per week. The average is about 7–8 hours per week. By way of comparison, the average child in this age group spends some 28 hours per week at school (McKechnie and Hobbs, 2001).

Summary of Section 2

The phrases 'child labour' and 'child work' are sometimes used interchangeably but often the phrase 'child labour' is used to differentiate between harmful and non-harmful work.

Numbers of child workers are only ever guesses, as reliable statistics are hard to come by.

Debates over child work have been raging for at least 150 years, and relate to how childhood is conceptualised and whether children are seen as economically useful or sentimentally priceless.

---

3 Sites of child work

This chapter has emphasised that children's work should be seen as broadly as possible to include not only paid work but also all forms of economic activity. The largest numbers of child workers are in majority-world countries and, in absolute numerical terms, most of them are in Asia (which has most of the world's population), although a higher proportion of children work in sub-Saharan Africa. Boyden et al. (1998) divide child workers in the majority world into four main categories, depending on where they work:

- **Child workers in rural areas**, mostly giving unpaid help to their families, predominantly in agriculture.

- **Domestic child workers and baby-minders**, working either in their own homes or as employees in other people's homes.

- **Child workers in the 'informal sector'**, in small shops and stores, small-scale building work and back-alley workshops; the most visible of these are children trading on the street.

- **Child workers in the 'formal sector'**, children working in comparatively modern, larger and more established industrial and commercial establishments.

3.1   The home and farm

The vast majority of child workers, both in the past in the UK and in the contemporary majority world, have worked at home with their parents and families, particularly in small-scale agriculture rather than in factories or sweatshops. Child work became a great concern of Victorian reformers, who were appalled at the idea of young, vulnerable children separated from their parents and working alone in factories or down mines, and campaigned vigorously against it. However, the majority of pre-adolescent workers in the nineteenth century and earlier were not employed in urban sweatshops or mills, but worked alongside their parents in the home or in small-scale manufacturing. Nevertheless, there remained a reluctance to admit that the work that these children did at home was economically useful or important, and such children were rarely included in the campaigns of those philanthropists, who tried to limit children's work in industry.

Today, the idea of children's work occurring in the home remains problematic for many reasons. There is still a sense of the home being a private, domestic haven in which children might help out or learn skills for the future, but this conceptualisation precludes the idea of work.

Figure 3 Two girls and their younger sibling in the East End of London in the 1950s. Until very recently, older girls were expected to look after younger children in the family and to help around the house

Home and work are different, separate constructs, and home is a retreat from the rigours of the workplace. As long as children are at home, the argument goes, they cannot work. Yet, as feminist scholars have long noted, there is always a tendency, when looking at work, to count only men's paid employment outside the house and to ignore both women's and children's work in the domestic sphere (Oakley, 1994). Until the late 1970s, there was almost no acknowledgement of children's contribution to the household economy or their ability to free other members of the family to take on economic work – just as women's work within the home, including the raising of children, was denigrated as 'housework' and not seen as proper work. The work of girls at home, carrying out domestic chores or babysitting other children, was especially undervalued, dismissed as 'playing' house or viewed as a form of life-training that would enable them to grow up to be good wives and mothers (Nieuwenhuys, 1996).

However, when researchers have looked at children's economic roles and have carried out detailed studies of children's time, they have found that children contribute substantial amounts to their households in economic terms. To give one example among many, girls of the Fulani of West Africa are expected, by the age of four, to be competent in tasks such as caring for their younger siblings and fetching water and firewood; by age six, they will be pounding grain, producing milk and butter, and selling these alongside their mothers in the market. In other places, goat and cattle herding is considered a job for young boys, and they are expected to follow their herds, look after them and ensure that they are fed. In many parts of the world, fetching water and firewood are children's responsibilities, and in almost all rural communities children are expected to feed chickens, sow seeds, pick out weeds from the crops and carry out many of the tasks necessary to grow food. In her studies of children in rural Bolivia, Sam Punch (2001) detailed the responsibilities falling on children's shoulders, including domestic work, agricultural tasks and animal care, which they started to undertake from around the age of three. She outlines a detailed age hierarchy in which children gradually take on more and more complex tasks as they get older and become more physically and socially competent.

All these activities may rightly be described by external observers as work, and yet the situation is complicated by the fact that many within their own community may not view children as useful or economically productive labour. One study in Java suggested that adults associated work with the activities done to keep a family together and the responsibilities that came with family life. Parents claimed that children did not work; they just spent several hours a day tending the ducks, caring for their younger siblings or collecting firewood (Hull, 1975). These parents looked on the work that their children did as a form of indulgence, without the pressures and duties that came with adulthood. It was only when children were involved with waged labour that their parents began to see them as actively contributing to the household. Housework was specifically discounted, and many parents claimed that children under 15 (i.e. those who did not work as labourers outside the family) were economically unproductive and a drain on household income. Children themselves can also undervalue their own work. In her study of child labour in the Zambezi valley, Pamela Reynolds (1991) watched a 14-year-old girl prepare a breakfast of porridge for herself and her younger brother, wash the plates from the previous night's meal and collect water twice from a source two kilometres away. Yet when

Figure 4 Agricultural work in Chad, Africa

questioned directly about what she had done that morning, she replied simply, 'Nothing' (Reynolds, 1991).

As long as children are working with or near parents there is a tendency to assume that their work is never harmful. One study of child labour in Thailand stated:

> It is customary for children in Thai families to always do some work for the family. This custom is particularly applicable to poor families, urban and rural alike. Children working in this fashion do not create an alarming problem. But once they step outside their household territory, they are no longer protected by their families.
>
> (Banpasirichote and Pongsapich, 1992, pp. 20–1)

Yet such statements must be treated with some care. Child work at home or in small-scale agriculture has its risks. Children may still be worked very hard and forced to do difficult and even harmful jobs. Both they and their parents may be subject to damaging or exploitative working conditions, and agricultural work can be tough, repetitive and dangerous. Looking after children all day, as well as preparing food, collecting water and washing clothes are all heavy work.

Figure 5   A child worker in Andhra Pradesh, India

Activity 3   Reading B

Allow about 35 minutes

Go to the end of the chapter and read Reading B, 'A child's work in Poompuhar', by Virginia Morrow and Uma Vennam. This reading reports on the lives of children in Andhra Pradesh in India. It focuses on one girl in particular called Ramya, who lives with her family and is obliged to work for them in the cotton fields for two or three months a year. The work involves pollinating cotton, work usually undertaken by children. After you have finished reading, answer the following questions:

- Do you see the activities that Ramya does, in both the field and at home, as work?

- How does Ramya herself see it?

Comment

The reading explains the various types of work that a child like Ramya has to carry out. Interestingly, she does not consider doing housework as work, although it is obvious that she has a large amount of domestic responsibilities. Instead, she sees work as what she has to do in the fields – work that she is not paid for and does not like doing but which is necessary to ensure her family's survival. However, the researchers who interviewed her clearly see her as working both in the fields and at home, and her work as directly helping not only her mother but her siblings as well. Ramya is clearly expected to have a mature understanding of how to manage family finances and undertake domestic chores. She shows a certain pride in this and, while she is very critical of the work she has to do in the fields, she is realistic about its necessity. She is very aware of the difficulties of combining work and education, which presents further difficulties in that neither her school nor her parents appear particularly sympathetic to the competing demands on her time.

Perhaps the most important point to come out of this case is the need for nuanced discussions. It is important not to over-romanticise child work at home or to assume that children who work with or for their parents are always protected. Many children carry out hard work for their parents and receive no money for it. Equally, however, it is important to acknowledge that many children must work for the family to survive, that parents do their best to look after their children, and that child work is not a sign of pathology within a poor family.

3.2   Child carers

Providing care for other family members exemplifies the difficult work that children must sometimes undertake at home, and is one area in which children's work in the minority world remains unregulated. Child carers are usually defined as:

> children and young persons under eighteen who provide care, assistance or support to another family member. They carry out, often on a regular basis, significant or substantial caring tasks and assume a level of responsibility that would usually be associated with an adult. The person receiving care is often a parent but can be a sibling, grandparent or other relative who is disabled, has some chronic illness, mental health problem or other condition connected with a need for care, support or supervision.

(Becker, 2010, p. 210)

The 2001 census showed that there were at least 175,000 children and young people aged under 18 in the UK who could be classified as 'young carers'. Overall, across the UK, 2.1 per cent of all children have unpaid caring responsibilities towards other family members. Another 9524 young carers are aged eight or nine, and 1055 of these are providing 50 hours of care or more each week. In total, around 35,000 young carers are of primary school age and nearly 4000 of these are caring for more than 50 hours per week (Becker, 2010).

Activity 4   Child carers

Allow about 10 minutes

Read the description below, given by 16-year-old Jimmy, of his experience as a young carer. Then comment on the following questions:

*   Was Jimmy working?
*   In what ways does this work challenge ideas about childhood?

Jimmy

When I think about all those years I cared for my dad it makes me angry, not because I had to care for him – I wanted to care for him – but because I was left alone to cope with his illness for so long.

I wasn't just doing ordinary tasks like other kids might do around the house. I was having to cook for him, beg for money and food parcels so I could feed him, take him to the toilet, clean him up when he couldn't get to the toilet – because he couldn't get up the stairs towards the end.

No one should have to see their parents like that, when they lose all their bodily functions. I loved my dad and I couldn't bear to see him losing his dignity – getting more ill before my eyes. But because I loved him, I wanted to be with him. I wanted to look after him. I just wish someone could have helped me and that those who interfered in our lives and made them difficult could have left us alone.

(Becker, 2010, p. 209)

Comment

Although Jimmy was not being paid for looking after his father, he was quite clearly working. Indeed, everything that Jimmy did as an unpaid carer, if it had been conducted by a non-family member (such as a nurse, social worker or personal assistant), would carry a monetary value and a charge. Yet it is also a very intimate form of work, which Jimmy was unwilling to let others do, and the line between care and the support that we all might give to emotional relationships is a fine one. However, care as a form of work is not seen to be part of a 'normal' childhood, and challenges the dominant construction of childhood as a time when children should be cared for by others rather than providing care themselves.

Figure 6 A child cares for his disabled mother

Children offer care to others throughout the world. In sub-Saharan Africa, the HIV/AIDS epidemic has led to what has been termed a 'lost generation' of parents leaving children behind to bring up their younger siblings or to look after their grandparents. Children are an active part of the care relations within families and are often regarded as an important resource. In Zimbabwe, a UNICEF worker described the care given by a teenage boy to his dying mother:

> During the last months of his mother's life Rindai (15 years) cared for her. His only sibling – an older brother – was away studying and could only come back home in the last two weeks before their mother's death. Their father had died two years previously of HIV/AIDS. Each day Rindai carried his mother outside to sit in the sun, took her to the toilet, and brought her food and drink.

His mother withdrew him from school and Rindai couldn't even go out to the shops and do normal 15-year-old things. … The experience made a big impression on him. He matured overnight.

(Robson, 2004, p. 227)

It has been estimated that 46 per cent of older adults in sub-Saharan Africa live with a grandchild, and it is often unclear who is caring for whom. Morten Skovdal (2010) conducted research in the Bondo district of Kenya, a district with high levels of poverty, an HIV rate of 13 per cent (twice the national average) and where one in nine children have lost both of their parents. Orphaned children are often taken in by guardians, usually a family member but one who is often ill themselves. Many of the children talked about needing to work in order to feed themselves and their family, many had full responsibility for their guardians and for younger children. All of the children performed the daily household chores and many nursed their guardians. Yet, just as young carers in the UK speak of their belief in the importance of caring for their families, very similar sentiments are expressed by children in sub-Saharan Africa. While the difficulties faced by the children should not be underplayed, it is important to listen to them talking about the difficulties, tensions and possibilities in their lives. For example, one of Skovdal's informants, 13-year-old Samuel, cared for his sick father and now cares for a disabled friend and the friend's sick mother. Yet Samuel says, 'All that I have done makes me happy. This is because I don't do bad things in the community, and the villagers love me seriously for that and the fact that I like helping sick people' (quoted in Skovdal, 2010, p. 99).

3.3   The street

Children carry out more visible work on the street, as newspaper vendors, shoeshine boys, rubbish collectors, beggars or petty traders. These children are often perceived as being out of place – neither at home with their families nor in school – and therefore as being at greater risk than other working children. However, being conceptually out of place also means they are often perceived as a nuisance or a threat, and many of their street activities – such as begging or small-time drug dealing – are illegal. This compounds the fear and distrust with which they are regarded. Street children often have to hustle to get work, putting them in conflict with those who do not want their car watched while they shop, do not want to give money for odd jobs, and do not want to buy chewing gum or cigarettes. Consequently, levels of violence against children working on the street are high. In Brazil, for example, members of the police and security forces have brutally beaten and even killed child street workers. When anthropologist Tobias Hecht interviewed one 15-year-old girl in Recife, Brazil, she told him:

> When we're sleeping we're woken up to kicks, clubs, buckets of water they throw on us – they mess you around in a thousand and one ways. Say you got money, two thousand, three thousand cruzeiros [a dollar or a little more] in your pocket, they take you to the police booth, snatch what you've got, smack your hands a bunch of times with a club, and send you out of the area.

(Quoted in Hecht, 1998, p. 127)

The risks come not only from the police but also from other street children, who may steal from them, and also from the middlemen from whom they have to buy the merchandise that they sell.

Figure 7 Young South American street vendors

Despite the risks that children face on the street, ethnographic research has suggested that the life of street children is not unremittingly bleak (Aptekar, 1991; Hecht, 1998). Furthermore, it has questioned whether the term 'street children' is the right one, as it suggests a split between children living at home and those who have left home and live and work on the streets. In reality, the situation is much more fluid. In

South America, many studies have shown that street children are not necessarily estranged from their families, and that work at 'home' and on 'the street' are not mutually exclusive. Many children work on the street but return home at night. Others stay out for several nights or weeks but return home regularly. Most important of all, they may remain fully committed to their families, especially their mothers, and try to send as much of their earnings as they can home to their parents. As Hecht points out, there are few opportunities for children of the urban poor in Brazil to earn money. Not all of them can stay at home and look after young siblings or the house; there is no family farm or small holding to work on; and, inevitably, children have to work. The household's survival 'ultimately depends on the ability of its members to secure from outside money or goods' (Hecht, 1998, p. 193).

Working on the street, therefore, is not a rejection of home but a way of supporting and reinforcing it. Yet opportunities are limited and competition is fierce: there are many poor, unskilled children trying to do the same types of work. Children may try to sell items that require little capital, such as popcorn, chewing gum or popsicles; but there are still start-up costs; children cannot afford the insulated boxes needed to keep ice lollies cold; and they are always in danger of being ripped off by their suppliers. Children can work doing odd jobs or running errands, but their services are not regularly needed; there is a lot of competition; and working adults may feel harassed by the children's demands. Begging and drug dealing are illegal and put children in conflict with the police, while scavenging for rubbish and selling on scrap metal to local dealers are dangerous and offer little financial return. In short, as Hecht argues, 'the informal sector opportunities open to children are competitive, sometimes dangerous, and offer only meagre financial rewards' (Hecht, 1998, p. 194).

In India, rag-picking is big business, with over 1 million people involved in the collecting and selling of scrap metals or plastics for recycling. As this is a job that requires no capital outlay and no skills, it is popular work for children. Children often begin to work at five or six years old, working alongside their parents. There are two categories of child rag-pickers in India: the 'street pickers' who collect rubbish in the streets, in public waste bins or from residential areas; and those who work on rubbish dumps, known as 'dump pickers'. These groups have different characteristics, so that street pickers tend to be boys, more mobile and often living away from their families; they tend to work for a middleman who takes a cut of their sales and pays a small amount back to them. However, dump pickers are more likely to live with, and work alongside, their families, in a relatively stable environment on, or around, the dumping ground. Girls are more likely than boys to be dump pickers, as it is perceived to be safer for them than working on the streets. They are also then available to help out at home and perform domestic chores (Pratham, n.d).

Figure 8   Child rag-pickers in Pakistan

The two examples discussed above – the street children in Brazil and the rag-pickers in India – both suggest the dangers of generalising about street working. While there are undoubtedly risks and the threat of violence, there are also opportunities for children to be entrepreneurial and to make money, despite a lack of qualifications or formal schooling. There is also a certain freedom: children can choose the hours they work; they are not always beholden to others; and they can be relatively independent. Working on the streets need not imply a breach with home; rather, it is another way of remaining tied to their families and to the home, and a means of supporting parents and siblings. In many cases, whole families live and work on the street, further complicating the division of home and street, and suggesting that there is no meaningful separation between child work in the domestic sphere and child work on the street.

3.4   Children and factories

While children who work in factories are fewer in number than those working in the fields, at home or on the street, they often receive a disproportionate amount of concern and attempts at intervention. There is a strong perception that factory work is particularly dangerous to children and completely at odds with contemporary ideas of childhood as a protected space in which children should learn and not earn. Certainly work in factories tends to involve longer hours and a more sustained level of effort than work on farms or in the home, and there is greater risk to children in terms of occupational health. Machines designed for and by adults can be difficult for smaller or younger children to operate, and may prove hazardous to children who have not been given the training to use them properly (WHO, 1987). More generally, conditions in many factories in the majority world are extremely poor for both adults and children, and health and safety legislation is non-existent. For example, the worst-ever industrial fire in Thailand occurred at the Kader Toy Factory, which made toys for Disney and Mattel among others: 188 people were killed and over 500 seriously injured. Most of the victims were young female workers under 18, from rural families; when they tried to escape, they found that the fire doors had been locked to prevent them from taking unauthorised breaks. Both adults and children face such risks on a daily basis in many factories in the majority world which produce goods for those in the minority.

Figure 9   A child worker in a garment factory in Dhaka, Bangladesh

The juxtaposition of poor children producing luxury or leisure goods for richer people in the minority world has fuelled a sense of outrage over children who work in factories. Recent years have seen consumer campaigns and calls for boycotts against countries or corporations who rely on child work to produce such cheap goods. In 1996, sports manufacturer Nike came under pressure after the June edition of *Life* magazine published a picture of a 12-year-old Pakistani boy called Tariq surrounded by the pieces of a Nike soccer ball which took him a whole day to sew together and for which he earned around $0.60. The result was a public outcry in the USA, which led to calls for a boycott of Nike products and various promises by Nike to pay closer attention to working conditions in their overseas factories. Similar boycotts have been instigated by US consumers, such as the 'Don't Buy Thai!' campaign, which ran from 1996 to 2000, in protest at the Thai government's failure to end the sexual exploitation of children.

Figure 10   Anti child labour protests in India

On one level, this is wholly admirable. Few people would argue against children being protected from hazardous work in factories, although in many cases adults are equally as vulnerable, and the problem is not necessarily one of the age of workers but the exploitative conditions under which they are employed. However, attempts to end children working in factories have often been counter-productive and result in hurting the very children they were meant to be helping. In 1992, a US Senator, Tom Harkin, proposed a ban on the import to the USA of all Bangladeshi products, especially clothes, made by child workers, after concern was raised about child workers in the Bangladeshi garment industry. Manufacturers in Bangladesh were terrified of the economic impact of this boycott, and swiftly sacked all child workers in their factories, employing only those over the age of 14. On the surface, this was a great success. Yet, when follow-up surveys were conducted some years later, it was found that children who could not work in factories did not go back to school nor did they go back to their families. Far from protecting children, the impact of the boycott drove them into more hazardous occupations such as brick chipping, rickshaw pulling and even prostitution (Rahman et al., 1999).

Activity 5 Reading C

Allow about 35 minutes

Go to the end of the chapter and read Reading C, 'Raising questions, questioning the answers', by Michael Bourdillon, Deborah Levison, William Myers and Ben White, an account of children working in a garment factory in Morocco.

When you have finished reading, comment on the following questions:

- What assumptions did the *World in Action* team make about child work in factories?
- How did this compare with how the children saw it?
- To what extent were the children being exploited by the factory owners?

Comment

The television team's investigation was based on the premises that child work in factories is necessarily exploitative and abusive, and children are always better off outside factories than working inside them. Images of children working in factories, especially ones supplying goods to British stores, are emotive. The team were representing these children as working for low wages in exploitative situations, totally incompatible with Westernised notions of childhood.

However, the children themselves saw things rather differently. While they agreed they were exploited and were fully aware of the pressures placed on them to work long hours without overtime, they did not want to lose their jobs. For them, the alternatives were much worse and, while the assumption remains that children who are thrown out of the factories will go home and finish their education, in reality this is likely to be untrue. Conditions of work may be hard and even exploitative, but working in the garment factories gave the girls freedom, independence and status within their families which they had not previously had before.

The children were able to voice their own opinions. Moreover, the authors here seem to suggest that, while factory work is bad, the options for other poor, badly educated children, especially girls, are much worse.

3.5   Children and school

The dominant minority-world view of childhood is that it is a time for play or schooling, not work. The United Nations Convention on the Rights of the Child emphasises that the proper place for children is at school or at home with their families. Indeed, while Article 28 states that all children have an inalienable right to go to school, there is no corresponding right *not* to attend. Not surprisingly, most people treat school and work as completely different activities. Fundamentally, they assume that schoolwork is not economically productive work. However, this view has been challenged in recent years. The sociologist Jens Qvortrup has argued that, in the modern economies in the minority world, children's 'work' in school not only is economically productive work but that it is children's most important productive work, especially compared with their paid employment outside school, which is relatively trivial – or, as he puts it, 'residual and anachronistic' (Qvortrup, 2001, p. 93). Qvortrup argues that children in school are productive workers: they are producing themselves as the future educated workforce. If a modern economy needs an educated labour force, then the production of that labour force is as much part of the economy as any other form of production. For some time, this has been widely accepted as far as teachers are concerned: teaching children in school is recognised as economically productive work. For Qvortrup, the same logic applies to children. Their work, as they learn in school, is economically productive too. This is not just a terminological quibble. If Qvortrup is right, children at school should not be seen as an economic burden on adult society. In the short term, they may incur economic costs to their parents and wider society, but they are also producing economic benefits, even if these can only be realised in the future (Qvortrup, 2001).

Qvortrup's argument is an intriguing one, and even if there is legitimate debate about how far schoolwork is economically productive, it is important, nevertheless, to acknowledge that children's education is often hard work – every moment of their day accounted for in the classroom, doing homework, studying for exams, taking part in extra-curricular activities or quests for self-improvement. Children are not

Figure 11   A primary school classroom in the UK

paid for this work, and it is often classified as education or self-improvement rather than work, but phrases such as 'schoolwork' or 'homework' do suggest some acknowledgement that childhood is not just a time for play but also a time for work, although this work must be carefully confined to the schoolroom. The dichotomy in children's lives is not between work and play, therefore, but between the sites of work. Child work in a factory is harmful and needs to be stopped, but child work in a school is beneficial and to be enforced.

Most writers, however, continue to treat 'child work' as something different from school, and child work in the sense of farming, domestic service and manufacturing or selling raises more acute moral and practical dilemmas. It is important to emphasise, however, that schooling is linked to work in other ways as well. For many working children, it is not the case that they *either* work in school *or* work outside it, but that they combine the two. The World Bank estimates that 50–70 per cent of working children attend school. Lieten and White (2001) suggest that the 'blind spot' for campaigners who want to abolish child work is that they 'consistently ignore the fact that most of the world's working children attend school' (Lieten and White, 2001, p. 6). In an international study looking at children's perspectives on school and work in Bangladesh, Ethiopia, the Philippines and Central America, Woodhead (2001) found that 77 per cent of the 300 working children studied felt that combining work and school was best for them. Most did not see work and school as alternatives in their present situation. Work, they said, was an absolute necessity while schooling was a desirable, but somewhat unrealistic, prospect.

> ### Summary of Section 3
>
> Children work in a number of different sites – the home, the farm, the street and the school.
>
> Most children work at home or in small-scale family agriculture, but the working children who cause the most concern are those on the streets or in factories.
>
> There is no distinct split between these sites – children may work in multiple places.
>
> Children may work long hours in all these sites, but their work is not always acknowledged as such because it does not involve paid employment.
>
> Factory work is often seen as the worst and most exploitative form of child work, but this is not necessarily how children themselves see it.

4 Evaluating children's work

So far this chapter has looked at different sites of work, detailing the places where children work and the types of activities they do. It has also suggested that these various types of work present some risks to children but also some advantages. This section will look at these in more detail, evaluating both the benefits and the hazards of child work.

Activity 6   Evaluating the positives and negatives of children's work

Allow about 30 minutes

This chapter has looked at various types of work that children do and where they do it. Draw up a table of the various places of work and the types of work children do in them and then write down all the positive aspects of each type of work and what negative aspects there might be.

Comment

Below is the table drawn up by the authors of this chapter.

Place of work	Type of work	Positive factors	Negative factors
Home	Babysitting Housework Cooking Making food to sell	Working with family Protection from negative outside influences Learning work and life skills Working under guidance Allows parents to go out to work	Unstimulating or inappropriate activities No time to go to school Loneliness and boredom Exacerbation of gender inequalities
Family farm or small holding	Sowing grain Feeding chickens Looking after livestock Herding cattle Collecting water	Working with family Stability and support from community Time to play Learning work and life skills Working under guidance	Hard work Loneliness, boredom Having to travel long distances from home and staying out overnight
Street	Going to market Watching or cleaning cars Petty trading Dealing drugs or cigarettes Selling sex	Opportunities for positive relationships with peers Less pressure on family incomes Children can be self-employed and entrepreneurial	Risk of violence Environmental risks (exposure to pollution) Risk of traffic accidents
Factory	Working on machines Weaving Hand stitching clothes Manufacturing goods for export	Learning a skill Earning money for either yourself or your family Appropriately regulated working environment	Exploitation and lack of legal or other protection Risk of accidents Limited opportunity to go to school Unreasonable parental expectations Coercive treatment

(Continued overleaf)

Table from Activity 6 continued

Place of work	Type of work	Positive factors	Negative factors
School	Reading Writing Learning to be a good citizen	Safe and healthy environment Children learn skills for the future Children enjoy learning Schools respect the child's interests and well-being	Incompatibility between the demands of work and school Bad conditions at school Unsympathetic teachers Schoolwork unrecognised as economically productive

What is interesting is that, in all cases, we could find both positive and negative aspects to all forms of child work. Even factory work, often considered the most dangerous and exploitative of all child work, could have beneficial consequences. Rather than talk about work as being either inherently good or absolutely bad, it makes more sense to think of children's work as being on a continuum whereby, like many other activities such as going to school, it can be both negative and positive. It is the conditions of work that are most important in deciding whether or not work is harmful, not the work itself. Factors that need to be considered include the number of hours worked, the time of day, the type of job undertaken and the child's experience in employment.

There remain, however, strong ideological and practical objections to child work. As long as childhood is idealised as a special and separate time in which children are segregated from the adult world, where adults work and children play, work will always be seen as an unnatural aspect of children's lives and one that takes childhood away from children. Paid work and money are not considered a legitimate part of a child's life; thus, the banning of all child labour is still viewed as a realistic goal by some activists.

There is overwhelming evidence that some working activities are physically, emotionally and psychologically hazardous to children. Nieuwenhuys (1994) notes that young girls working as domestic servants often have little protection against sexual and physical abuse by their employers. Many of the world's working children do so in agricultural settings where there is risk of exposure to dangerous pesticides and heavy machinery (McKechnie et al., 1998). When children become soldiers, or work as prostitutes or drug runners, the risks to their physical or psychological development are high.

Figure 12   Bhima Sangha is a union of, by and for working children, founded in 1990 in Karnataka, India. It has a membership of 13,000 working children in both rural and urban areas.

These hazards are all serious problems and no one is suggesting that all work, in all circumstances, is good for children. However, in other instances, the impact of children's work may be less about the specific work undertaken and more about the work situation itself. As UNICEF has argued, 'in every country, rich or poor, it is the nature of the work children do that determines whether or not they are harmed by it – not the plain fact of their working' (UNICEF, 1997, cited in Liebel, 2004, p. 5). Not all work is exploitative or dangerous, and the children themselves may not necessarily see work as negative. There are potential benefits to the child, such as autonomy, economic gains, life skills or the passing on of family traditions.

There are many instances of children reporting that they *want* to work. Examples can be found in the working children's movements' organisations of Latin America and Africa (Liebel, 2004). These organisations are usually run by working children aged 12–16, who work in the 'informal' work sector in cities. The organisations have, typically, been set up as a result of adult humanitarian organisations, but are run and administered by children themselves who wish to be recognised as workers. Children see these organisations as the best way to protect their working conditions while enabling them to keep working. Many working children have created small syndicates or cooperatives or unions. In Paraguay, for example, shoeshine children allocate themselves workplaces in the morning or afternoon so that their peers can attend school during the other half of the day (Liebel, 2004). Given this, Liebel questions the widely held view that children in poor economic circumstances do not want to work and are passive victims of economic circumstance. More often, he argues, children wish to work but to do so by their own will and under safe and reasonable conditions:

> The children see in their work not merely a burden or a necessity, but also a chance to learn things that school does not offer them. They say: 'Our work helps us to educate ourselves'; it serves 'to take up the experience of adults, to learn to defend ourselves, to make ourselves more independent, to master life, to prepare to be someone in life'. What many working children like is not always the work itself, but the fact that it enables them 'to be together with others'. The children who work in the streets frequently say: 'We find friends and can play with one another.' They also like 'sharing work with others'. For many children in the countries of the [majority world], work is an opportunity to get together in groups, either to help each other with their work, or to defend their interests and rights.
>
> (Liebel, 2004, pp. 2–3)

Summary of Section 4

Each type of work that children carry out has risks but usually has benefits too.

It may not be work itself that poses a risk to children but working conditions.

Children themselves often want to work and contribute to their families, and they see work as a way of learning useful skills.

---

5 Conclusion

This chapter has shown that work is a fact of life for many children, especially those in the majority world, whose work makes a vital contribution to the family and, indeed, to the wider economy. However, working children also challenge the ideal of childhood as a carefree and protected space, separate from the demands of business; the tension between the useful and useless child is not a new one. This chapter has argued for a more balanced understanding of children's work, setting the risks against the benefits, and the hazards against the positive factors. It has also suggested that work in itself need not be inherently wrong, and that children and young people should be able to work in some circumstances. However, children still have the right to be protected from abuses in the workplace, whether these occur in the factory or in children's own homes. Before outsiders make value judgements about their work, however, children's own opinions must be sought, the alternatives available to them carefully considered, and the contexts and conditions in which they work taken into full account.

References

Aptekar, L. (1991) 'Are Colombian street children neglected? The contributions of ethnographic and ethnohistorical approaches to the study of children', *Anthropology and Education Quarterly*, vol. 22, no. 4, pp. 326–49.

Banpasirichote, C. and Pongsapich, A. (1992) *Child Workers in Hazardous Work in Thailand*, Bangkok, Chulalongkorn University Social Research Institute.

Becker, S. (2010) 'For love, not money: children's unpaid care work in modern Britain', in Brockliss, L. and Montgomery, H. (eds) *Childhood and Violence in the Western Tradition*, Oxford, Oxbow.

Boyden, J., Ling, B. and Myers, W. (1998) *What Works for Working Children*, Florence, Rädda Barnen and UNICEF International Child Development Centre.

Cunningham, H. (2000) 'The decline of child labour: labour markets and family economies in Europe and North America since 1830', *Economic History Review*, vol. 53, no. 3, pp. 409–28.

Hecht, T. (1998) *At Home in the Street: Street Children of Northeast Brazil*, Cambridge, Cambridge University Press.

Hull, T. (1975) *Each Child Brings its Own Fortune: An Enquiry into the Value of Children in a Javanese Village*, unpublished PhD thesis, Canberra, Australian National University.

International Labour Organisation (ILO) (2010) *Facts on Child Labour* [online], Geneva, ILO, http://www.ilo.org/wcmsp5/groups/public/@dgreports/@dcomm/documents/publication/wcms_126685.pdf (Accessed 30 November 2011).

International Labour Organisation (ILO) (2011) *Children in Hazardous Work: What We Know, What We Need to Do* [online], Geneva, ILO, http://www.ilo.org/wcmsp5/groups/public/—dgreports/—dcomm/—publ/documents/publication/wcms_155428.pdf (Accessed 30 November 2011).

Liebel, M. (2004) *A Will of Their Own: Cross-cultural Perspectives on Working Children*, London, Zed.

Lieten, K. and White, B. (2001) 'Children, work and education: perspectives on policy', in Lieten, K. and White, B. (eds) *Child Labour: Policy Options*, Amsterdam, Aksant Academic.

McKechnie, J. and Hobbs, S. (2001) 'Work and education: are they compatible for children and adolescents?', in Mizen, P., Pole, C. and Bolton, A. (eds) *Hidden Hands: International Perspectives on Children's Work and Labour*, London, Routledge Farmer.

McKechnie, J., Hobbs, S., Lindsay, S. and Lynch, M. (1998) 'Working children: the health and safety issue', *Children and Society*, vol. 12, no. 1, pp. 38–47.

Nieuwenhuys, O. (1994) *Children's Lifeworlds: Gender, Welfare and Labour in the Developing World*, London, Routledge.

Nieuwenhuys, O. (1996) 'The paradox of child labor and anthropology', *Annual Review of Anthropology*, vol. 25, pp. 237–51.

Oakley, A. (1994) 'Women and children first and last: parallels and differences between children's and women's studies', in Mayall, B. (ed) *Children's Childhoods: Observed and Experienced*, London, Falmer Press.

Pratham (n.d.) *Child Ragpickers* [online], http://pratham.org/images/Paper_on_ragpickers.pdf (Accessed 30 November 2011).

Punch, S. (2001) 'Household division of labour: generation, gender, age, birth order and sibling composition', *Work, Employment and Society*, vol. 15, no. 4, pp. 803–23.

Qvortup, J. (2001) 'School-work, paid-work and the changing obligations of childhood', in Mizen, P., Pole, C. and Bolton, A. (eds) *Hidden Hands: International Perspectives on Children's Work and Labour*, London, Routledge Farmer.

Rahman, M. M., Khanam, R. and Absar, N. U. (1999) 'Child labor in Bangladesh: a critical appraisal of Harkin's bill and the MOU-type schooling program', *Journal of Economic Issues*, vol. 33, no. 4, pp. 985–1003.

Reynolds, P. (1991) *Dance Civet Cat: Child Labour in the Zambezi Valley*, Harare, Baobab.

Robson, E. (2004) 'Hidden child workers: young carers in Zimbabwe', *Antipode*, vol. 36, no. 2, pp. 227–47.

Skovdal, M. (2010) 'Children caring for their "caregivers": exploring the caring arrangements in households affected by AIDS in Western Kenya', *AIDS Care*, vol. 22, no. 1, pp. 96–103.

UNICEF (1997) *The State of the World's Children*, New York, UNICEF.

Woodhead, M. (2001) 'The value of work and school: a study of working children's perspectives', in Lieten, K. and White, B. (eds) *Child Labour: Policy Options*, Amsterdam, Aksant Academic.

World Health Organization (WHO) (1987) *Children at Work*, Geneva, WHO.

Reading A
From useful to useless: moral conflict over child labour

Viviana A. Zelizer

Source: *Pricing the Priceless Child: The Changing Social Value of Children*, 1985, Princeton, NJ, Princeton University Press.

The exclusion of children from the marketplace [in the USA] involved a difficult and prolonged battle lasting almost fifty years from the 1870s to the 1930s. It was partly an economic confrontation and partly a legal dispute, but it was also a profound 'moral revolution.' Two groups with sharply conflicting views of childhood struggled to impose their definition of children's proper place in society. For child labor reformers, children's early labor was a violation of children's sentimental value. As one official of the National Child Labor Committee explained in 1914, a laboring child 'is simply a producer, worth so much in dollars and cents, with no standard of value as a human being … How do you calculate your standard of a child's value? … as something precious beyond all money standard.' On the other hand, opponents of child labor reform were just as vehement in their support of the productive child, 'I say it is a tragic thing to contemplate if the Federal Government closes the doors of the factories and you send that little child back, empty-handed; that brave little boy that was looking forward to get money for his mother for something to eat.'

The child labor conflict is a key to understanding the profound transformation in the economic and sentimental value of children in the early twentieth century. The price of a useful wage-earning child was directly counterposed to the moral value of an economically useless but emotionally priceless child. In the process, a complex reassessment of children's economic roles took place. It was not just a matter of whether children should work or not. Even the most activist of child labor reformers were unwilling to condemn all types of child work, while their opponents were similarly reluctant to condone all child labor. Instead, their argument centered over conflicting and often ambiguous cultural definitions of what constructed acceptable work for children. New boundaries emerged, differentiating legitimate from illegitimate forms of economic participation by children.

It was not a simple process. As one perplexed contemporary observer noted: 'To work or not to work – that is the question. But nobody agrees upon the answer ... Who among the controversialists is wrong? And just what is work anyway? When and where does it step across the dead line and become exploitation?' Child work and child money were gradually redefined for the 'sacred' twentieth-century child into primarily moral and instructional tools. While child labor laws regulated exclusively working-class children, the new rules for educational child work cut across classes, equally applicable to all 'useless' children. ...

In defense of the useful child

In a letter to the editor of the *Chicago News*, a Reverend Dunne of the Guardian Angels' Italian Church bitterly criticized the 1903 Illinois child labor law as a 'curse instead of a blessing to those compelled to earn their bread by the sweat of their brow.' The priest ridiculed a law that transformed the noble assistance of a working child into an illegal act: 'He must not attempt to work; he must not dare to earn his living honestly, because in his case ... that is against the law.' ... Opponents of child labor legislation defended the pragmatic and moral legitimacy of a useful child. As a controversial article in the *Saturday Evening Post* asserted: 'The work of the world has to be done; and these children have their share ... why should we ... place the emphasis on ... prohibitions ... We don't want to rear up a generation of nonworkers, what we want is workers and more workers.' From this perspective, regulatory legislation introduced an unwelcome and dangerous 'work prohibition': 'The discipline, sense of duty and responsibility, ... which come to a boy and girl, in home, on the farm, in workshop, as the result of even hard work ... is to be ... prohibited.' The consequences would be dire: 'If a child is not trained to useful work before the age of eighteen, we shall have a nation of paupers and thieves.' Child labor, insisted its supporters, was safer than 'child-idleness.' ...

For working-class families, the usefulness of their children was supported by need and custom. When parents were questioned as to why their children left school early to get to work, it was often 'perplexing' for the mother to assign a reason for such an 'absolutely natural proceeding – he's of an age to work, why shouldn't he?' As one mother who employed her young children in homework told an investigator: 'Everybody does it. Other people's children help – why not ours?' Studies of immigrant families, in particular, demonstrate that the child was an unquestioned member of the family economic unit. For example, in her study of Canadian workers in the Amoskeag Mills of Manchester, New Hampshire, Tamara Hareven found that the 'entire family economy as well as the family's work ethic was built on the assumption that children would contribute to the family's income from the earliest possible age' ([Hareven, 1977, p. 63]). While generally older boys were more likely to become wage-earners, boys under fourteen and girls were still expected to actively assist the family with housework, childcare, and any income obtained from odd jobs.

Government reports occasionally provide glimpses of the legitimacy of child labor: [a] mother boasting that her baby – a boy of seven – could 'make more money than any of them picking shrimp'; or an older sister apologizing for her seven-year-old brother who was unable to work in a shrimp cannery 'because he couldn't reach the car to shuck.' Work was a socializer; it kept children busy and out of mischief. As the father of two children who worked at home wiring rosary beads explained: 'Keep a kid at home, save shoe leather, make better manners.'

Child labor legislation threatened the economic world of the working class. In 1924, one commentator in the *New Republic* predicted the potential disruption of traditional family relationships: 'The immemorial right of the parent to train his child in useful tasks ... is destroyed ... Parents may still set their children at work; children may still make themselves useful, but it will no longer be by right and obligation, but by default of legislation ... .' Many parents resented and resisted this intrusion. A 1909 investigation of cotton textile mills reported that 'fathers and mothers vehemently declare that the State has no right to interfere if they wish to "put their children to work," and that it was only fair for the child to "begin to pay back for its keep."' In New York canneries, Italian immigrants reportedly took a more aggressive stand. One study reports a quasi-riot against a canner who attempted to exclude young children from the sheds: '[He was] besieged by angry Italian women, one of whom bit his finger "right through."' Parents routinely sabotaged regulatory legislation simply by lying about their child's age. It was an easy ploy, since until the 1920s many states required only a parental affidavit as proof of a child worker's age. For a small illegal fee, some notary publics were apparently quite willing to produce a false affidavit.

Middle-class critics also opposed child labor legislation in the name of family autonomy. Prominent spokesmen such as Nicholas Murray Butler, president of Columbia University, warned that 'No American mother would favor the adoption of a constitutional amendment which would empower Congress to invade the rights of parents and to shape family life to its liking.' An assemblyman from Nevada put it more succinctly: 'They have taken our women away from us by constitutional amendments; they have taken our liquor from us; and now they want to take our children.'

In defense of the useless child

For reformers, the economic participation of children was an illegitimate and inexcusable 'commercialization of child life.' As one New York City clergyman admonished his parishioners in 1925: 'A man who defends the child labor that violates the personalities of children is not a Christian … .' The world of childhood had to become entirely removed from the world of the market. Already in 1904, Dr. Felix Adler, first chairman of the National Child Labor Committee, insisted that '… whatever happens in the sacrifice of workers … children shall not be touched … childhood shall be sacred … commercialism shall not be allowed beyond this point.' If the sacred child was 'industrially taboo,' child labor was a profanation that reduced 'the child of God [into] the chattel of Mammon.'

The persistence of child labor was attributed in part to a misguided economic system that put 'prosperity above … the life of sacred childhood.' Employers were denounced as 'greedy and brutal tyrants,' for whom children were little more than a 'wage-earning unit,' or a profitable dividend. Any professed support of child labor was dismissed as convenient rhetoric: 'A prominent businessman who recently remarked that it is good for the children to work in industry is a hypocrite unless he puts his own children there.'

Reformers sympathized with the financial hardships of the working class, yet, they rarely understood and seldom condoned working-class economic strategies. Instead, parents were depicted as suspect collaborators in the exploitation of their own children. 'If fathers and mothers of working children could have their own way, would they be with the child labor reformer or against him?' was a question asked in *The American Child*, a publication of the National Child Labor Committee. Others were more forthright in their indictment: 'Those who are fighting for the rights of the children, almost invariably, find their stoutest foes in the fathers and mothers, who coin shameful dollars from the bodies and souls of their own flesh and blood.' A child's contribution to the family economy was redefined as the mercenary exploitation of parents 'who are determined that their children shall add to the family income, regardless of health, law, or any other consideration.' As early as 1873, Jacob Riis had declared that '… it requires a character of more disinterestedness … than we usually find among the laboring class to be able to forgo present profit for the future benefit of the little one.' At the root of this harsh indictment was the profound unease of a segment of the middle class with working-class family life. The instrumental orientation toward children was denied all legitimacy: '… to permit a parent … at his or her will to send a child out to work and repay himself for its maintenance from the earnings of its labor, or perhaps … make money out of it seems … nothing short of criminal.' Child labor, 'by urging the duty of the child to its parents,' obliterated the 'far more binding and important obligation of the parent to the child.' This 'defective' economic view of children was often attributed to the foreign values of immigrant parents, 'who have no civilization, no decency, no anything but covetousness and who would with pleasure immolate their offspring on the shrine of the golden calf.' For such 'vampire' progenitors, the child became an asset instead of remaining a 'blessed incumbrance.'

Advocates of child labor legislation were determined to regulate not only factory hours but family feeling. They introduced a new cultural equation: if children were useful and produced money, they were not being properly loved. As a social worker visiting the canneries where Italian mothers worked alongside their children concluded: 'Although they love their children, they do not love them in the right way.' A National Child Labor Committee leaflet warned that when family relations are materialistic, 'It is rare to find a family governed by affection.' By excluding children from the 'cash nexus,' reformers promised to restore proper parental love among working-class families. 'It is the new view of the child,' wrote Edward T. Devine, editor of *Charities and the Commons*, a leading reform magazine, 'that the child is worthy of the parent's sacrifice.'

Thus, the conflict over the propriety of child labor between 1870 and 1930 in the U.S. involved a profound cultural disagreement over the economic and sentimental value of young children. While opponents of child labor legislation hailed the economic usefulness of children, advocates of child labor legislation campaigned for their uselessness. For reformers, true parental love could only exist if the child was defined exclusively as an object of sentiment and not as an agent of production.

Reference

Hareven, T. (1977) 'Family and work patterns of immigrant laborers in a planned industrial town, 1900–1930', in Ehrlich, R. L. (ed) *Immigrants in Industrial America*, Charlottesville, University Press of Virginia.

Reading B
A child's work in Poompuhar

Virginia Morrow and Uma Vennam

Source: *Children Combining Work and Education in Cottonseed Production in Andhra Pradesh: Implications for Discourses of Children's Rights in India*, Working Paper No. 50, 2009, Oxford, Young Lives.

Ramya (not her real name) is 12 years old … She is one of five children, four girls and a boy. Ramya's case shows how child work is not necessarily directly caused by poverty. Ramya's father works as the village secretary … (considered to be a powerful position locally, as most decisions about social security services are made by secretaries, for example, whether a household is classified as being below the poverty line and receives a white card entitling them to a range of benefits such as allowances of rice and oil). Her mother manages the home with support from her paternal grandmother, who lives next door, as her father is busy with his job. The father makes the major decisions about the children, though the mother is consulted. Apart from the father's job, the family depends on the family land on which seed cotton and tobacco are grown. Like most children in the village, Ramya works in the fields from August to November. She described her day as starting as early as 7 am and going on until 7 pm. She misses school for two to three months of the year and finds it difficult to make up for lost classes. Her parents know that she dislikes working in the fields and the long walk (3.5km) to the fields. Being the youngest of four girls, she is spared from doing the bulk of the household work, though she described sweeping up, fetching the milk and numerous other chores. Ramya understands the need for her to work on the family's farm, and she is quite open about her dislike towards farm work as it is very difficult and makes her tired after the long day. She also considers this as a major obstacle to her ambitions. …

She described going to the fields on an 'empty stomach', plucking the flowers for half an hour:

> Then we cross the flowers from 8 till 12 … we usually have breakfast at 11 am. My mother gets it, she follows us to the fields with the food, then we eat, and work on flower buds. It will be 6:30 pm, we will pack up all the things and return home, all of us

come together, mother, me, aunt, brothers, sisters (i.e. cousins) and my sister and three daily wage workers together.

She complained that the walk is scary, the road is narrow, and she is scared of the insects in the field. But she also described talking while walking and how she mostly talked with 'the lady who comes as wage labourer on our farm ... she is always smiling, she also talks nicely and makes us talk also'. She described watching TV (not at home, in the neighbourhood), having supper, and then studying for half an hour, then going to bed. 'I try to read, but I feel tired; I miss school, so I don't know what is happening at school.' Her father is too busy to help her with homework. Her mother understands her problems about work: 'If I say "I don't like to go to the field", everyday, she understands it and does not force me. If I want to go to school, she will allow me. But she doesn't let me during the cotton crop season.' ...

... [Cotton] pollination work is a daily job and involves a great deal of labour. ...

> It is very hard ... there is pain in the legs, we walk every day, I feel pain in the legs too ... we have to do the same work everyday, even if it is hot. At that time I cover my head with a towel, sometimes I get a fever, but mostly it is only hands and legs that ache. I feel tired of the long day, and do not feel like doing anything after reaching home. Not even studying.

The interviewer asks her about what she thinks and feels about the work she does.

> This field work, be it cotton or tobacco work. For these works we have raised loans, we will have to repay the loans, we work and repay the loans. Father took a loan for our sisters' marriage; we performed their marriages at the same time [2 sisters were married on the same day last year]. We have taken a loan of 1 lakh rupees for their marriage. ... I have to work, though it is hard work; we have to clear the loans.

The loans are both from the bank and from informal sources, who finance agricultural operations, which is a common practice in these communities. Ramya talks about buyers coming to the village and purchasing the crop. Ramya is not technically a debt-bonded labourer, as she works on the family farm and not for wages. She talks about the family's inability to hire many labourers, as this would increase the expenses. Ramya has a clear understanding of financial arrangements and why she needs to work. She also described other activities she undertakes for her family:

> I have to do all the small jobs, like going here and there to collect money given as small loan by my grandmother; they will send me to collect that money. I will have to do all that granny asks me to do; she will send me to get money, she will send me to the shop, she will send me to ask if anybody wants to buy blouses. My granny sells these; she has a small shop [next door].

She also takes care of her sister's baby (now 4 months old) when she returns from school, while her sister does the domestic work. She doesn't watch much TV now because she has to keep the baby at home. In terms of household chores, as mentioned, she helps with sweeping: 'I don't feel bad about it, it's our home, it looks good clean, *it should be clean and tidy and it's our job and should be done by us only*, that's why I like to do it, everybody at home *has to take on responsibility*' (emphasis added). She talks about her brother (aged 11) and describes how he comes to the fields sometimes,

> but does not do any work … but at this age, I used to go to the fields and do work … he is the youngest of all, only son after 4 girls, he is pampered a lot, as he is the only son, mother and father both pamper him. I also feel he is small, he cannot work. But sometimes I get angry; when he troubles me, when the work is hard, I compare [the fact] that he is not going, but I have to. But I don't say anything; I like him as a small brother …

When asked for her views about school, she described how she dislikes being scolded and beaten if homework is not done or school attendance is not regular.

> I feel very bad when teacher scolds me. I like to be regular in school, do home work, but I can't do it all, it is difficult. But there

is no choice, I have to do all the work that mother and grandmother say. Now that my two sisters are married I have to share work; they say I am now old enough to do all this. …

Before examinations, even at that time, the work is from dawn to dusk … a few days to [attend] school and a few days to do tobacco work. Even at that time, I had to work from morning to evening. We go at 7 am and pluck it, return home by 9 am or 10 am, and we take a bath and wash thoroughly. It is very pungent, It is like a burning sensation on the hands. We take a bath, and wash thoroughly, and have food, then sit to stitch tobacco.

When asked 'did it affect your studies and seventh grade examinations?', Ramya replied, 'it affected a lot. I would have been in school regularly, prepared better and scored more marks in the examination'. She described her plans for education, but here she is caught in a vicious cycle – she wants to carry on studying to tenth grade, but when she does go to school she is scolded by teachers because she is not attending regularly – 'we are scared of it' yet 'we will have to obey parents and go to the fields'. She explained that she has asked her mother to come and speak to the teachers in the school, but her mother never comes. 'If I insist on her coming she may ask me to stop school, so I just keep going; teachers also know by now about this system, it has become a routine in our village.' She would like to become a teacher, 'if the people in the family let us [me], I will study until degree' and described how she and three friends all want to become teachers. She named a teacher 'who is the inspiration. We like her, she teaches well.'

On the other hand, the school itself is not in a good physical state. The buildings are old, there is no furniture in the classrooms and children sit on the floor. The school is due to have a new building, but the construction has not been undertaken because of inadequate funds. The high school is therefore located in the same premises as the earlier upper primary school. The children do not mind all these inadequacies, but the water and lack of toilets do affect the older girls and their attendance at school (particularly those coming from the neighbouring villages). …

She expresses strong opinions about school and work and said: 'Children of my age should be in school only, no work, no field work.

They can help in domestic work at home, because this is petty work and can be easily managed … *We should help* at home, if alone it is very strenuous for mothers at home, we have to share the work with the mother'. …

Ramya's parents were reluctant to speak openly about their daughter's work, downplaying the amount of time she spends working and citing the fact that 'labourers don't turn up' as a reason for children having to work. Her mother, however, considers her participation as an inevitable result of the need to reduce the cost of hiring labour. Her parents complained that she is a weak child and can't work in the fields for long, and that it is better if she gets educated. 'She is tiny for her age, not yet attained puberty, all her friends have.' …

What do we learn from [Ramya's] account? [She] shows a clear understanding of [her] work role …, [her] domestic tasks, and of the difficulties [she] face[s] in combining school and work. [Her] expressed desire to support [her] mother … highlights the interdependency of family members, particularly mothers and daughters, and the ways in which children contribute to the domestic economy. Nieuwenhuys (2005, p. 169) argues that children who work are involved in 'wealth creation' (or at the very least subsistence), and she emphasises the importance of recognising the 'interdependence between the two areas of social life … childhood and the market … Children play a key role in constituting and maintaining forms of wealth that are passed down from generation to generation'. She utilises the notion of generalised reciprocity … to explain how 'sets of social rules and divisions of tasks ensure that … new generations of children are taken care of and acquire assets, resources, knowledge and relationships that will enable them to repay, as adults, their debt to the older generation' (Nieuwenhuys, 2005, p. 175).

Ramya describes how obedient girls are, and how housework is 'our job', and clearly recognises her own responsibilities to her family: as Nieuwenhuys (2005) notes, submission is the most evident way to be a 'good child' (p. 176). Child labour/work is conceptualised as problematic because it is perceived as conflicting with the over-riding aim of 'being a child', in other words, to become educated. This paradigm leads to a societal devaluation of children's contributions, and hence fails to acknowledge interconnections between family members, generations, and others in the community … .

Reference

Niewenhuys, O. (2005) 'The wealth of children: reconsidering the child labour debate', in Qvortrup, J. (ed) *Studies in Modern Childhood*, Basingstoke, Palgrave Macmillan.

Reading C
Raising questions, questioning the answers

Michael Bourdillon, Deborah Levison, William Myers and Ben White

Source: *Rights and Wrongs of Children's Work*, 2010, New Brunswick, NJ, Rutgers University Press.

In Europe and North America it is widely assumed that factory work is bad for children, a clear case of harmful 'child labor'. In this [reading] we introduce an example of working children in Morocco which disturbs such common assumptions and attitudes about child work. This example leads to reflection and questions on how children's interests relate to adult interests, on the way we understand childhood, on children's rights, and on the kinds of information we need to understand children's work.

'When I was fired, I cried for two weeks': how interventions went wrong in Morocco's garment industry

Toward the end of 1995, a team from British Granada TV's *World in Action* investigated the labeling of garments made in the Sicome factory in Méknès, Morocco, and found that many girls between the ages of twelve and fifteen were working in the factory. Representatives from Marks and Spencer, the well-known chain that retailed the garments in Britain, quickly visited the factory. At the end of 1995, many of the girls were summarily dismissed, allowing Marks and Spencer to announce in January 1996, two days before the Granada program was aired on British television, 'Marks and Spencer has conducted a full investigation … and absolutely no evidence has been found to support this claim … no young person under the age of 15 years is currently employed there' (Zalami et al., 1998, p. 32). Superficially, the matter appeared resolved; there were no longer any under-age girls working in the factory.

The girls and the families, however, saw things differently. This is how Amal, a girl from Méknès, described her experience of finding a job at the age of thirteen in the Sicome clothing factory, and losing it the following year.

> I started work at Sicombe in 1994 and was fired in
> December 1995. My starting salary was 210 dirham ($21). My job

consisted of trimming threads with scissors from finished garments. Sometimes I used to draw the lines on fabrics …

We used to begin work at 7.30 A.M. (the company bus picked us up from the neighbourhoods at 6.30 A.M. and brought us back in the evening). We had a lunch break from 1 to 2 P.M. and we worked very often until 8 P.M., but we were never paid for overtime. The working conditions were extremely tiresome and our supervisors used to insult us and tell us, 'If you don't like it, leave: there are plenty of other girls waiting at the gate to be hired for less money.' When the Europeans came to visit, one of the supervisors used to ask me and other young girls to hide.

One day, as I was leaving at the end of the day, they called me into the office and one of the accountants, Shadia, asked me to sign a paper. When I signed it, she told me that I had just signed my resignation papers. They gave me severance pay ($90). I told her I did not know what I had signed, but she told me that I was the one who wanted to quit. Then she said to come back in a year and we will probably hire you …

I wanted to study but I did not have the money to buy school supplies and books. Now it is too late for me to go to school. I would not mind learning a skill in order to get a job. I need to work to help my family. The only person working now is my elder sister, who is a maid living in a home in the city …

(Zalami et al. 1998, p. 44: paragraphs have been re-ordered)

Amal's account raised a number of questions. Why were she and other girls working in the factory, and why were they fired? The action of the Granada team was based on the assumption that factory work was bad for Amal and her friends, and that their proper place was at home or in school. Were these assumptions valid? Was the girls' employment illegal? And what were the consequences of their dismissal?

A Moroccan researcher, Fatima Badri Zalami, met Amal and eleven other girls who had been dismissed from Sicome, and heard their stories. Her report reveals the complexities of the situation and helps us understand the importance of knowing about the contexts of children's work.

In the mid 1990s, Morocco's textile and garment industries accounted for about 40 percent of Morocco's export revenues and employed mainly young female workers from poor rural and urban families. Work was nothing new for Moroccan girls in low-income households, who traditionally started to take on household chores from the age of five. They were usually confined to the house or its immediate surroundings, while boys were free to roam. In the 1990s, however, increasing numbers of young women joined the paid work force. Girls no longer wanted to stay at home, doing household chores and waiting for a husband. They found paid work outside the home a liberating experience, boosting their self-esteem and freeing them from the total control of their family. Their contributions to family income improved their status in the family. Work gave girls access to a world that they could not experience at home, including friendships and entry to the labor market. This experience would provide a chance to postpone marriage and improve their standing with their husbands when they married.

Unemployment among high school graduates was high, and the girls saw that extended schooling did not guarantee access to good jobs. So, with their parents' encouragement, they tried to enter the job market early. The Moroccan government encouraged young people to opt for vocational training. As in many other societies, young people had traditionally learned their trades and made themselves employable by working at apprenticeships. Morocco's laws allowed young people between the ages of twelve and eighteen years to take two-year apprenticeships (extendable sometimes to a third year), and offered them some legal protection. The laws specified that the employer should teach the apprentices a trade, that this training should not be longer than eight hours per day, that apprentices should be allowed to attend professional classes, and that they should be paid according to regulations.

The girls gave many reasons for seeking paid factory employment. Some of them had been victims of gender discrimination, pulled out of school to help at home while their brothers were able to pursue their studies. One girl had dropped out of school because she was failing, and others had also been doing badly in the formal education system, which they saw as inadequate, irrelevant, rigid, and failing to provide sure access to a job. Economic pressures and family debts obliged families to seek extra income, and household heads – especially women – relied on their children to share responsibility for the family livelihood. Although it was not always dire necessity that drove the girls to work, their income made important contributions to family welfare.

Amal and about 100 other young girls worked under apprenticeship contracts in the factory alongside several hundred adult workers, producing pajamas and other garments on contract to one of the suppliers to Marks and Spencer. When they started to work at Sicome, all the girls had reached both the legal minimum age for apprenticeship in Morocco and the age for employment in light work in developing countries permitted by the ILO Minimum Age Convention (no. 138 of 1973). They were therefore legally employed.

On the other hand, the girls' accounts make it clear they had been systematically exploited in the factory. Sicome regularly contravened the provisions of the apprenticeship law: the girls received little professional training, they worked standing up for long hours, they were usually paid wages lower than those specified in their contracts, they were not paid for overtime work, and they did not receive adequate health benefits. Some of the young girls left the factory of their own accord because of the way they were treated.

Most girls nevertheless saw advantages in factory employment. Their main alternatives were jobs in the informal sector, such as street vending, or in domestic service where pay was worse and conditions may be very harmful … Many young people worked in home-based or cottage industries, where they had no legal protection and sometimes suffered permanent damage (for example, from inhaling fumes from the glue they used). An apprenticeship in a garment factory offered a rare opportunity for formal-sector employment, which the education system no longer guaranteed. Conditions in factories producing for export were certainly not ideal, but they were better than in enterprises producing for the local market. Employment in the export sector was consequently relatively prestigious work. The girls' earnings, though small, gave them some financial independence. In spite of the bad treatment at Sicome, it was the preferred employer in Méknès by both girls and their parents, providing the girls with a relatively safe work environment and safe free transport to and from work. Viewed from this perceptive, the textile industry represented the best among available options, providing girls with work that was considered culturally appropriate.

When their employment was suddenly terminated without any period of notice, the girls lost all these advantages. For Amal and her friends, dismissal meant a reduction in family incomes. The employer, not the children, was responsible for violating the regulations on working conditions for the apprentices, but it was the children, not the employer, who suffered the consequences of dismissal. It is widely assumed that if children are stopped from working, they will go to school, but these girls could not and did not return to school, for reasons they were not in school in the first place, and because it was difficult once out of school to obtain re-admission. They were effectively robbed of a relatively secure, formal-sector job, in what was considered the most desirable form of employment for low-income women. All were desperate to find alternative employment. Some of the girls formally apprenticed at Sicome remained at home, helping with household chores and making buttons, a time-consuming and poorly paid task, which the girls say damages their eyesight. Others found less attractive jobs, while at least one became involved in prostitution. Some may eventually have been re-employed at Sicome, but with the same poor working conditions as they suffered before they were dismissed. The intervention by the TV team and foreign corporation affected only work for the export market, which in the eyes of the local community was the best and most sought after work. Outsiders had no influence over, nor any apparent interest in, the less advantageous forms of work to which girls were driven.

How should we view the employment of these girls? …

It is too simplistic to try to classify all kinds of child work dichotomously into 'good/safe' work that can be permitted and 'bad/harmful' work to be abolished, based on ideals prevalent outside the community concerned. In the case we have presented, the situation of the girls could be seen as exploitative and harmful, but it is not necessarily factory work as such that is harmful: the problem lay in the working conditions and relationships with employers and supervisors. Not all factory workers are mistreated, and poor working conditions can potentially be improved. When compared with alternatives realistically available to the girls (such as drudgery at home, or early marriage, or worse employment elsewhere), even factory work in poor conditions seemed good. When we assess the place of work in the lives of children, we need to ask what alternatives are realistically available.

Reference

Zalami, F. B., Reddy, N., Lynch, M. A. and Feinstein, C. (1998) *Forgotten on the Pyjama Trail: A Case Study of Garnet Workers in Méknès (Morocco) Dismissed from Their Jobs Following Foreign Media Attention*, Amsterdam, Defence for Children International/International Society for the Prevention of Child Abuse and Neglect.

Chapter 6

Using visual data in research on childhood

Martyn Hammersley

Contents

In this chapter, you will:

- examine the role of visual data in research on childhood
- gain an understanding of the variety of forms that this type of data can take
- look at some of the basic principles guiding the interpretation of this type of data
- consider how researchers' use of it should be assessed
- learn about the ethical issues surrounding visual data.

1 Introduction

When investigating issues to do with childhood, researchers can draw on many types of data. Yet, across all fields of social research, there has been a tendency to rely very heavily on just a few sources, questionnaires and interviews in particular. In recent years, however – in the field of childhood studies especially – there has been increased use of other kinds of data, including what has come to be called 'visual data' (see Pink, 2006; Thomson, 2008; Rose, 2012). These include the use of photographs and video recordings, but also such things as drawings, maps and even material objects of various kinds.

In this chapter, we will consider the kinds of material included under the heading of 'visual data', what is involved in analysing them, how audiences respond to visual images, and some of the distinctive ways in which their use gives rise to ethical issues.

2 Forms of visual data

What counts as visual data is not entirely straightforward; as we have already indicated, they can take many forms. Furthermore, it is not clear what the defining features of this category are, even though the phrase clearly picks out some kinds of material that share distinctive features.

Activity 1   Examples of visual data

Allow about 30 minutes

Look back through earlier chapters in this book and list any examples of what you would take to be visual data.

Are there important differences between these examples that would suggest subcategories?

Comment

A range of kinds of visual data has been used or mentioned in earlier chapters. These include:

- an artefact (Jay's box, Chapter 1)
- maps of their local areas produced by children and young people (Chapter 1)
- photographs taken by researchers (Chapter 2)
- ultrasound screening images produced by hospitals (Chapter 2)
- architectural plans of school buildings (Chapter 4)
- photographs of school buildings (Chapter 4).

One set of categories that could be used to distinguish between these examples is:

- data already available for researchers to use
- data produced directly by researchers themselves
- data produced by others at the request of researchers.

A rather different set of subcategories could be based on the type of material involved – for example, moving images, still images, and artefacts. There are no doubt other ways of categorising examples of visual data: it could be argued that plans and maps are fundamentally different sorts of image from photographs. The important point is that while all these types of material are usually categorised as visual data, they vary considerably in character in ways that may be relevant when using them for research purposes.

As Activity 1 makes clear, the category 'visual data' is quite diverse: the differences among what it includes are perhaps as striking as the similarities, and it is important to recognise them. In particular, we might want to draw a distinction between visual data that consists of images or representations of various kinds, on the one hand, and material objects, on the other. These seem very different from each other in character, although there are those who question this distinction. For example, the French social theorist Jean Baudrillard (1994) argues that we now live in a world that consists entirely of images, and that those generated by the mass media effectively constitute the reality in which most people live, with the internet, video games, and so on, playing a similar role. Indeed, he denies that there is any longer a true reality 'behind' these images.

Nevertheless, in my view this is an important distinction, although each of the two subcategories that we identified – images and objects – includes much diversity. Thus, 'material objects' includes: buildings and the spaces that they enclose, as well as those that surround them; gardens, their layout and furniture; household equipment from heating boilers to doorstops; toys; and so on. Moreover, just think what variety of objects comes under the heading of 'toys'. We also need to remember that there is an important sense in which images *are* themselves material objects, as with photographs displayed on the mantelpiece of a home or children's drawings and paintings stuck on the fridge door in the kitchen. At the same time, as already noted, our experiences of the world of objects are often mediated through images of one sort or another: for example, toys for children are increasingly viewed online before being purchased.

Partly because of this diversity and the fluidity in its meaning, the term 'visual data' needs careful handling. A useful way of trying to clarify terms whose meaning is uncertain or vague is to consider on what implicit contrast, or contrasts, their use relies. The most obvious interpretation of 'visual data' is that it relates to what is seen, as opposed to what derives from the other senses, especially what we hear. Thus, one contrast for 'visual data' is what we might call 'aural data' – in other words, what people say about the world, notably in interviews, and what they say in the course of pursuing various kinds of social interaction. This certainly picks out a relevant and important difference in the sort of data that researchers might use, although it does not capture all of what is meant by the phrase 'visual data'. After all, on this definition, transcripts would seem to count as visual (since most of us look at them rather than listen to them), even though they are a representation of aural data. Another contrast that helps to define the meaning of 'visual data' is with 'textual data' – in other words with linguistic communication, whether in oral or written form. So this category relates to images and objects rather than text. While these two contrasts broadly indicate the boundaries around visual data, they should make clear that those boundaries are rather fuzzy. Furthermore, in practice visual data are often closely intertwined with other sorts of data. Researchers have increasingly recognised this, emphasising the importance of paying attention to ways in which visual data are related to other kinds, including those deriving from the other senses (see, for example, Dicks et al., 2006; Pink, 2009; Kress, 2010).

Activity 2   Links among types of data

Allow about 40 minutes

Look at Figure 1, which is an image from a website.

Figure 1   A web page from the *Parents* website

Consider these questions:

- What different types of data can you see within this image?
- What would you say are the relationships between these types of data?

Comment

As our discussion of what 'visual data' means indicated, what exactly counts as belonging to this category, and why, can vary. It is worth noting, first of all, that what you are looking at here is an image, in a book, of a website as it existed online when this chapter was being written (it has almost certainly changed in some respects by the time you are reading this). While this image includes pictures and drawn design features, it also incorporates quite a lot of textual material, and you may notice that the website also offers some aural material in the form of children's songs.

There seems to be a strong relationship between the visual and textual elements in this website. The images are no doubt intended to capture our attention, but in large part they seem designed to lead us to particular items of text. At the same time, the textual elements comment on the images in various ways. The biggest picture, showing the four children, is closely related to the text to the side of it, partly obscured, which is about birthday parties. Even more obviously, the picture of the woman carrying a child in a sling relates both to the text alongside it, which reads 'Win this', and to a competition that the magazine is running.

As Activity 2 reminds us, very often we find visual images and text positioned together, and they are frequently designed to 'speak' to one another: a caption is intended to tell us how to read an image, while images are often designed to illustrate stretches of text, or they may simply be intended to draw our attention to these. With this in mind, we can ask why particular bits of text and particular images are placed in one position rather than another, what their functions are in relation to one another, and so on. In much the same way, objects may well include textual elements: for example, vases and crockery often have the maker's name and some other information on the bottom; and many objects come with instructions for their assembly or for their use.

We should also recognise that we can look at written text itself as visual data – in other words, as a material object. Figure 1 reminds us of this: it contains forms of text that vary quite considerably in character. As well as noting where the text is positioned, we can also ask about the size of the fonts used. Generally speaking, the larger the text the more important we are likely to take it to be, or at least we will probably tend to give it attention first (even if we remember that it is sometimes essential to 'read the small print'!). We should also ask why some text is in black while other colours are used elsewhere. To some extent this may be to provide variety, but there may be other kinds of significance too. The particular variety of font employed (Arial, Times New Roman, Cambria, etc.) could be important, since fonts can be seen as carrying different messages (e.g. some appear quite formal, others more informal and 'friendly'). We might ask why some text is in bold, italics or capitals. Again, this is likely to reflect how keen the person who produced the website is for us to read a particular piece of text. Often, of course, the text that is most striking is designed to capture our attention and lead us to read other text that may not be so immediately attention-grabbing.

We should also remember that visual and aural data often go together. Thus, video recordings include sound as well as images, and both are aspects of the same scene being recorded. Similarly, where researchers invite children to produce visual material of some kind (drawings, scrapbooks, video-diaries, etc.), they often carry out interviews too, in order to access the meanings that shaped the production of this material. These interviews produce aural data that may then be turned into textual data through transcription, as well as being analysed in association with the visual data.

Clearly, visual data can be of great importance in research on childhood, as well as on other topics. Some commentators have argued that, in the past, the value of visual data has been neglected or suppressed (Law and Whittaker, 1988), this perhaps reflecting the ambivalent attitude towards the visual that has been characteristic of modern Western culture, at least in some quarters (Jay, 1993).

Summary of Section 2

Diverse kinds of material come under the heading of 'visual data', and various subcategories can be identified.

The meaning of 'visual data' is largely given by the contrasts with aural and textual data.

However, all these categories are fuzzy round the edges; very frequently, not only are different types of material found together, but they are also closely interrelated, performing a variety of functions together.

---

3 Analysing visual data

One early and influential general approach to analysing images was given the label 'semiotics', a term that refers to 'the study of signs'; this approach represents an attempt to apply forms of analysis to non-verbal signs that were originally developed in linguistics, the study of language (see Bignell, 1997). Semiotics arose from a recognition that we 'read' all manner of non-verbal features of our environment as carrying messages or implications – pointers on clocks, images in advertisements, the clothes people wear, and so on. For example, part of the debate about the 'sexualisation' of young children concerns the 'messages' that different kinds of clothing send, not least in suggesting that they are adults. Clothing is also central to the study of youth cultures, where distinctive forms of dress are often used to signal membership. In short, it is not only verbal language that carries messages; these can be conveyed non-verbally, and not just through gesture and facial expression but also through the design of various sorts of image, object and place.

A prime requirement for semiotic analysis is careful attention to features of the images or objects being studied, and to physical and semantic relationships among these features, as well as between different images and objects. Rose (2012) refers to this as 'compositional interpretation'. It is important to note that this sort of analysis requires us to overcome the kind of mundane, functional attention that we use much of the time in everyday life, in which our awareness of the presence of, and relations between, images and objects is below the level of consciousness: we do not notice or pay attention to them. Instead, for the purposes of research, we need to look very closely at the objects or images concerned, concentrating on their features and how these are arranged, to ask why we tend to interpret them in the ways that we do, what would be significant changes in their meaning, how the relations among them vary across contexts, and so on.

Advocates of this sort of research challenge the view that images simply represent the world, as in the naïve idea that photographs are direct representations of the people and/or places pictured *as they truly are*, or the assumption that the design of objects simply reflects the purposes they are intended to serve. Instead, it is argued that there are 'grammars', or sets of conventions, governing how images are constituted and interpreted, as well as how objects are designed; and that these are culturally variable. For example, there are what might be called different 'genres' of image: there are usually big differences between the type of photograph taken and presented as part of a family album, those taken by the police of someone suspected of a crime, and those taken as part of a fashion shoot.

This sort of variation in conventions and genres has led to the notion of 'visual cultures' (Barnard, 2001; Sturken and Cartwright, 2001; Evans and Hall, 2005): to the idea that research can be focused on identifying the cultural conventions that shape the production and use of particular sorts of images and objects (and also of spaces). This is an idea that gains particular significance in the case of children and young people, not least because there are often major generational differences in the objects and images that are given attention, and in how these are interpreted. Given this, researchers may need to devote considerable ingenuity and effort in seeking to gain access to the sometimes distinctive understandings of children and young people (see, for example, Bragg and Buckingham, 2008). Being aware of different 'visual cultures' is also important when it comes to understanding how the meaning of images of children functions in the mass media and online.

Activity 3   Semiotic or compositional analysis

Allow about 40 minutes

Look carefully at Figure 2, another screenshot of a website, this time that of UNICEF UK.

Figure 2   Home page from the UNICEF UK website

Complete the following tasks:

1   Outline, in a couple of sentences, your first impression of the main messages conveyed by this website presentation. Pay attention to which items you notice first.

2   Identify what you take to be the main components of this presentation in terms of photographs, blocks of text, design features, etc.

3   Look now at the largest photograph. Describe the features of this in a few sentences. Can you identify any messages that you think this photograph is designed to convey?

4   Finally, compare this photograph with the one in Figure 3 below, which is one of the pictures in a sequence of three that the website runs through automatically. What do you think are the main differences between these two photographs in the messages that they convey?

Children's emergency in East Africa.
Your donations have helped halve the number of famine zones, but hundreds of thousands of children are still at risk.

Figure 3   A second image from the the UNICEF UK home page

Comment

Here are my responses, necessarily reflecting to some degree and in particular ways who I am in terms of gender, social background, etc., just as your interpretation will, in certain respects, reflect who you are:

1   The main message of the web page, I would say, is about the famine in East Africa and the need for donations: the largest of the photographs is designed to draw attention to this issue, while the associated text provides more details. Of course, the image and text relating to this message are located within a frame that signals that this is the UNICEF website, and the website provides information about other material available on it.

2   At the top of the web page is the UNICEF banner; below this is the main photograph and the block of text relating to it. The text is on the left, includes a headline, and is white on a grey background, making it stand out. It is hard to say whether the eye is drawn first to the photograph or to the text, but clearly each complements the other. Below the text is a sequence of smaller pictures. In the bottom half of the website image, there is a 'welcome' banner, and then below that, on the left, is more information about the famine, some of which is highlighted in red. On the right-hand side, other resources available on the website are signalled: video, photographs and audio. There is also a set of buttons that the site's users can click on to support the organisation in various ways. Below this some other current stories are presented.

3   Looking at the main photograph (Figure 2), I am struck by the fact
    that the child is fully clothed: my impression is that this has often not
    been the case in advertisements seeking contributions to famine relief
    – for example, where the pictures are designed to reveal the effects
    of starvation, such as bloated stomachs. I also find it unusual for a
    child so young to be wearing beads, and my impression is that this is
    African dress. By contrast, the child is wearing a top with a bear on it
    which a child of this age might be wearing in many countries across
    the world. Perhaps there is an intended balance here between
    othering the child as African (from the point of view of minority-world
    audiences) and rendering the child as 'just like children in one's own
    society'. The child is shown with (what we take to be) the mother,
    indicating that this is no orphan, although no father is present. I
    presume that the child is a girl, but, given my lack of knowledge of
    the culture of Niger, I don't know whether young boys might also wear
    beads. The expression on the child's face is, to me, one of despair
    and perhaps pain, but not resignation or agony. I also notice that the
    child doesn't look into the camera, in the manner of some previous
    advertisements for famine relief organisations.

4   In the second photograph (Figure 3), again we have mother and child,
    but this time they are both looking out at the audience. Their
    expressions seem to me to be requesting help, although this is not
    strongly signalled – they are not pleading. It could even be that the
    image is intended to represent how they are *after* relief has been
    provided.

Activity 3 was designed to provide some indication of how we might set
about analysing visual data and any textual material with which it is
associated. This kind of semiotic or compositional analysis focuses
primarily, if not exclusively, on images or objects themselves, their
characteristics, and relationships to text. There is great value in this,
both in drawing attention to features that we are normally unaware of,
and in stimulating exploratory ideas about why the images or objects
have the features that they do, why these are arranged in the manner
that they are, why they are interpreted how they are, and so on.
However, you may have noticed that my interpretations in the activity
frequently involved inferences about the process by which the image or
object was produced – for example, attributing intentions or purposes
to designers and perhaps also, by implication at least, expectations about
how audiences will respond to the image or object and what effects it
might have on them.

There is clearly an issue about whether such conclusions can be 'read off' from the features of images or objects themselves. We might be able to do this if we could assume that the design of images and objects is a clear indication of the functions they were intended to serve, and that it determines the message received by, or its impact on, audiences. However, these assumptions have increasingly come to be challenged, and this has prompted research into the processes by which images and objects used as visual data were produced, and into how they are interpreted by audiences. When thinking about the use of visual data in research on children and young people, we need to pay attention to both production and reception. We will look briefly at each of these processes in turn in the next two sections.

Summary of Section 3

An influential way of analysing visual data is semiotic or compositional analysis.

This involves examining the features of images and objects, and their relationships with one another and with textual material.

The aim is to identify the ways in which these features and relations operate so as to convey particular messages, and the underlying 'grammar' involved.

This kind of analysis often involves, explicitly or implicitly, making inferences from images or objects so as to draw conclusions about why they were designed in the way they were and what their effects on audiences will be.

---

4 Production processes

It is easy to forget that the sorts of image and object (and text) that we come across routinely in everyday life are the product of complex production processes. We usually interpret them quickly for our own purposes, without stopping to think about why and how they have been produced. Yet in fact a great deal of work goes into their production, this often involving assumptions about the purposes for which, and the contexts in which, they will be viewed or used.

When thinking about visual data, an important distinction must be drawn between that produced specifically for research purposes, on the one hand, and that produced by others but used by researchers as data, on the other (e.g. the website material we have been looking at). We will consider each of these types of data separately.

4.1   Researcher-initiated data

Researchers studying children and young people sometimes take photographs – to document living or working conditions, for example, or the character of classrooms or homes. It is now quite common for researchers to make video recordings of social interaction in particular settings in order to capture more detailed and accurate records than could be produced by relying on audio recordings or written field notes alone. In addition, researchers may invite children to take photographs or make video recordings that can then be used as research data. Allan (2005) used what she refers to as the 'photographic diary method' in order to study how 'high-achieving girls' managed and negotiated their identities in school. She gave them disposable cameras and asked them to take photographs to illustrate their lives in school. In much the same way, researchers may ask children to make drawings, produce maps, create scrapbooks or make video diaries as a way of gaining access to their experiential worlds (Hart, 1979; Bragg and Buckingham, 2008; Leitch, 2008; Noyes, 2008; Thomson, 2008; Clark, 2010; Clark and Moss, 2011).

When we read research reports where these sorts of data have been employed, we need to think about how they were produced and what the implications might be for the way we should interpret and assess conclusions reached by researchers, rather than taking either interpretations or conclusions at face value.

Activity 4   Interpreting video recordings

Allow about 40 minutes

What issues do you think we might need to bear in mind when interpreting researchers' use of video recordings, and in assessing research conclusions based on such data? Think about what can, and cannot, be captured by video recordings, and about what is involved in making them.

Comment

There are at least three issues I can think of:

1 Video recording people can significantly affect their behaviour, so that what they do when they know they are being videoed may be rather different from what they would otherwise do (this is sometimes referred to as 'reactivity', pointing to the fact that people react to the behaviour of the researcher). At the very least, if people know they are going to be filmed they may dress more smartly, but they may also consciously try to behave in the manner that they take to be appropriate to the circumstances, whereas they may be less concerned to do this on other occasions. Of course, much depends on whether people know they are being filmed, how the video recording is carried out, how long it will last, what other pressures are operating on them at the time, whether videoing is normal or unusual in the setting, and so on. We should remember too that most other forms of observation will also involve the danger of reactivity; video recording is not unique in this respect, although it may bring about a higher level of reactivity than that generated by the presence of an observer alone or even by audio recording. The key point is that we need to be aware of how video data may have been shaped by the way it was produced.

2 Video recordings made within a situation do not include everything that was going on there: much will be 'out of shot'. Not only may this be important in itself, but it may affect what we see on the screen; and learning about what was out of shot may change our interpretations of what has been captured on the video. Imagine seeing a video of a lesson in a classroom, showing the teacher and children, but later discovering that, besides the researcher, the head teacher and some parents had also been behind the camera, watching the lesson. Would that affect how you interpreted what you saw?

3 Video recordings always take place at particular times as well as in particular places. Indeed, because processing and analysing such data requires a great deal of time, researchers using this method often observe over shorter periods than those relying on audio recordings or field notes. This means that what we are seeing in the data may represent only a very small sample of what the people videoed do in this setting, and, aside from the effects of reactivity, this sample may not be representative of normal patterns. Yet, unless we remember this, we may tend to assume that it is typical, that it tells us what happens most of the time in that situation. Indeed, when

watching video data, there is often a strong tendency to make this assumption.

These points – about reactivity, selectivity and sampling – also apply when researchers ask children or others to take photographs or make videos. But here there are other factors shaping the production process too. For example, what participants photograph or video may be influenced by what they think the researcher wants and/or by what they believe is appropriate in the circumstances; they may also set out to shock or surprise, or use the activity to serve their own purposes. This docs not mean that data involving high levels of 'reactivity' are of no value, but rather that in interpreting them, as with any data, we must remain aware of how they may have been shaped by the process of production and the contexts in which this took place. Of course, we will not always have detailed information about this, but we can make reasonable assessments of what factors may have been involved and try to allow for them.

4.2   Already available data

Thinking about how visual data was produced is also important where research relies on images or objects that were already available rather than produced by the researcher. It is even more likely that here we may forget what has gone into their production, since they are often highly polished products specifically designed to encourage us to take them at face value. Yet, producing them often involves complex processes that may employ a large number of people performing a variety of tasks. Only occasionally is the scale of this brought home to us – as, for example, when we watch the credits at the end of a film and are surprised by the number of people who took part in its production and the many roles they played, some of these being obscure in character. By contrast, while watching, we were probably oblivious to the film's production processes. Moreover, even where only a few people or only one person is immediately involved in the production of images and objects – as in the case of a child's drawing – we should not assume that the production process is simple or unproblematic. Skills are required, but also interpretations of the purposes and conventions surrounding the images or objects concerned.

Some of the complexities of producing video programmes are outlined by Kehily and Maybin (2011) in discussing the making of television programmes for the previous version of the module with which this book is associated. While the aim in these programmes was to 'give children a voice' (Kehily and Maybin, 2011, p. 267) and to provide 'vicarious access to [their] embodied experience across a range of social and cultural contexts' (p. 268), both voices and experience were, inevitably, highly mediated. This reflected not only the range of people – from academics to producers and technicians – involved in making the programmes, but also the affordances and distortions built into the technologies employed to do this.

It is essential to remember, then, that the already available images and objects that researchers use as data have been produced in particular ways and for particular purposes. For example, photographs have been taken from particular angles, with a view to showing some aspects of a scene rather than others, to include some people and not others, and so on; and, of course, the scene may have been prearranged in various ways. In addition, the images may subsequently be modified or manipulated in ways that are hard to detect, the most obvious example being when someone is 'airbrushed' out of a picture, or someone who was not actually present is put in. Similar considerations apply with films and television programmes, which are usually 'edited' in a whole range of ways.

Often, those designing images will give considerable thought to how best to convey the intended message while avoiding unwanted messages. For example, in the case of the UNICEF website, it seems likely that a delicate balance was sought between maximising the impact on an audience so as to motivate them to contribute to the relief fund, on the one hand, and not reinforcing stereotypes of the people who need relief, on the other. In the past, charities seeking to stimulate aid giving have often been accused of stereotyping, as, for example, in the case of advertisements for Shelter, the charity for the homeless in the UK, during the 1960s and early 1970s (see Grosvenor and Hall, 2012).

Another point to note here is that while many images and objects are intended as products to be consumed by an audience, others are generated as devices to assist in carrying out work of some kind, and are shaped by the characteristics of this. However, these may also sometimes be used for other purposes. For example, ultrasound screening in pregnancy, as discussed in Chapter 2, is designed to facilitate medical monitoring, but in some countries the images produced have come to play a key role in the process of becoming a parent, notably being associated with finding out the sex of the baby.

Furthermore, printouts of the images are retained by parents and sometimes displayed in their homes. We can see here how multiple meanings of visual images are generated in processes of production and use.

Given the complexity of production processes, there are a number of questions that we may need to ask when thinking about the use of already available visual data by researchers. Here are some of them.

---

1   Who was involved in the production process, in what roles and contexts?

2   What purpose(s) and interests governed that process?

3   Who were the intended audience(s), and how distinctively were these audience(s) envisaged?

4   What conventions or genres were assumed in producing the images or objects concerned? Was there a particular genre within which the producers were working?

5   What resources were drawn on in producing the images or objects (and in what alternative ways might these resources have been deployed)?

Activity 5   Interpreting displays

Allow about 20 minutes

Consider the case of display boards in schools in terms of how the displays are produced, who is involved in the production and who the audiences are.

What do you think might be the answers to the questions listed in the box above, when asked in relation to school display boards?

Comment

Here are my speculations:

1   Teachers, support assistants, children/young people and perhaps parents as helpers are likely to have been involved, although one might suspect that the teachers would exercise control over what material appears and how it is presented. In some cases, examples of children's work displayed may have been 'co-produced' with teachers or support assistants.

2   An interest in displaying the range and quality of what is done in the class or the school is likely to be involved.

3   Besides other people in the school, new parents and Ofsted inspectors may also have been anticipated audiences.

4   It is difficult to say what conventions or genres were assumed, but there are probably conventions commonly used in producing and 'reading' school display boards, these also drawing on broader notions of what would count as good work for children of particular ages and of particular kinds.

5   Again, it is hard to tell what resources were drawn on, but these will be shaped by the limits of what can easily be displayed physically on a board of a particular kind, and the time and materials available. It is possible that time spent on producing displays could detract from the learning that takes place in the class or school.

Summary of Section 4

There is a danger of our forgetting that all images and objects are the result of production processes of one sort or another; and knowing about these may be relevant for how we evaluate images and objects as research data.

We can distinguish between visual data that was specifically produced by, or at the instigation of, a researcher and that which was produced independently of the research process. The processes of production are likely to be different in each case. In some cases, researchers ask children to produce visual data through drawing, photography or video recording.

An important consideration that we must take into account in evaluating the first kind of data is reactivity: for example, how people producing photographs, videos, etc., at the invitation of the researcher, and the people being photographed and videoed, may react to this process in such a way that their behaviour no longer tells us how they normally are, what they usually do, and so on.

In evaluating the use of data that were already available for the researcher to use, we need to take account of how these were produced, by whom, with what purpose, for what audiences and with what resources. These facts may be important if we are to be

able to draw sound conclusions about what these data can reliably
tell us.

5 Reception of visual material by audiences

Increased attention on the part of researchers to the 'reception' of
images was partly generated by developments in the study of texts. At
one time, there was a tendency to assume that the impact of a text or
image on audiences could be 'read off' from its characteristics, because
these were assumed to control its reception. For example, it was argued
that advertisements could be constructed in such a way that they had a
standard, powerful and predictable effect on audiences. In reaction
against this view, many commentators subsequently came to argue that,
in fact, the meaning of images and texts is to a large extent constructed
by audiences. In other words, audiences should be seen as engaged in
the active creation of meaning, with this process determining their
responses to any image (albeit often largely unconsciously). An
important implication of this argument is that the interpretations that
people make of the same image or object are likely to vary across
cultures and contexts.

One aspect of this process of 'construction' is that audiences will
interpret images in terms of some set of background assumptions about
by whom, how and why they were produced. On this basis, they may be
either accepted at face value as authoritative or dismissed as
propaganda. Another aspect of the reception process is that people
interpret images, and texts too, in terms of particular cultural
conventions, or by implicitly or explicitly comparing them to other
images of a related kind. For example, in the case of the UNICEF
website that we looked at earlier, I compared the photograph associated
with the famine appeal with my memories of other photographs used in
aid campaigns.

It is also important to remember that people may respond to images in
different ways, depending on the context in which they experience them.
For example, how images are interpreted will be affected by the sort of
activities in which audiences are engaged when they come into contact
with them, and perhaps whether they are alone or with other people.
While images are sometimes used for entirely instrumental purposes or
treated as background to unrelated activities, at other times they may
'stop people in their tracks' and prompt reflection and thought.

Debate over whether the meanings of texts and images are predetermined, or the extent and ways in which they are constructed by audiences, has prompted a considerable amount of research on audiences, especially in relation to film and television. Not surprisingly, it was found that the sense that audiences make of any particular text or image can vary according to how interested they are in it, why they are interested in it, what expectations they had about it, in what context they view it, what film or TV genres they are familiar with, and with which other people (if any) they discuss it. At the same time, it was often found that there was a predominant message 'received' or 'constructed' by most audience members, and that this could be related to specific characteristics of the image or object or text concerned (see Fenton et al., 1998).

Most research on audiences has been concerned with television. A range of research methods has been used to try to understand audience reactions, from focus groups being shown a television programme followed by a discussion about it, through interviews with family members about the television programmes they watch (Morley, 1980, 1986), to participant observation in people's homes (Lull, 1990; Walkerdine, 1990) or in other settings where television viewing is discussed (Gillespie, 1995).

Activity 6 Investigating audience responses

Allow about 40 minutes

What methodological problems do you think there might be in using focus groups, interviews or participant observation to document audience interpretations of/reactions to visual material?

Comment

As regards focus group or interview data, first of all we need to remember that what we have here are accounts provided retrospectively, and many factors may shape what is remembered and how it is portrayed. Furthermore, the greater the gap in time between viewing the visual material and gathering the data, the more significant the retrospective character of the accounts is likely to be. A second point is that people are producing accounts in researcher-initiated contexts, and the nature of these contexts may shape the character of what they say in significant ways. In interviews, the informant is likely to take account of what he or she believes the researcher will be interested in hearing or will want to hear, how the interviewer has responded to earlier answers, and so on. Furthermore, what people say in focus groups will be affected by what others in the group have said about how people think others will react to what they might say, and so on. Where the researcher listens to people talking about television programmes in other settings, at least some of the reactivity will be reduced; but we should remember that even here they are speaking on particular occasions to particular people, and what they say will be shaped by these and other aspects of the context, rather than simply displaying context-invariant attitudes.

In the case of participant observation in people's homes, similar points arise as with the use of video recordings for research purposes. The presence of the researcher is likely to have a reactive effect: people may pay more attention to the television than they would otherwise do, they may talk about the material more than they would usually, and they may be influenced by what they think the researcher's views are, and by her or his behaviour. How much time the participant observer spends with the people concerned will have an effect on this, of course. Typically, the effect of the presence of a participant observer may be considerable at the start but tends to decline quite rapidly over time, as people begin to take her or his presence for granted or even to forget it. The length of time will also determine how well the researcher is able to get an accurate sense of the range of people's normal behaviour.

We cannot assume, then, that it is possible to 'read off' from the character of some image or object how audiences will react to it. Investigations of audience response suggest that there will often be considerable variation. However, no method can give us direct access to the way audiences interpret visual material, although focus group, interview and participant observation data can reveal some of the complexities involved.

Summary of Section 5

The 'reception' of images and objects, and of texts, has been conceptualised in two sharply contrasting ways: some commentators argue that the characteristics of visual or textual material determine how audiences will respond to it, while others insist that audiences effectively construct what they are responding to.

Another approach is somewhere between these two extremes: attending to the role that the characteristics of images or objects or texts might have in shaping audiences' responses, while at the same time recognising that the latter will vary, depending on background assumptions and the contexts in which reception takes place.

There has been some research on audiences, using data from focus groups, interviews and participant observation. These methods provide rather different perspectives on how people respond to images, objects and texts, although they are subject to potential error in the same way that other sources of data are.

6 Ethics and visual data

Ethical issues, of one kind or another, and of varying degrees of severity, arise in all forms of social and educational research. Generally speaking, these are identified in terms of a small number of key principles, such as requiring that harm to participants be avoided or minimised, that their autonomy is respected (e.g. through seeking informed consent), and that their privacy is protected.

In some of its forms, the use of visual data involves few serious ethical problems. This is generally the case where what are being collected and analysed are publicly available images or objects. However, it is worth noting that where children or young people are encouraged by researchers to produce collections or collages of material from magazines or from what is available on the internet, ethical issues may arise about sexual and other content. Other forms of visual data can raise much more difficult ethical issues. Taking photos and making videos of children have become extremely sensitive activities in many societies. Moreover, if some of the resulting images are to be included in research reports, then there are serious questions about how those pictured can be protected from harm and their privacy preserved. After all, unless precautions are taken, they are likely to be immediately recognisable to many who already know them, and perhaps will also become identifiable by others.

A common strategy for dealing with these problems is to seek informed consent for taking photographs or making videos, although it is generally recognised that this does not resolve or avoid all the difficulties. Of course, informed consent is not a simple matter, and especially not when children are to be photographed or videoed. One issue here concerns whose permission is required. In schools, for example, the permission of the head teacher – and perhaps even of school governors, or of a local authority – may be necessary for taking photographs or filming, but probably also that of parents and perhaps that of the children themselves. And, of course, there is scope for conflict here: if one party gives permission while another refuses, there is the question of whose decision should be given priority – as, for example, when children want to be included but parents refuse permission.

There are also questions about what counts as informed consent, and in the case of visual data, some technical knowledge may be required if someone is to be judged well-informed. As Prosser (2000) comments, discussing professional filming:

> The subjects, not steeped in filmic knowledge, would be unaware of the techniques and ploys of directors going about their art. Moreover, … the outcomes of filming cannot be preordained.
>
> (Prosser, 2000, p. 126)

And he adds (quoting Gross et al., 1988, p. viii):

> How rare it is that image-makers show us to others as we would like to be seen … .
>
> (Prosser, 2000, p. 127)

Prosser illustrates the problems surrounding images as 'true representations', and also how audiences can be misled, by using the example of one of his own photographs: of a child sitting alone on a wall at the back of a school playground, with the caption 'Pupil on walkabout'. He writes:

> The boy was regularly found on a Friday afternoon hiding in the school's fuel storage area or in the cloakroom (usually under a mound of coats). He explained how each Friday the physics teacher told him to 'get lost', so he did. The photograph was taken to illustrate his predicament. …
>
> In the past, documentary photographers … have developed what can be described as 'pseudo-objective' photography. … This style

was used [in this picture] and raises a number of general ethical questions. ... one ethical responsibility of researchers is to report conceptions and procedures on which a research report is based. However, given that photographs are constructions, to what extent is it possible for photographers to account reflexively for the influence of aesthetic considerations? I was aware that using the 'standers and sitters' style, coupled with chiaroscuro lighting, would produce an 'arty' image. Equally, I was aware that the central positioning of the boy, the pathos of the figure and the gloominess of the place would evoke an overly emotional response in the viewer. In conveying a sense of isolation and depression I was representing an interpretation that was unsupported by data and had no substantive basis. This was not a case of incompetence (I knew what I was doing), more a case of the artistic style, drama and sensationalism of an image being given priority over academic integrity.

(Prosser, 2000, pp. 122–4)

How images will be produced, therefore, and how they will be interpreted by audiences are matters about which those approached to give informed consent, and sometimes even the researcher too, will often not have reliable knowledge.

The issue of how to obtain informed consent from children and what weight to give it – as against the judgements of parents or school authorities or, for that matter, of the researcher – is a contested one. Questions are raised, on the one hand, about how far children (of various ages) are capable of judging the likelihood of harm; it is often argued that adults in relevant caring roles are better placed to do this. By contrast, other commentators emphasise the need to respect the autonomy of children, and warn against any tendency to underestimate their capabilities in making such judgements. They may also argue that much preoccupation with harm arises from an increasing tendency for public opinion in Western societies to be 'risk averse'.

Generally speaking, in research dealing with children, informed consent is obtained from the children as well as from relevant adults, and this is believed to be especially important where the research involves the use of visual material. However, much depends on particular circumstances.

Activity 7   Is informed consent always required?

Allow about 20 minutes

Consider the following questions, noting down your thoughts:

- Is it always necessary to gain permission to photograph or video children?

- Is covert photography or videoing always unjustifiable?

Comment

Covert research is often ruled out as unacceptable in principle (Bulmer, 1982), and especially where children are concerned. However, as with most other ethical issues relating to research, we must resist general proscriptions (and prescriptions). There is some uncertainty about whether permission is required to take photographs and videos in public settings – for example, on the street or in a park. Indeed, non-researchers do this routinely and usually without asking the permission of those included in the shots. Given this, we might ask why researchers would need to seek permission in settings of this kind. Some commentators would deny that there is any need for this. Others argue that this is only necessary where the photographs or videos are to be made public via research reports or conference presentations. But some insist that permission must always be sought when photographing or videoing children, even in public settings.

There are also exceptional circumstances where it could be argued, even when the setting is not public, that photographing or videoing children covertly is legitimate. Take, for example, the case of an orphanage where the conditions in which children live are judged to be seriously abusive, or a youth camp run by an extreme nationalist or religious group. In these cases, might we not question whether it would be ethical for a researcher to give the adults concerned the right to withhold permission? After all, in such circumstances, permission might well be refused, thereby preventing documentation of the lives of the children involved. Moreover, if filming without the permission of these adults were to be attempted, gaining permission from the children could make them vulnerable to punishment, and might make it obvious to the authorities what is taking place. Some would conclude that covert filming would be legitimate in this case.

It is not uncommon for there to be dilemmas of this kind in research, as there are in the work of other occupations and in everyday life. One implication is that we should be cautious about accepting unconditional rules about what is and is not ethical, even though it is important to keep ethical principles in mind.

As I have hinted, there are sharply conflicting perspectives on research ethics. At one extreme, there are those who believe that all harm must be avoided, that autonomy and privacy must be fully respected, informed consent carefully obtained and frequently revisited; and/or that the people being studied should be included as equal participants in the research process, or even allowed to determine its course (Mertens and Ginsberg, 2009). In reporting on a study of young children entering preschool, which employed video data, Flewitt (2005) argues that research must be seen as a process of 'sharing', that this is essential if proper respect is to be given to people. This is particularly important, she argues, where those people are vulnerable, as in the case of very young children. She comments:

> Sharing decisions [in the course of negotiating initial and ongoing consent, participant consultation during data analysis, and in addressing issues of anonymity when re-presenting visual data in research write-ups] in no sense absolves the researcher of ultimate responsibility for decisions taken, but by listening to and respecting all participants' wishes, it can at the very least help to balance the unequal power balance between researcher and researched.
>
> (Flewitt, 2005, p. 554)

Other researchers go even further in this direction. For example, also in the context of research on children, Graue and Walsh suggest that researchers should '[enter] the field as though on one's knees, requesting permission to be there. This posture is not merely an entry ploy but a posture that one maintains throughout the entire research' (Graue and Walsh, 1998, p. 57).

However, a rather different view is taken by those who argue that research is a pragmatic process in which it is rarely possible to meet the highest ethical standards. This is partly because these often conflict in their implications, but also because adhering to them would make completing research projects impossible or very difficult. They may also reject the claim that it is better to 'compromise the research rather than compromise the participants' (Price, 1996, p. 207), or that 'our primary obligation is always to the people we study, not to our project or to a larger discipline' (Denzin, 1989, p. 83). It could be argued that these statements from Price and Denzin amount to ethical perfectionism; in other words, they forget that the world is not a perfect place, that most people are not primarily concerned with behaving ethically but are instead preoccupied with pursuing their own goals or protecting their own interests. This kind of pragmatic stance is rare in childhood studies today, but we might ask whether many of the ethical pronouncements about research in this field, such as that of Graue and Walsh quoted above, are not premised on an overly 'romantic' view of the child as inherently good, and as vulnerable and powerless, when this might be questioned.

The ethical issues relating to research involving children are the same as those concerning adults, but how we interpret those issues, and what would and would not be acceptable, will vary. For example, in thinking about informed consent, we should recognise that adults vary in their possession of relevant kinds of knowledge and capability. Furthermore, the particular social locations that they occupy within societies may generate vulnerabilities or prevent them from freely deciding whether or not to consent to being researched. In some cases, the dangers involved may be little different from those of research with children.

The strategies that researchers use to deal with ethical concerns are broadly similar whether children or adults are involved. And, of course, in most research on childhood, adults are part of the focus alongside children. In her research on child prostitutes in Thailand, Montgomery took great pains not only to ensure the anonymity of her informants, but also to keep secret the location of the village in which she had done her research, and the identity of the non-governmental organisation through which she had gained access. Such was the sensitivity of the topic, particularly at the time she was doing her research, that this was essential if there were not to be damaging consequences for all of those whose lives she documented, both children and adults (Montgomery, 2001).

As we noted earlier, a major issue about the use in research reports of visual data, especially when it has been generated by researchers, is that it may reveal the identities of those studied, perhaps thereby invading their privacy or opening them up to potential harm. Of course, there are means by which the danger of participants being recognised from photographs or video recordings can be reduced. Flewitt (2005) mentions fuzzying faces, or reducing the pixel count across whole images, so as to protect identities, particularly in the case of children. It is also possible to produce sketches of video stills and photographs so as to indicate body positioning, physical environment, directionality of movement, and so on.

However, these techniques are not without problems, and have themselves been challenged on ethical grounds as 'an example of the "Othering" of young children in research' (Nutbrown, 2011, p. 3). As this author comments, 'that's what the media does with photographs of people accused of crime' (p. 4). Furthermore, such devices often destroy the point of the picture:

> Take, for example, a picture of a 4-year-old, her painting apron thickly covered in paint, paint up to her elbows, deep smile on her face, staring with shining blue eyes straight into the camera lens. Through my adult eyes what I see in this image is her joy, her discovery, and her 'immersion' in this experience. If pixilated, this rich image would be turned into an unrecognizable blear of brown and blue – or worse – just her face would be distorted in this way – the picture would leave me with nothing to interpret and this 4-year-old girl would be masked to me and, to my mind (if a picture is a thousand words), 'voiceless.'
>
> (Nutbrown, 2011, p. 8)

She continues:

> Pixilation takes something drawn from a life truth (the face of child covered in paint, the toddler with paint all over her legs) and turns it into a lie.
>
> (Nutbrown, 2011, pp. 8–9)

Interestingly, there is a parallel here with the textual strategies sometimes used to preserve anonymity, as with Sikes's (2010) use of fictional composite accounts of teachers accused of sexually abusing pupils. In all these cases, questions can be raised about what is lost, the dangers involved, and what would and would not be ethical.

Summary of Section 6

The use of visual material in research raises ethical issues in distinctive forms, and this is particularly true in childhood studies.

Widely espoused principles such as informed consent are quite complex in character and may lead to difficult decisions, for example, about who is sufficiently informed to consent, or what to do when there is conflict between the decisions of carers and of children themselves regarding research participation.

One of the problems with visual data is that it may render those pictured easily recognisable. However, the strategies commonly used to avoid this, by obscuring their faces, have themselves been criticised.

Difficult ethical evaluations may be involved in research, and there are some important differences among researchers in how they approach them.

---

7 Conclusion

In this chapter, we have looked at some of the issues involved in the use of visual data for research purposes, and particularly in studies involving children and young people. We noted that the concept of visual data is marked out by contrasts with aural and textual forms of data, but that the boundaries around these categories are fuzzy. Furthermore, as commonly used, the category of 'visual data' is quite heterogeneous. It covers photographs, videos, plans/diagrams, maps, drawings, as well as material objects of many kinds. It is also important to recognise that visual, aural and textual data are often closely interrelated rather than operating in an entirely independent manner.

We emphasised the distinction between visual data produced by researchers for research purposes, or produced by others on the instigation of researchers, and the use of already available images and objects for analytic purposes. Somewhat different considerations are involved in interpreting and assessing these kinds of data. Yet others arise where researchers ask children to produce visual data in the form of drawings, photographs or video recordings.

A very common form of analysis of visual material is what is often referred to as semiotic or compositional analysis. This demands careful attention to and interpretation of images and objects themselves, how they are located in relationship to one another, and how this shapes the meanings they convey. However, we stressed the importance of investigating both production and reception processes, and that these can be culturally and contextually diverse.

In the final part of the chapter, we looked at some of the ethical issues associated with the use of visual data in studying children and young people. In this field, ethical issues take on distinctive forms and have led to forthright statements about what is required and what is unacceptable. These tend towards what we referred to as the perfectionist end of a wide spectrum of views that can be found among social scientists, and these may overlook the dilemmas and complexities involved in research. In particular, there are issues around informed consent: when this is necessary, and what it means to be informed and to freely consent. There are also questions about whether children should be considered capable of giving informed consent and, if so, at what age, as well as questions about how to deal with the various adults who play roles in relation to them. Another key problem arises from the fact that photographs and videos make it hard to preserve the anonymity of participants and places, and may thereby entail threats to harm or the infringement of privacy. While there are strategies that can be used to maintain anonymity where photographs or video images are employed in research reports, these can have undesirable implications or consequences. There are no easy answers, but it is important not to exaggerate the severity of the dangers involved.

References

Allan, A. (2005) 'Using photographic diaries to research the gender and academic identities of young girls', in Troman, G., Jeffrey, B. and Walford, G. (eds) *Methodological Issues and Practices in Ethnography*, Amsterdam, Elsevier.

Barnard, M. (2001) *Approaches to Understanding Visual Culture*, Houndmills, Palgrave.

Baudrillard, J. (1994) *Simulacra and Simulations* (first published in French in 1985), Ann Arbor, MI, University of Michigan Press.

Bignell, J. (1997) *Media Semiotics: An Introduction*, Manchester, Manchester University Press.

Bragg, S. and Buckingham, D. (2008) '"Scrapbooks" as a resource in media research with young people', in Thomson, P. (ed) *Doing Visual Research with Children and Young People*, London, Routledge.

Bulmer, M. (ed) (1982) *Social Research Ethics: An Examination of the Merits of Covert Participant Observation*, London, Macmillan.

Clark, A. (2010) *Transforming Children's Spaces: Children's and Adults' Participation in Designing Learning Environments*, London, Routledge.

Clark, A. and Moss, P. (2011) *Listening to Young Children: The Mosaic Approach* (2nd edn), London, National Children's Bureau.

Denzin, N. K. (1989) *Interpretive Biography*, London, Sage.

Dicks, B., Soyinka, B. and Coffey, A. (2006) 'Multimodal ethnography', *Qualitative Research*, vol. 6, no. 1, pp. 77 96.

Evans, J. and Hall, S. M. (2005) *Visual Culture: The Reader*, London, Sage.

Fenton, N., Bryman, A., Deacon, D., with Birmingham, P. (1998) *Mediating Social Science*, London, Sage.

Flewitt, R. (2005) 'Conducting research with young children: some ethical considerations', *Early Child Development and Care*, vol. 175, no. 6, pp. 553–65.

Gillespie, M. (1995) *Television, Ethnicity, and Cultural Change*, London, Routledge.

Graue, M. and Walsh, D. (1998) *Studying Children in Context: Theories, Methods, and Ethics*, Thousand Oaks, CA, Sage.

Gross, L., Katz, J. S. and Ruby, J. (eds) (1988) *Image Ethics*, New York, Oxford University Press.

Grosvenor, I. and Hall, A. (2012) 'Back to school from a holiday in the slums! Images, words and inequalities', *Critical Social Policy*, vol. 32, no. 1, pp. 11–30.

Hart, R. (1979) *Children's Experience of Place*, New York, Irvington.

Jay, M. (1993) *Downcast Eyes: The Denigration of Vision in Twentieth-century French Thought*, Berkeley, CA, University of California Press.

Kehily, M. J. and Maybin, J. (2011) 'A window on children's lives? The process and problematics of representing children in audio visual case study', *Journal of Children and Media*, vol. 5, no. 3, pp. 267–83.

Kress, G. (2010) *Multimodality: A Social Semiotic Approach to Contemporary Communication*, London, Routledge.

Law, J. and Whittaker, J. (1988) 'On the art of representation: notes on the politics of visualisation', in Fyfe, G. and Law, J. (eds) *Picturing Power: Visual Depiction and Social Relations*, Sociological Review Monograph 35, London, Routledge.

Leitch, R. (2008) 'Creatively researching children's narratives through images and drawings', in Thomson, P. (ed) *Doing Visual Research with Children and Young People*, London, Routledge.

Lull, J. (1990) *Inside Family Viewing: Ethnographic Research on Television's Audiences*, London, Routledge.

Mertens, D. and Ginsberg, P. (eds) (2009*) The Handbook of Social Research Ethics*, Thousand Oaks, CA, Sage.

Montgomery, H. (2001) *Modern Babylon? Prostituting Children in Thailand*, New York, Berghahn.

Morley, D. (1980) *The Nationwide Audience: Structure and Decoding*, London, British Film Institute.

Morley, D. (1986) *Family Television: Cultural Power and Domestic Leisure*, London, Routledge.

Noyes, A. (2008) 'Using video diaries to investigate learner trajectories: researching the "unknown unknowns"', in Thomson, P. (ed) *Doing Visual Research with Children and Young People*, London, Routledge.

Nutbrown, C. (2011) 'Naked by the pool? Blurring the image? Ethical issues in the portrayal of young children in arts-based educational research', *Qualitative Inquiry*, vol. 17, no. 1, pp. 3–14.

Pink, S. (2006) *Doing Visual Ethnography: Images, Media and Representation in Research* (2nd edn), London, Sage.

Pink, S. (2009) *Doing Sensory Ethnography*, London, Sage.

Price, J. (1996) 'Snakes in the swamp: ethical issues in qualitative research', in Josselson, R. (ed) *Ethics and Process in the Narrative Study of Lives*, Volume 4, London, Sage.

Prosser, J. (2000) 'The moral maze of image ethics', in Simons, H. and Usher, R. (eds) *Situated Ethics in Educational Research*, London, Routledge Falmer.

Rose, G. (2012) *Visual Methodologies: An Introduction to the Interpretation of Visual Materials* (3rd edn), London, Sage.

Sikes, P. (2010) 'Teacher–student sexual relations: key risks and ethical issues', *Ethnography and Education*, vol. 5, no. 2, pp. 143–57.

Sturken, M. and Cartwright, L. (2001) *Practices of Looking: An Introduction to Visual Culture*, Oxford, Oxford University Press.

Thomson, P. (ed) (2008) *Doing Visual Research with Children and Young People*, London, Routledge.

Walkerdine, V. (1990) *Schoolgirl Fictions*, London, Verso.

Acknowledgements

Every effort has been made to contact copyright holders. If any have been inadvertently overlooked the publishers will be pleased to make the necessary arrangements at the first opportunity.

Grateful acknowledgement is made to the following sources:

Figures

Cover image: Mother and Child Shopping, © Holzhandler, Dora (Contemporary Artist)/RONA Gallery, London, UK/The Bridgeman Art Library; page 6: © Imaengine/Dreamstime.com; page 12: © Rostislav Ageev/Dreamstime.com; page 16: © Craig Colvin/Dreamstime.com; page 22: © Ron Zmiri / Dreamstime.com; page 23: Flag Parade, The Playgound (Joseph Lee Memorial Library, National Recreation and Parks Association, Ashburn, Virginia); page 24: © Gopal Bhattacharjee/Dreamstime.com; page 28: © Roger Hart; page 30: © aprile_Lucia/www.adirt.it; page 36: From 'Young people and territoriality in British cities' by Keith Kintrea, Jon Bannister, Jon Pickering, Maggie Reid and Naofumi Suzuki, published in 2008 by the Joseph Rowntree Foundation. Reproduced by permission of the Joseph Rowntree Foundation; page 37: From 'Young people and territoriality in British cities' by Keith Kintrea, Jon Bannister, Jon Pickering, Maggie Reid and Naofumi Suzuki, published in 2008 by the Joseph Rowntree Foundation. Reproduced by permission of the Joseph Rowntree Foundation; page 59: © Gloria Upchurch; page 60 (top): © Martin Woodhead; page 60 (bottom): © Christopher Walker; page 63: © Harry Kerr/Getty Images; page 68: Copyright © 1982 by Michael Ondaatje. Reprinted by permission of Michael Ondaatje; page 77: © Mary Jane Kehily; page 81: © Mary Jane Kehily; page 83: © Wellcome Photo Library, Wellcome Images Historical photo, children's ward, circa 1930. This file is licensed under the Creative Commons Attribution-Noncommercial-NoDerivatives Licence, http://creativecommons.org/licenses/by-nc/2.0/uk/; page 115: © Sonya Etchison/Dreamstime.com; page 123: © Ahmad Zaihan Amran/Dreamstime.com; page 130: © Steve Estvanik/Dreamstime.com; page 131: Image reproduced by permission: Source Ashoka Changemakers.com; page 135: © Nicholas Rjabow/Dreamstime.com; page 136: © Chloehall/Dreamstime.com; page 138: © Manuel Gutjahr/iStockphoto; page 169: © Fei Xie/Dreamstime.com; page 173: © Architectural Press Archives/RIBA

Library Photographs Collection; page 174: © RIBA Library Books & Periodicals Collection; page 176: © British Pathé; page 177: Clay, F., (1929), Modern School Buildings Elementary and Secondary, Batsford. Reproduced by permission of Anova Books; page 179: piazza – Diana Municipal Preschool © Preschools and Infant-toddler Centres – Istituzione of the Municipality of Reggio Emilia, (Italy); page 182: © Samrat35/Dreamstime.com; page 185: © British Pathé; page 187: © Alison Clark; page 188: © David Snyder/Dreamstime.com; page 190: © Jianbinglee/Dreamstime.com; page 194: © Zatletic/Dreamstime.com; page 219: Lewis Hine, courtesy of Library of Congress, http://www.loc. gov/pictures/item/ncl2004001219/PP; page 222: Photography Collection, Miriam and Ira D. Wallach Division of Art, Prints and Photographs, The New York Public Library, Astor, Lennox and Tilden Foundations; page 224: © John Drysdale; page 226: © Giacomo Pirozzi/Panos Pictures; page 227: Reproduced with permission. © Young Lives 2009. Young Lives is an international childhood study following the lives of 12,000 children in 4 developing countries over 15 years. www.younglives.org.uk; page 230: © SHOUT/Alamy; page 232: © Dieter Telemans/Panos Pictures; page 234: © roger parkes/Alamy; page 235: © Stan White/Alamy; page 236: © AFP/Getty Images; page 239: © Johm Walmsley/Education Photos; page 243: Flag hoisting of Bhima Sangha, a union of working children. Courtesy of CWC's Archives; page 270: © Meredith Corporation; page 275: © UNICEF; page 276: © UNICEF.

Text

Page 44: Reprinted with permission from Urban Geography, Vol. 17, No. 3, pp. 205-220. © Bellwether Publishing Ltd., 8640 Guilford Road, Suite 200, Columbia, MD21046. All rights reserved; page 51: Ward, C. (1990) 'Adapting the imposed environment', The Child in the City (2nd ed.), Bedford Square Press. Copyright © Colin Ward, 1978, 1990. Reproduced by permission; page 95: Bauer, E. and Thompson, P. (2006), *Jamaican Hands Across the Atlantic*, Ian Randle Publishers. Copyright © 2006 Elaine Bauer and Paul Thompson; page 100: Clarke A. J, (2004), 'Maternity and materiality: becoming a mother in consumer care', in Taylor, J. S. et al (eds), Consuming Motherhood, Rutgers University Press. Copyright © 2004 Rutgers, The StateUniversity of New Jersey; page 105: Hall, T. (2006) 'Out of work and house and home: contested youth in an English homeless hostel', ETHNOS, Vol. 71:2, pp. 143-163, Routledge Journals, Taylor and Francis, on behalf of the Museum of Ethnography. Reprinted by permission of the publisher (Taylor & Francis Ltd, http://www.tandfonline.com); page 149: Matthews, H., Taylor, M., Percy-Smith, B. and Limb, M. (2000) 'The unacceptable flaneur: the shopping mall as a teenage hangout', *Childhood*, vol. 7, no. 279, Sage Publications; page 160: "Fashion Gender and Consumption," in Liberalization's Children, Ritty A. Lukose, pp. 66-81. Copyright, 2009, Duke University Press. All rights reserved. Reprinted by permission of the publisher. www.dukeupress.edu; page 203: Burke, C. (2005) 'Contested desires: the edible landscape of school', Paedagogica Historia, vol. 41, nos. 4 & 5, Taylor and Francis. Copyright © Stitchting Paedagogica Historica, reprinted by permission of Taylor and Francis Ltd, www.tandfonline.com on behalf of Stitcting Paedagogica Historica; page 206: Pike, J. (2008), 'Foucault, space and primary school dining rooms', Children's Geographies, vol. 6, no. 4, pp. 413-422, Taylor and Francis. Reprinted by permission of Taylor and Francis Ltd, www.tandfonline.com; page 211: Whitty, G. and Wisby, E. (2007) Real decision-making? School councils in action. Department for Children, Schools and Families Research report DCSF-001. Nottingham: Department for Children, Schools and Families, 78-80; page 248: Zelizer, V. A. (1985), 'From useful to useless: moral conflict over child labor', Pricing the Priceless Child: The Changing Social Value of Children, Princeton University Press. Copyright © 1985 by Basic Books; reprinted by arrangement with Basic Books, Harper Collins Publishers, Inc; page 253: Reproduced with permission. © Young Lives 2009. Young Lives is an international of childhood study following the lives of 12,000 children in 4 developing countries over 15 years. www.younglives.org.uk; page 259: Boudillon, Michael et al. Rights and Wrongs of Children's Work. Copyright (c) 2010 by Michael Bourdillon, Deborah Levinson, William Myers, and Ben White. Reprinted by permission of Rutgers University Press.

Index